CW00860480

C H A D,
A CELEBRATION *of* LIFE ~
BEYOND A MOTHER'S MEMORIES

Arista

BALBOA.PRESS

A DIVISION OF HAY HOUSE

Copyright © 2020 Arista.

All rights reserved. No part of this book may be used or reproduced by any means, graphic, electronic, or mechanical, including photocopying, recording, taping or by any information storage retrieval system without the written permission of the author except in the case of brief quotations embodied in critical articles and reviews.

Balboa Press books may be ordered through booksellers or by contacting:

Balboa Press
A Division of Hay House
1663 Liberty Drive
Bloomington, IN 47403
www.balboapress.com
844-682-1282

Because of the dynamic nature of the Internet, any web addresses or links contained in this book may have changed since publication and may no longer be valid. The views expressed in this work are solely those of the author and do not necessarily reflect the views of the publisher, and the publisher hereby disclaims any responsibility for them.

The author of this book does not dispense medical advice or prescribe the use of any technique as a form of treatment for physical, emotional, or medical problems without the advice of a physician, either directly or indirectly. The intent of the author is only to offer information of a general nature to help you in your quest for emotional and spiritual well-being. In the event you use any of the information in this book for yourself, which is your constitutional right, the author and the publisher assume no responsibility for your actions.

Print information available on the last page.

ISBN: 978-1-9822-5078-2 (sc)
ISBN: 978-1-9822-5080-5 (hc)
ISBN: 978-1-9822-5079-9 (e)

Library of Congress Control Number: 2020912929

Balboa Press rev. date: 08/13/2020

A Story of Life

~ ~ ~

This book is dedicated:
to my son, Chad,
and
all the Children
he now holds hands with;
and
all the Children
who will have Lives and Dreams
because of Them

CONTENTS

FOREWORD

I met Arista through the publisher of Reggie's book *Quiet Grace*. From the moment we spoke, I knew we would be friends for Life, Mothers losing a Child- what greater bond could we have together. But when she told me about *The Chad Foundation for Athletes and Artists,* I was thrilled. Finally, we had somebody doing something to help save young lives from Sudden Cardiac Death by screening them with Echocardiograms <u>before</u> they play sports. And, she wanted to provide a screening for the athletes at Reggie's former high school, Dunbar High, here in Baltimore and she did: the doctors and technicians from Johns Hopkins Hospital would conduct these tests. Arista spoke, I spoke, and the Doctors spoke to the Student Body about the importance of prescreening athletes to identify risk factors like HCM, hypertrophic cardiomyopathy, which took Reggie and which we now know is genetic. One in five hundred births can have this abnormal gene. I cannot tell you how important it is that we screen athletes and youth before the start of their sports seasons and also to have the portable AED (Automatic External Defibrillator) available at every sporting event. CHAD, through the generosity of Agilent Technologies [now Philips], donated an AED in Reggie's honor to Dunbar High School. I myself played basketball on those gym boards, and my talented son Reggie followed. I wish you all could have known Reggie. He loved children, and when he became a Boston Celtic, he gave back to the children of his community through basketball clinics and a Turkey Giveaway every Thanksgiving in Baltimore and every Christmas in Boston while he was alive. On behalf of Reggie and Chad and all those young people who did not have the benefit of early screenings or an AED, please support The Chad Foundation to help save young hearts and lives.

IF TEARS COULD BUILD A STAIRWAY, AND
MEMORIES BUILD A LANE, I WOULD WALK RIGHT
TO HEAVEN, AND BRING YOU HOME AGAIN.

-AUTHOR: UNKNOWN

Friend till the End,

Peggy Ritch
Proud Mother of Reggie Lewis, All Star-Boston Celtic,
21 November 1965 to 27 July 1993

PART I

CHAD
A Celebration of Life

CHAPTER 1

The Phone Call

I remember the credit card held tightly between my thumb and index finger. It was near closing time at Bloomingdales NYC on a Saturday in April. I was finishing up with the last customer, and then I could go home and work on my screenplay. Yea! Life was good. I had worked hard to establish myself as a makeup artist in the cosmetic industry. I could work as a resident artist 3 or 4 days a week in a permanent position, which allowed me the vehicle to sustain my art as an actor/ writer. My sons were doing well on the west coast- living on their own in the City of Angels and pursuing careers in the film industry. And *finally,* after many years of raising my three sons, I was living in New York City, pursuing my own career as an artist. In the past few years, I had written, produced, and performed in my 1st off-off-Broadway stage play, *All About Sneakers.* Audiences really loved this little play, and now the screenplay version looked like a promising indie film. However, in about 1 minute, my life was about to change forever: the phone was about to ring, delivering the call every parent dreads, is in denial of ever receiving, and can't imagine how those parents who do receive it can survive. Me? Well, I didn't really worry about it too much because, in my mind, I had made a pact with God– anybody but my 3 Sons. *I* had made the pact, and as I hadn't heard anything to the contrary: I assumed it was consensual.

But today, the proverbial tower was about to fall- all those false notions we tell ourselves were about to be swept away. Funny what you remember on this earth-shattering, life-changing moment: the little cubby hole where the cash register was located, the customer's credit card stuck between two fingers, like a car that becomes frozen in its tracks unable to move as it sees that roaring train heading straight for it. A conductor once told me that after such a train accident, the person's hand might have to be pried from the steering wheel- with the help of a tool, it was stuck that tight.

This day, as I heard that speeding locomotive coming straight for me, I dropped the phone but held on to the customer's card. My legs buckled, leaving me near the floor, but that card was still glued to my thumb and forefinger as I heard the calm voice on the other end of the phone speaking words I could not comprehend. You are enduring the greatest shock of your life, but by all means, don't lose the customer's card. The voice was that of my former husband, Carl, and the Father of my children. He had never called me at work before, but today he was telling me that Chad, our eldest son, was playing football and there was an accident and after somewhat of a pause, he said… "He didn't make it…" He didn't make what? I thought, and said, "What are you talking about, he didn't make it—a touchdown?" In the same calm voice, he repeated it in more detail. Collin and Curt, our other sons, had gone to the hospital– to identify… "WHAT ARE YOU TALKING ABOUT??" My voice roared in volume. The owner of that card was watching the scenario, and it didn't look good; her card was still stuck to my fingers, and all she wanted to do was retrieve her merchandise and go home. But I was trying to decipher some altered state of conversation, and it took complete precedence.

He told me in different words. This time it hit home, and my emotions surfaced like a tsunami, engulfing everything. There was no warning, and editing was not an option. The President of the United States could have been standing next to me; there would have been the same reaction. "HOW CAN YOU TELL ME THIS? WHAT ARE YOU SAYING??" I still am unable to process what I am hearing. I cried, I bent over, I didn't know where the phone had gone; was it still in my hand, just no longer on my ear? And the woman standing on the other side of the counter was no longer there, and then suddenly, a colleague from the neighbouring counter appeared. Francis was a nice man: I always liked him. I handed him the phone. His face was turned away from mine, but I could tell by his shoulders and the way his hand covered his mouth, it was true.

When he turned back, the first thing he did was embrace me; the proud mama, always talking about her sons, showing pictures. Why Chad had even stopped by the counter at Christmas on what would be his last trip to New York and our last family holiday together, and Francis remembered the handsome young men that were my Sons. All of the cosmetic associates knew how close we were. How could she possibly handle this news was on his mind as he tried to be the buffer of these sad tidings. This day, this phone call would remain with him for a long while. When he turned back, he spoke to me gently but with a sense of purpose. I had to get home as quickly as possible as plane reservations had been made, and then he put the phone in my hand again because I needed to listen to the details. Of course, Carl would have taken care of all the details even in this- his most tragic moment. When he was 20, he was going on 40. Dependability was his second nature. But it was Francis's manner, both compassionate and firm, and the inkling of the thought that I had to get to my other sons that caused me to take the phone from him again. What my sons were going through was inconceivable; I must get to them.

Suddenly one of the flagship retail behemoths of the world turned its business face aside and became very human. The floor manager came to handle the counter immediately. My manager, returning from her break, accompanied me home at once to help me pack. She lived on Long Island, not a short distance away. -It didn't matter to her. When my neighbor Francis returned to his own counter, as in La Prairie, he took the card from my fingers, but the fingers remained in the same position for several seconds. Here was a person in myself who was not used to being led, but this day I was so grateful for those people who took the reins during the next few hours. The tower had fallen, and the lightning and thunder, though invisible in their magnitude, were felt by all, and they were the brave souls guiding

3

me through the maelstrom. I vaguely remember being led out of the store arms around me, someone else calling a cab for us.

When we reached my apartment Karen, my manager, packed my suitcase. How does one go into a strange closet and start choosing clothing?? She did an excellent job, however, for when I arrived in Los Angeles, it seemed I had all the right clothes to wear. It's true, we New Yorkers wear a lot of black, but Karen had also packed other colours. Chad would have been happy. He would not have wanted me entirely in black. He was the most positive person I've ever known.

I remember a moment on the plane. Even though it was night, I wore my sunglasses continuously, for my eyes were swollen from crying. I remember asking the flight attendant for ice. She brought it quietly and disappeared. People sense when something is wrong and give you the space and respect you need. It is so appreciated for in this circumstance, one becomes oblivious to all, even one who is usually conscious of social demeanor in public. I was glad it was a night flight and that the plane didn't appear to be full. Then, one like an animal that had been recently attacked could retire to a place of solitude and lick its wounds in private.

When I found myself seated on the plane- I could not remember what airport, the ride there, or who was sheltering my suitcase. Carl had made all the arrangements, and I was just on some conveyor belt being led through this murky, surreal state. As the plane's ascent began, I felt this terrible pain suffuse my entire being: no more delaying, no more turning back, no more time. This plane, with every motion, was taking me to meet, face to face, this horrific loss. Sharen, Carl's wife, must have sensed my anguish, for, at this moment, she reached across to take my hand, and we held hands across the aisle as the plane took off... to face the most difficult moment of our Lives.

CHAPTER 2

Chad's Home, The City of Angels

The first memory I can recall of reaching Los Angeles was entering my sons, Curt and Collin's apartment. It was a small, stucco building typical-style of the Hollywood '60s. It was located in the Brentwood area near the San Diego Freeway, which the denizens refer to as the "405."

Less than 6 weeks later, my son Curt would call me from this very room, and we would go through another senseless tragedy- the deaths of Ron Goldman and Nicole Brown Simpson. That day as my son talked to me on his cell phone, one could hear the deafening whir of the helicopters above his apartment tracking the white Bronco of O. J. as it made its way down the 405. Curt walked to the freeway and saw people on the viaduct, cheering, "Go, O.J.!" For a moment, we both thought the world had gone mad. A few days later, my youngest son, Collin, would call me at Bloomingdales, where I had returned to work a month before. He wanted to tell me that the Dr.'s name on Chad's autopsy report was the same Doctor who performed the autopsy on Ron Goldman and Nicole Simpson. Yes, it was; Collin was very observant. (He also remembered the words on his brother's autopsy: the cause of death - "idiopathic dilated cardiomyopathy," a medical term which would change our lives.)

I thought of how Ron Goldman resembled my own sons, who would have been the same type of person to drop off a customer or friend's sunglasses. And if confronted with this horrendous situation would have also fought to the death to save a Life, including their own, and especially if it was someone who could not fend for themselves. My heart ached for those families – only we could know... and I wanted to write to them and add my empathy and prayers, but I could see they were being inundated with those who cared, and I knew they would be okay.

But for the moment, this night that I entered my sons' abode, we held together as a Family to embark upon the saddest journey of our lives. My youngest son hugged me and said, "…Sorry, Mom." He was in such utter shock. How could the youngest be called upon to identify his older brother? - There was barely thirty-four months between them, and 17 months between Chad and his middle brother. They were like stair steps; they had grown up together in 5 states. When Chad was 7, and they were 5 and 6, Chad referred to his brothers as "The Three Musketeers," and said they would always be together. How is it possible one could be missing now??

Collin had been managing a small restaurant chain, "City Wok," in Studio City when he got 'the call.' It was Keven, Chad's best friend, who had been playing in the football game with Chad when he collapsed coming out of a huddle. He had not been hit, just collapsed, face down. He tried to turn over, and someone helped him. He tried to get up, but Keven told him to stay down, "It's okay, buddy, just stay down." Chad's last words were the spirit of who he was, "I'll be okay."

Then Jason, the coach, took over, and when there was no more breath detected, he began CPR. Later, when I would have the opportunity to speak to Jason personally, he would tell me it seemed like an interminable amount of time he had administered CPR to Chad. According to the log, it was 16 minutes before the paramedics arrived. There was a firehouse right across from the field, but at that time in 1994, AED's (Automatic External Defibrillators) were not standardized equipment in a firehouse. When the paramedics arrived, they tried to revive Chad with their paddle defibrillators. We now know every minute that goes by without the benefit of an AED decreases survival chances by 50%. What a stressful experience it must have been for the coach, trained in this life-saving technique, and today, the 23rd of April, he was called upon to use it to try to save a young athlete's Life.

It's almost like the coach's Hippocratic Oath. I know in speaking to Jason, there was a lifelong bond of sorts that transpired between us; he was the person who last touched my son, trying to breathe Life into him. That, too, must have been a life-altering experience for him. So many are affected when a young person leaves the Earth much before their time. I have been unable to visit that spot– the grassy, final place where my Son last lay on Earth, and I probably never will. Chad loved to play sports: from his sports closet in his and Maria's apartment to the black grease, spread asymmetrically under the eyes, to the immaculate uniform he always wore and the absolute respect he held for the game and its rules. - This is the place where he should have gone down.

When Curt and Collin came out west a few years prior, to pursue their acting, it gave them time to be with their older brother. They could play lots of sports from Wiffle ball in a hole dug for a new apartment, which, to Chad, was just another Wiffle ball stadium, to being weekend warriors in baseball, volleyball, and football. To this day, I see Chad's Friends missing that male camaraderie and love for sports that they shared together and would have always shared for many years to come. Thus, when such a call would come to a brother, I, as a mother, can't imagine what that means… and the youngest, who has an impeccable work ethic, throws down the towel and says, "I have to leave, my brother died." My brother died, and I have to go to the hospital and identify him… What does this mean? How is one able to do this, but he did. I remember this child at 4 burying a frog in our backyard in St. Louis *'cause,'* he said, "It *senigraded.*" Why does this child have to go do this? Why couldn't it have waited until the mother and father got there? That should have been our responsibility. Why did our Sons have to do it? These are the questions one asks.

And when I embraced my middle son Curt, there would be more questions to ask, hurtful ones. The first thing Curt said was, "…Sorry, Mom." It took me back slightly that my sons were saying those words to me, shouldn't I be saying that to them? They were always such sweet, thoughtful sons. But it was the second question he asked that stopped my heart. "Mom, why did Chad's body start turning blue, and it got so hard. I tried covering him with blankets... – He was so cold…" I felt my hands balling into fists to prevent them and me from shaking. And it took all my power to appear calm and not unduly affected as I felt like screaming at full tilt to the heavens. But instead, I answered in a quiet, compassionate voice, "Honey, how long were you there with Chad?" There was a beat as he thought a moment, "Six-seven hours... I couldn't leave." God was holding me up that moment because otherwise, I would have surely fainted. Livid is not all-encompassing enough to describe my feelings accurately. –How could this hospital let my son sit there for 7 hours and witness the deterioration of his beautiful brother? When my biological father had passed from cancer, the family was allowed 10 minutes to say their goodbyes and then was whisked out of the room. There were time constraints in place for a reason. The body would soon begin its natural decomposition process.

Chad's body was a temple. He always tried to take care of it and eat well. He never took a puff of a cigarette or drank a drop of alcohol— certainly not drugs or steroids his entire life. It was just his code, and, ironically, he was always saving himself for the older years. He planned on being healthy and vital and playing sports for many years to come. It was bad enough losing a brother, but to witness what he was seeing was unnecessary and cruel. Curt had nightmares for years about these images.

With fists still clenched, I hugged him again and told him, "I'm so sorry you had to see this. You should have been taken out of the room…" I knew I would write to the Mayor of Los Angeles as soon as I got home. This should never happen again to any family, especially a young person. I did write that letter. The Mayor at the time, Mayor Riordan, was very kind and apologetic. He forwarded my letter on to the appropriate health authorities who made an unscheduled inspection visit, citing the hospital for two infractions, 1) not offering to counsel, and 2) violating the time limit before a body must be taken to the morgue. This would be the 1st letter of many written to prevent parents and families from going through the most significant loss of your Life, your child, when and if it can be prevented.

That night in the City of Angels, as I struggled to sleep in fitful starts in Curt's bed which lay upon the floor: I awoke crying, and if awake or still asleep, I saw and felt my Son, Chad, hovering and enclosing his arms around me from behind. He wore his favourite colour, a blue Oxford shirt, and on his back were the "wings" of an Angel.

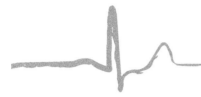

CHAPTER 3

What they become...
when you let them go
~ Carolco Pictures

The moment the elevator door opened, I knew I was stepping into a strange and wondrous place, much like *Oz* when Dorothy stepped through the massive door with her stalwart Family, who had made the ominous journey by her side. Today, I was accompanied by Chad's Father, Carl; his youngest brother, Collin; and, steadfast, Cousin Mike. And like the *Wizard of Oz*, we were greeted by extraordinarily kind, caring denizens who took your arm and welcomed you. Now, they would be your shelter and your sanctuary. Even the President of the studio was there to welcome us along with Chad's boss. In my unreal state-of-mind, I thought how wonderful to meet Chad's boss, but why was the "head" of the studio there as well? Chad was the *Assistant* to the General Counsel, *not* an executive. But I was to learn that all these special people from top to bottom and their lovely house would act as a way station, which would help prepare us for the *major crossing to come...* And they would be there for us as long as we were in their Land – a Land that had come to know my son, Chad, very well, and I was to find he had made quite an impression.

Carolco Pictures was an indie film production house that produced some major blockbuster action films in the '80s and '90s. Chad had told me that Carolco had done the post for the Brandon Lee films... Funny how lives intersect: a segment I had written and hosted in New York, entitled, *Asian American Artists: Stereotypes and Alternatives,* was re-aired on WNYC-TV specifically for the Brandon Lee Tribute. Brandon, the son of the most celebrated martial artist, Bruce Lee, died young also; his demise was due to a freak accident while filming, just a little over a year before.

The studio was located on a sunny corner of Sunset Boulevard on the fringe of where some of the bigger studios are found. Once you entered the top floor of their offices, you could see a vista of the land of Hollywood through the high glass windows prominent throughout. It was much like another industry counterpart, 3,000 miles away – SAG, the Screen Actors Guild offices, which rise to view the city it belongs to – New York. Chad informed me there were other studios in his building as well. I remember once he called to tell me he had said hello to Sylvester Stallone in the elevator and that he was very nice. A few days later, I would find a *Cliffhanger* hat in Chad and Maria's apartment, which I now have along with his Detroit Tiger's cap, which I had given him, his "A" cap, and his baseball team cap. Funny, too, how *Cliffhanger* was one of the last films Chad, his brothers, and I watched together. It was during our last Christmas together in New York… All these memories become so vivid now.

And then I found myself being led with arms about me into the President's corner office with its elegant wooden desk, dark-paneled walls, and warm appointments that made the ambiance welcoming. Just as in *Oz,* there came a gentle, steady stream of warmhearted people- all Chad's co-workers. But instead of tending to my nails and wardrobe, they were caring for my heart and spirit with their heartfelt stories of Chad: how he always made them laugh even if they were in a bad mood, and that he was such a great, creative writer!

So many of Chad's work-friends reiterated how he had written them individual notes: emails, post-its, cards, and the amazing thing is they had all kept them. One lovely colleague said she would be glad to go around and collect copies of all these personal notes and present them to me at the Wake. Well, of course, I would like that, though I had no idea what I was in store for! I also thought to myself how interesting that men and women would want to keep notes Chad

had written to them… I did not know what a precious gift I was about to receive in his writings. For later, when I would have a chance to read each one individually, I was so grateful they had shared them with me. It gave an inside look into the young man my son Chad had become: his caring about each person, his unique sense of humour and utter cheekiness, his ability to admit mistakes and let others know how much they are appreciated, and his creative writing that I/we will always cherish. His writings on the Native Americans I found especially compelling. The last movie I saw with Chad was *Geronimo,* and in New York, I had written my first off-Broadway play with a beautiful Native theme woven within. As I looked to the co-mingling of my son's words, so creative and personal, I defer to his boss, R.G., who could not have said it better, "I wish I could have known what could have been."

I had the great pleasure of meeting Chad's boss and talking at length to someone who had gotten to know my son and taught him on an everyday basis. Although privy to the charm and charisma of Chad, he could also rein it in as he saw the raw, innate potential which he could help cultivate. R. made me aware that he saw qualities in Chad that would have made him an excellent attorney. Coming from the General Counsel, I thought that was a special vote of faith in Chad's abilities. In fact, they had discussed it. He had told Chad arrangements could be made so that he could work part-time while he went back to school. Chad had been contemplating it. To me, R. was like the surrogate father-figure on the west coast. We, Chad's Family, were all on the East coast at this time caring for the younger brood – and he seemed to have taken Chad under his wing to guide him and nurture his talents.

R. was also aware of Chad's creativity and unique sense of humour. He told me, oh yes, he had heard about the legendary "email" sent out by Chad to one specific person. Only Chad not entirely down yet with qualifying who gets the email sent it out en mass to the whole studio by accident. I never saw the entire contents of the infamous electronic missive. But his boss told me, Chad got savvy very quickly and got it off the system before his superior had returned from vacation.

I know Chad's feelings were reciprocal as evidenced by a birthday card he wrote to his boss, and I would be privy to read:

> *"Dear R.,*
> *May Life now from this moment forward be one Substantial*
> *Musical.* May your life consist of *"Can-Can* meets *Oklahoma,"*
> think of yourself in the *South Pacific* on a raft reading *Kon-Tiki,*
> sipping a pina colada. When work gets you down, take a ride
> to the *West Side* to hear a story about those *Sounds of Music*
> you'll be hearing. Enough already of the corniness (is that even
> a word?) you say? Can I say and how many differnt ways will I
> be able to show it – my gratitude for you, the *"Lionheart."* One
> day I'll repay your kindness just you wait and see.
>
> Happy Birthday,
> Chad"

At this warm and welcoming establishment, I did break once. It was when I saw my son, Collin, his father, Carl, and Cousin Mike gathering all the items from Chad's desk and walls. Tissues were at the ready, and being used by everyone… Chad's office was a large, corner, 6 x 8-foot space with modular, gray fabric walls. Above his desk, there was an 8.5" x 11" piece of paper on which Chad had posted pictures of his heroes/heroines/icons. Later, when I got back to NY, I would take the time to look with care at each image, for these were the people on Earth your child admired and held in esteem: Joe Dimaggio, Joe Montana, Dan Marino, and Robert Duvall in the 1st row. Pictures of the Brewers'- Molitor, Yount and Gantner, Nolan Ryan, Anne Archer, Jeanne Tripplehorn, Clint Eastwood, and Gene Hackman were in the 2nd row. And, in the last row, was Mickey Mantle, Paul Newman, and Ted Williams.

They were all icons of the sports or entertainment worlds. Even the female actors were interesting choices. Many were the legendary Athletes & Artists of the world. Of note: Chad was also a 3-way winner for the Oscar Pool, just a few weeks before he left us. He scored 14 out of 16 categories correctly, such as Emma Thompson in *Howard's End*, Al Pacino in *Scent of a Woman*, and best film,

Unforgiven. Two of the actors, Clint Eastwood and Gene Hackman, were on his 'wall of fame.' (When I named Chad's organization, "The Chad Foundation for Athletes and Artists," I'm not sure I completely understood why. It was rather evolutionary, and the moniker just found its way to becoming what it was. Chad truly was an athlete and an artist – in his mind/body/spirit.)

A few days later, Chad's co-workers and friends at Carolco would present me with a simple black binder at the wake. It was one of the most precious gifts I have ever been given for its contents were filled with years and moments that my son Chad had lived on his own, in his own way, finding his own voice, expressing his own unique person through his written words. It was if I was being presented with a biography of my son's life- *Since I left Home, Mom.* A mother can only try to do the best she can, and then she must set her fledglings free to live on their own terms; hopefully, they will be ingrained with a moral compass and respect and love for all humanity. I am forever grateful for this Gift. For when these fine people opened the door that day and shared their personal gifts of Chad's writing with me, I was able to see the special young man my son was growing into and how many people he had touched.... each so personally.

In reading a simple email requesting a meeting, methinks my progeny was a throwback to the days of Lancelot wearing 21st-century attire and scribing on 21st-century scribeware. (I do confess to buying knights' armour for him and his brothers when they were little, maybe...)

> *"HEAR-YE, HEAR YE,*
> *By the powers vested in me as the 5th in line to the Throne of King Gold... and as the Duke of Debauchery, I bequeath all worldly possessions in the name of the Empire but with one request: that all of the King's Court convene in his Chamber (minus the maid) for a ..."*

...Now granted this type of vernacular would not be 'acceptable' in the corporate culture of other major cities. But then that's the beauty of California- a land of fertile imagination and freedom to play with convention, and Chad did play…

There was an email he wrote to his female colleague when he learned there were tickets for the *Tonight Show*, guesting Kathy Ireland, Elle Macpherson, Rachel Hunter, and Tori Amos.

> *"P.,*
> *I tried calling you at light speed but no answer, I left a message,*
> *though. It's safe to say you can ice Those tickets, I'm all over*
> *them.*
>
> *Your new best friend, Chad"*
>
> *(20 minutes later)*
>
> *"P.,*
> *I think I love you. I'll be down soon. Bye Darling, Ha, Chad"*

~   ~   ~

All the sympathy cards I received were so unique and individualized, like the one from A.S. She reflected that each one there had such personal memories of Chad. For her, Chad had asked about her background, and she had shared with him that her father is Irish/Scottish and her mother, Filipino/Spanish. And Chad had mentioned, he, too, had a similar background, and he would laugh at what it was like to grow up being different- the pros and cons. But she said she could tell Chad was happy being who he was. However, I think the most important thing she shared was a thought that all of his Carolco friends and colleagues felt. Chad made them assess all their lives, what they may be doing or not and inspired them to live one day at a time – Living Life to the fullest in so many ways, each and every day. She said Chad always had a good word to say to someone, and they all were happy to have the memories and experience.

Everywhere he went he left his unique mark, even on the "Requisition for Supplies List":

- *1 AK47 Cuban made, Russian Designed Assault rifle/Binder*
- *C. A. Butrum*
- *Sideout visors/Killer Loop sunglasses/ K & M sheet protectors,*
- *C.A. Butrum*
- *Huge thick black Binder/1 Stallion For Stud, C.A. Butrum*
- *A lot of Gray envelopes/some grapes and apples with cereal,*
- *C..A. Butrum*

(Psst! Chad loved grapes, as you shall see, from a very early age. Those grapes will be a reoccurring theme.)

~ ~ ~

And a simple post-it he penned to brighten someone's day:

> "*T.,*
> *You know what you are, a breath of Fresh air in a smoke-enshrouded Room. Your that ray of sunshine on a cloudy day, your a dandy lion on a sea of weeds but most of all your my pal. –Chad*"

~ ~ ~

–And this birthday card he gave to a friend… It was like seeing Chad at 5 years old when he learned to read, staring at a 7" historical marker for the longest time and envisioning things we could only imagine. Now, he was 25, looking at a simple photograph on a greeting card, but seeing the world, the texture, the life within it. – It was just the picture of a house in a distant land. Through the windows without glass, birds can be seen in flight amidst a few men in flowing robes who traverse the clay earth. Another square abode lies beyond… It was fascinating what Chad saw and regaled. ~

"C.,

Beautiful picture isn't it, while in India on Caravan (showing property, a real estate inside joke), my entourage pulled off the beaten path for some native cuisine and jungle entertainment. After lunch, called Supper there, I layed down for a catnap, referred to in Holland as 40 winks. When I awoke I was flabbergasted to actually view The Swallows (seen clearly in the photograph) returning to San Juan Capistrano. I was truly taken aback to discover that they flew all the way to India for the winter, though. Notice if you will the "grout" between the cobblestones, the craftsmanship imported from Nepal yet done by Sikhs, off in the distance. You notice Gandhi's compound or Summer House, which when we woke up we swam to and C., I have to tell you, really not all that it's cracked up to be!

Now on to a reality check, you've quite a sense of humor and wow what a laugh you possess. Hopefully, this Birthday will bring you some of the presents you desire and deservedly so...namely a tall, dark and handsome man, named Sir Ivanhoe or Lancelot. You're a big help around here, and may things go smoothly for you, health, spirituality, etc.

Best of Luck,
PS Happy Birthday, C. A. Butrum"

~   ~   ~

And talk about grounding!

"D.,

...and every once in a while, when I need to be reeled back in and grounded, you provide the impetus. Good luck with the working out. I hope you stick with it. Don't forget the voice, you missed your calling, voiceover, DJ, etc. Oh, yea, hope you find a Keven/John Nordic type.

Respectfully, Chad Butrum"

Guys too saved his cards, like his Racing Partner who was about to become a Father:

*"My Dearest Race Partner,
I'm convinced you and I should enter the "Paris to DaKaar-"
Rally with all the miles we logged together. Possibly, an alterna-
tive we could take a jaunt across this great Country of ours,
but you would definitely have to take me through the "Lone
Star State."*

   *Don't forget quickly to enlist a small army of teachers to
train your "Boy" for his entrance into a top-notch Pre-school.
Football, Baseball, and Volleyball will follow as soon as he's
able to walk. It's important to start him early if he's to be a
Leader for the formative years of "5" are essential.*

Best of Luck, Racer-X aka C.A. Butrum

*P.S. Too bad about Nirvana
P.P.S Thanks for granting me Lifetime D.J. rights in your car."*

(You don't think…know they are listening…but they are. I had
mentioned that last sentence, which Chad wrote above, a few times
in his lifetime. He had absorbed it like a sponge, and it became part
of him. And he disseminated it to others when the time was right.)

~ ~ ~

And this lovely missive he wrote which contains one of the tenets
Chad's Foundation is built upon:

"Dancer,

*I think of this often, what am I to do? Your lunches are always
full of errands and such, and I can't get away like I once could.
This is a dilemma which needs to be tackled with all our might.
We need to roll up our shirtsleeves and put some elbowgrease
into it. With the intestinal fortitude of a linebacker wreaking
havoc in the back-field playing with reckless abandon. This
must be our battle cry, "Remember the Alamo," if you will
indulge me. A typhoon of paperwork awaits us. – I say we go
to the lagoon where long walks and sunny days await, where
tropical drinks are the rule of thumb, of course, mine being*

non-alcoholic but you still able to dabble in bohemian libation since I would be driving."

Ivanhoe"

~   ~   ~

Wow, and sending his girlfriend's resume in for a job… If I were the HR recruiter, I think I would have saved this, too, oh my-

"PLEASE TAKE INTO CONSIDERATION THAT WHATEVER MY GIRLFRIEND LACKS IN PROFESSIONAL EXPERIENCE SHE MORE THAN MAKES UP FOR IN ATTITUDE, PERSONALITY, AND PERSEVERANCE. INCIDENTALLY, I'M ASSISTANT TO THE GENERAL COUNSEL FOR 2 YEARS. BEFORE THAT ANSWERED DIRECTLY TO THE VICE PRESIDENT OF POST PRODUCTION. I TELL YOU THIS NOT [TO] EMBELLISH BUT TO MAKE A POINT A RESUME DOESN'T REFLECT EVERYTHING, MINE DIDN'T.

And lastly, Chad had great respect for the Native American ancestors and abhorred the atrocities they had undergone. *Geronimo* was the last film we saw together. I'm glad one of the last pieces of creative writing that he penned to a friend reflected the plight of the 'first keepers of the Land.'

"Broke Neck,

I say yes to the big winds from the North West, they tell of good things to come for long hair and white eyes. It is one of uncertainty yet the shaman say have belief in the Creator and his wise ways, be it not for him there would be no mother planet he wills this union and so do I. "GO to where the two rivers meet in the land of the big sun where the snake reigns supreme, and ask your creature brother whether the deity sides with the redman or white eyes? You and your sister from the North are of the Earth just as the rivers meet to become one, you to will become one. The Valley of the Sun will lead in time of darkness use Tree of Two Branch as a Sceptor to point you in right direction. Ghost Dance of Kiowa Commanche will begin

20

as the bright one closes eye on Creator's land where Buffalo and Bear once lived.'

Crazy Horse
Chief Kiowa Commanche
Northern Texas Territories 1878"

~   ~   ~

"Broke Neck,

I am the one they call CRAZY HORSE a great warrior, the Plains Indian is the greatest light cavalry the world has ever known. I came by my name in battle with the BLUECOATS General Beauregard's men engaged my warriors at sunrise in the Valley of the Big Sky at a place the miners refer to as Hole in the Wall. We defeated the man who spoke with forked tongue, and his scalp adorns my wigwam now. You speak bad medicine for little brave from the North. I am battle tested and will not take lightly your accusation.

I am Crazy Horse Chief of the Comanche from North Texas, I rule my tribe from Texas to Wyoming. Cochise fellow chief of the Kiowa from Kansas to Arizona concurs. The drums of war now beat do not side with the White-eyes. Broke Neck, you are from the great Sioux nation but make no mistake. We will blow in from the South like the lands have not seen before all settlers will be no more, then back will come to the buffalo. We will do away with the Iron-horse that brought the blue coats and settlers. It will be as it was before the time of Big Sun Two Rivers and the snake reigned supreme. I am Crazy Horse who are you."

~   ~   ~

It was as if this little Kingdom that I came upon when the elevator door opened was really a modern-day Kingdom with 21st century players. "R. the Lionheart," was the King and Carolco, the Court – brought back to a time when the court jester, here named Chad, kept everyone in a good mood and the dual poet/scribe delivered missives that people actually kept and treasured. Chad, I loved your Kingdom if it lasted only for a few moments in time – it truly was a Camelot.

CHAPTER 4

The Bridge Days

Somehow the word "Wake" seems foreign to me. It conjures up images of people in the mid–19th century: Men dressed in woolen-suits and women attired in long-skirted dresses of the day. They are either sitting very somber and spiritless in the decedent's home or quite spirited, raising many a pint to honour the Life of their friend/family member in a grand final party of sorts. But for me, this interim period- the prelude to the 'Wake,' was akin to what I call 'The Bridge Days.' It marked a transition point for my Family and me. It was much like an arc-shaped bridge that we would cross together. Holding hands, we felt the rising incline with each step we took, until, finally, we would reach the summit. And, then, we would begin the gradual descent to the other side, to a world that was now forever changed.

In this segment of our passage, there was another word that seemed equally remote, and that was 'autopsy.' Somehow, that seemed more relevant to CSI episodes than to daily Life. However, when I had called the Los Angeles City Morgue to speak to the doctor and order copies of Chad's autopsy, he explained to me why such a procedure was necessary. They just wanted to make sure there had been no foul play, and that Chad had not been hit or hurt. We were all so stunned that a young person who had never consumed a drop of alcohol, smoked a cigarette, or taken drugs his entire Life could just fall down and die. Here was a young, healthy person who exercised, played sports, and had a healthy mental attitude about Life. The only chronic ailment we knew he had as a child and teen was asthma - never a heart problem. Therefore if an autopsy could help to identify the cause, then we wanted it performed so we could have answers. This meant, however, that we would have to wait several days before the actual funeral could take place.

It now seemed we were to continue the journey by ourselves, leaving temporarily behind the comfort of Carolco Friends who would rejoin us at the Wake on Thursday of that week. This time we found it was Chad's Friends and Family who rallied around us - the brothers, Curt and Collin, Maria, Chad's 4-year companion, and myself.

Chad and Maria's apartment was comprised of several rooms in a two-family dwelling located in the San Fernando Valley, a sprawling suburb made up of many smaller communities. *The Valley,* as it is known by Los Angelenos, was located on the other side of the Santa Monica Mountains in the northwestern portion of LA. The gray stucco dwelling where they lived had a long, wooden staircase that led up to their 2nd story apartment. In the open porch that skirted the back portion of their abode, there was the customary barbecue grill that hosted many a party. Chad always loved "HOME," the beauty and comfort it gave his Life, and the stability and anchor it provided. It was one of the most important things to him, and Maria had continued that valued tradition. He always mentioned to me what a beautiful 'home' she had created - "Chad's Sanctuary." It was his cocoon from the world which Maria had made just for him. Of course, he had carved out his own personal touches, like the all-important Sports Closet, which contained nothing but his sports equipment. TV & Sports, and TV & Sports, and let us not forget the film portion – Chad watched John Wayne movies…a lot.

It was here that the Chad saga continued. And I, as a mother, had the privilege of seeing firsthand where her Son lived, loved, and played, and experienced the happiness and challenges of Life. Chad had always kept the souvenir pictures from the trips and escapades he had taken with Maria and her Mom, Joan. Joan was born in England and, as a child, had lived through the frightful bombings of London in World War II. Her entire city was under siege, and she remembered running for the underground shelters the moment the air raid sirens pierced the sky... be it any time of the night or day. You can rest assured that Chad probably knew Joan's entire History from the day she was born; he was the roving reporter of History and heritage, and no one young or old escaped his millions of questions.

Once, he was at Cousin Mike and Donna's home in Northridge playing ball in the backyard. He hit the ball over the fence into the neighbor's yard. –Well, that was a considerable timeout for that game. Finally, one of his friends queried, "Why is Chad talking to that stranger for an hour and a half?" ...Insatiable curiosity he had. There was always something more to know and find out- about every person he encountered.

Once, Joan had sent me a picture that depicted the Hill-Palmer House in Chatsworth, California, where she had taken a trip with Chad and Maria. She had written on the back, "Chad, Maria, & I visited this historic house. We had a great day there. Chad's enthusiasm for History was impressive." His love for the classics, History, and England would be recurrent themes in his Life. When I looked at their bookcase, I noticed a book I had given Chad for Christmas. -This was another custom I initiated when they were very young, to give each of my boys a gift of a book as one of their Christmas presents. (It continues through their adult lives.) This book I had chosen for Chad was about the Civil War, one of his best-loved periods in History. When I opened it and saw what I had written on the title page, I broke again. – I mention this because I have found it is not the expected moments, such as anniversary dates or birthdays, but the zingers from left field that you aren't expecting or prepared for that grab you by the throat and shake your foundation.

But step in friends like Louis Milito and Keven Simmons, true stalwarts of Chad and the Family for many years, submerging their own feelings for the moment to bring levity to the situation. What would Chad want us to do? – He wouldn't want us to be standing around moping, and certainly not crying, so we took to the residential street behind their apartment and played his number one game—baseball. Keven gave the ball to Mamacita (that was what I heard Kev call me), and I pitched a strike, right down the middle! "Will you look at that arm! He called out. HA!" The team was made up of Curt, Collin, Maria, Kevin, Louis, myself, and I think Uncle Eric. – The boys' Grandma Edlund had had a very late baby in Life, which made for a very young uncle the boys could cavort with. This was like stepping into another time capsule of Chad's World: reliving his Life from what he ate for breakfast, what canyon he drove to work, where he played sports, and what he wore from the trendy retro bowling shirts of the day (pressed meticulously of course) to his classic oxford button-down collar shirts and penny loafers.

And after playing a good game of ball, we went to the movies – to see – *The Chad and Maria* videos. And aren't we grateful to the creator of that priceless medium? It allows us to replay the moments of our Lives in perpetuity, again and again, for generations to come. We saw Maria's and Chad's latest assault on Ladyface Mountain, a family trek that began years ago when our family first moved to Agoura. Only now, the brothers were replaced with a partner, "Come on, Maria, you can do it! One foot in front of the other!" There was the hysterical archaeological video reporting of the supposed petrified accouterments of dinosaur parts they found on Anacapa Island. Each of them was holding rounded boulders, and recounting to camera in vivid description what they were... (Today, the pair would have made an exceptionally charming travel-host-duo on the *Travel Channel*.) And then there was the amusing one in which they are displaying their new Halloween costumes. – Chad was "Army Man" in green fatigues, a beret, and army boots, and Maria was "Teenage Enema Nurse" complete with the pole gadgetry. They had even carved the Halloween pumpkin with Chad's birthmark. No surprise in the video, Chad was making Maria late to the Halloween Party because *he* was watching... what else, a John Wayne movie. Yes, Chad was a classic man and, in some ways, a drawback to a very different place and time.

– There was a harrowing video that Chad had taken of the 1992 LA earthquake. The aftermath was devastating, and Chad had gone right into many of the fallen buildings filming up close. Because of the climate, housing in LA is not made of the heavy, durable materials found in the East and Midwest. His video showed piles of floors and ceilings collapsed upon each other like layers of cement pancakes, which had taken much of the Life within them with it. Maria told me later how terrifying it was when the actual event occurred: Chad had wholly covered her with his body. Then in the quaking dark, he guided her to stand under the doorjamb as one is supposed to do during an earthquake. Whilst all around them, they could hear everything falling and shattering to the floor, from the cupboards in the kitchen to the hangings on the walls. I can remember that day trying to reach them, and all the lines were jammed. It was a nerve-wracking time, just as it would be several years later when my sons would be trying to reach me 3,000 miles away on the east coast on another tragic day, 9-11.

But the best and most memorable of the Chad and Maria videos was *The Last Dinner Party* tape. – It depicted the pure happy innocence of young Life living Life: eating, drinking, merriment, tomfoolery, and dancing, one of Chad's best-loved things in Life! What a beautiful sight it was to see Maria and Chad dancing in the kitchen to Sinatra's, *New York, New York*. In Chad's World, one must have music, dancing and, food… and for Chad, his only drink, "Milk."

There is one point in the video, where Chad is rappin' and dancing–while still seated and still chewing on his steak (for *a long time*), and there is a big glass of milk in front of him. Next to that, is his friend's beer bottle. That moment became a 'seminal' moment in time, a moment that would define my Life from that moment on. – I knew instantly what I would do in seeing that image: I would create a foundation that would inspire youth to live as Chad did - vibrantly and with generosity of spirit, without substance abuse - "Healthy Body/Mind/Spirit." The next day I would call Chad's boss, who, after a brief moment, thought of a way to make this a reality. Perhaps the legal corporation that handled all of Carolco's affairs would help us form the structure of the foundation. And they did. They are the first of many Angels that would help us form and implement Chad's very own charitable foundation, *"The Chad Foundation for Athletes and Artists."*

Speaking of Angels, it seems these spiritual beings would always be a part of this journey. For as I lay with my eyes open that night, attempting to sleep, I found my gaze wandering about my Son's bedroom in the dark, stopping at the images of sweet little cherubs that decorated the room in several places. These tiny symbols of love brought comfort, and I was so glad they were there as I looked down and saw the lovely, red-haired Maria, sleeping in the crook of my arm. She had not been able to sleep in their bed since Saturday when Chad left us, and so I, his Mother, slept in his place and cradled his partner in my arm. While my other Sons and their Friends slept in their living room on couches, chairs, and the floor. They were probably unaware they were being comforted by the spirit of their brother and friend that was still present in this room - his home.

It was like that scene in *Oz* when the good witch is spreading her brilliant stardust over the meadow to protect the sojourners. It was as if we, too, were being calmed by some caring, gentle force that abates the gale for a moment to soothe the weary souls of the travelers to close their eyes and sleep. Maybe it was Chad helping us all. For he knew in the broad light of day, especially the next few days, we would all need our maximum greatest sustenance to go through the modern-day Wake, the Funeral Day, and also helping Maria to find her next home. I think she had come to that decision as soon as it had happened. She would not be able to live in their apartment anymore, and without question, we would all help her sort things out. And the brothers would ultimately help her move into another place. As timing would have it, it was near month's end in April, so it was possible to move more easily without added financial duress. The next day would begin the daunting task, a task all of us will face at one time or another. – How does one choose to keep or not to keep that which once belonged to your Loved One and their Life?

In ancient times, a pharaoh's tomb would have held the trappings of the regent's Life in all their splendour… and splendiferous they were. But today, stepping into one's home is like stepping into one's individual Castle. One witnesses the total of their Life, even a young Life who was just beginning to build the foundation of his own house and dreams. What pictures were on the wall? What books on the shelf? What foods to nourish in the cupboard? What did the closets hold behind their closures? And what about your private vault, where lies the personal keepsakes you thought no one else might see? It was here in a simple, business accordion folder of the day where I found the treasures of my 'Son,'- not a gold treasure chest emblazoned with jewels. Yet, these treasures, too, were priceless. –They were the connections of the Soul that we had left each other, an eternal bond between Mother and Child that could never be broken.

I had recently attended a SAGAFTRA screening of the film *Interstellar* and found the storyline intriguing. But it wasn't until Jessica Chastain, the talented leading actor in the film, spoke to us afterward that I began to see the clarity of the film's message unfold. What made this film so exquisitely unique is that the scientific world is starting to acknowledge the extraordinary, inviolable connection that exists between parent and child. And that it is this Love- this infrangible tie is what would save the world. Perhaps it's the only thing that can… for the Love between parent and child is not bound by time or space. -Well, at least that's what I heard her say, and I've never forgotten it since.

I often wondered what the legacy would be that I would leave my children—being an Artist, it did not bode well for the prospects of material wealth… But it was here in this simple, sturdy paper box, replete with pocket dividers- that each new treasure was revealed. Here lay the heart of a mother and child and the riches that they had shared together. The jewels of hope and promise, support and wisdom, forgiveness and flaws, but most of all, unconditional Love.

Among the most precious was an article I had sent him. At the top, it was titled, "Jacki-O Brings Up Two Children…" One of the pictures in the article was of Jackie and her son, John, Jr., walking arm and arm at the Shriver/Schwarzenegger wedding. (That last name will appear again in later chapters.) John, Jr. appeared tall and handsome as ever in his suit and tie, escorting his beautiful Mother. I had inlaid in the magazine article a picture of Chad in his graduation suit and tie, also looking very handsome. At the bottom of the article, I had written, "Chaddie, that picture [of John, Jr.] above reminds me of you." (As I looked at this article today, and as I write the words of this book, I noticed on the envelope in which I sent Chad the letter, there were two stamps of a military man. Of course, that had not been intentional, and I had never noticed it before. Today, I thought let me google this person; maybe it's one of Chad's most-liked generals. The man's name was Alden Partridge. He was not a general but a captain. He had been the first from his birth town, Norwich, Connecticut, to attend the Military Academy.

However, it was the next few sentences that I found absolutely fascinating in his bio. *"It has been said of him by one who knew him well in his youth that he was never known to utter a vulgar or profane word or a by-word, or to use tobacco in any form."*[1] - I had never known anyone to do the above, until my Son, Chad. Although I'm sure there are many more who subscribe to this code, this is the first 'other' name I have read about. Also, Captain Partridge was an educator. His foundational tenet was 'mens sana in corpore sano,' which in Latin means a sound mind in a sound body. The tag-line of Chad's foundation is "Healthy Body/Mind/ Spirit." Well, all I can say is, I guess a very appropriate stamp found its way to his letter. One of Chad's friends told me later, regarding his code of never using any foul language, that once he had offered Chad ten bucks to say the s_ _ _ word. No deal. A girlfriend once told me, she tried to trick Chad by kissing him with some celebratory champagne in her mouth. He spat it out and washed his mouth. – He was a different kind of dude, my Son, Chad… and yet he never tried to impress his code of conduct on any of us.

Then there was a little gem that stuck to my hand when I pulled it out - a crazy little 'sticky note' I had sent him and forgotten all about. It had in the bottom corner, pictures of cartoon dinosaurs with shades on, and on the left side of the note, a palm tree served as the note's border. The line at the top read, "Now You're Playing with the BIG GUYS... & Gals (which I had added). The body of my note read:

> "Dear Chaddie,...One giant 'dinosaur step' for Mommy. We're shooting next week, upstate! Wish you were here, LoveLoveLove Mommy & Maria too."

It was accompanied by the Backstage notice, casting for my screenplay, *Earthen,* which we were shooting some spec scenes from in upstate New York. He had kept it. - He will never know how much that meant to me. Just like his brothers, he was always the greatest supporter of my dreams.

...And perhaps the most meaningful to a Mother, and I hope to a Son, our Family Crown Jewels. Set only in ink and paper, it was a 5 page, single-spaced typewritten letter which I had sent to Chad. Bless his heart, he had saved every page. Being a parent, as we know, is the most arduous role in Life; being a parent on both coasts makes it even more challenging. But like his very sage superior and friend from Carolco wrote, he was glad he told Chad while he was with him. I, too, am so happy I had the foresight and maturity to tell my Son while he was still with me...

> *"Dearest Chad,*
> *...... "growing up" doesn't necessarily mean going to a traditional school for 4 more years, preparing for a traditional job, but what it does mean is "growing on" to different experiences, different people of different backgrounds, skills, countries, different ways of approaching things, doing things –growing away from childhood friends, environs, if necessary. It's always taking/making that 1st step that is the hardest- so make it a fun one. I want to hear that you just pulled into the VA Hospital for an adventure, that you enrolled in an acting class one night a week, that you ventured to take a step, however small, however different.*
>
> *I want nothing more but to see you take that 1st step, just as I saw your 1st step in walking, this is your 1st step in "Living." Take that 1st step, and you're Home free! No matter how many times you fall down, or go down a path that leads nowhere,*

31

you'll always get back up again – because you'll love that new-found sense of freedom, of walking, exploring, venturing out in the world on your own, all by yourself with no one holding your hand. Go at your own pace, but take the bulls by the horn, Taurus, and put that foot FORWARD ON NEW GROUND!

You come from strong stock, Chad, and a rock foundation. The house may no longer be there, but the foundation is-for Life, yours, mine, your children, and theirs. – My legacy to you and your brothers is the foundation I built. It's there for you and will see you through whenever you need to use it.

And lastly, do you remember how bad I felt when I slapped your little face that time in St. Louis when you told your relative she got fat, AND how inside I told you how I had been so wrong and I promised you I would never do that to you again. I would never be disloyal to my child. Well, this long, long epistle is just to remind myself of that, and the promise I made to myself AND TO YOU. ....BUT he's 20! But he should be..... and my answer is my Son is not a robot or a pre-fab mold, but he is a very special individual, a unique human being who grows at his own rate. And I'll support and nurture and wait for him, and be there waiting, nurturing and supporting every new leaf. And one day, it will become a great big beautiful tree that I can sit under in awe of how this little seed that grew in my tummy became this magnificent human being. With care and Love and courage and risk, it became a beautiful thing of its own – a Chad, no one else in the world like it.

Let this be a well-needed shower of sunshine and Love for the tree that is the most special tree to me in the whole world because it is my 1st!

I love you Chad, Forever,
Mom"

It was here in his personal vault that Chad left the key to his heart for his Mother to find. It was here in this simple, stucco domicile that Chad's Brothers, Family, and Friends saw the light and love of an everyday young American preparing for Life. It was apparent by the treasures that he saved - that he Loved, and Honoured his Mother and Father, his Brothers, the core of his existence …and his surrogate families in the later years. He learned about the exterior existence- canyons, and mountains, and athletics, and how to be a Man from his Father. He learned about the interior landscapes – Spirit, Morals, Art/Culture, and the care of mind/body and soul from his Mother. He learned about Life-long companionship and joy and the meaning of the word "brother" from his two brothers, Curt and Collin. He learned about Love and Partnership, and Man and Woman from his 4-year companion, Maria. He learned about enduring Friendship, the meaning of camaraderie, and the special bond of men through Friends for Life: Louis, Keven, Sean, and Michael, who would bear him on their shoulders, along with his brothers to the next world. We, each of us, took something special from Chad's last home on Earth. Before we closed that door forever on this ordinary young man's chamber, we filled ourselves with the treasure chest of memories and mementos to fill our minds and spirits for all the days to come.

We were reaching the arc of the 'Bridge' and soon would we begin the final descent, but there was one more door we had to go through before the "Sun/Son" would rise, and that was the, appropriately named, "Wake." The building that housed this door was cream-colored, as I recall, with dark-brown wooden trim, kind of like the Tudor architecture, which we all felt such a kinship to. It was warmer in invitation than most facades which housed a commercial establishment. Like so much of the journey had been, it was as if we were stepping off of some unseen conveyance vehicle that knew the stopping points without being told.

The most striking thing that met your eyes as you first entered was the astonishing profusion of flower arrangements! I have only been to a few funeral parlors in my lifetime, and they had seemed to have let's say, 10 to 20 floral arrangements per room. Here, in the foyer alone, there must have been 30 to 40 floral arrangements. Looking down the hallway, you could see there were baskets of multi-colour flowers of every size lined up against one entire wall. Non-ending, it went all the way to the exit sign at the far end of the building. Every room was filled with 40 to 50 arrangements– sitting on desks, the floor, standing proudly on their tripod stands.

The chapel, too, was abundantly laden with flowers from the altar to the rafters, and the circular floral arrangements were placed between every pillar and pew, almost as if they were standing guard. The Director of the parlor told me later, they had been in business since 1940, and this was the most flowers they had ever received in their History. – They even had celebrity funerals here, but never this profusion of flowers. He told me he finally had to inform people not to send any more flowers. They were already giving the surplus away to every home or hospital they could think of. – It was the beautiful send-off humankind provides when they must send one of their own off way before his time… in the blossom of his youth. – Perhaps that's why there were so many full-grown flowers….to represent all the years there would have been… Chad's Father was the President of a radio advertising firm that represented 250 stations across the U.S. I think it would be safe to say that close to 250 stations, if not all, sent their floral respects. I would also say that they all sent their respects to a Father whom they knew loved his Sons.

As my foot entered one doorway, I saw friends from Carolco and Chad's boss, and I think again, the President of the studio. When I mentioned how awestruck we were by the magnitude of flowers, he pointed out the gift from Carolco. It was breathtaking; it must have been nearly 4 feet high. It was delicately arrayed in smaller white flowers that found their way to the very base of the arrangement in the most natural way as if they were emanating from the ground– no vase in sight. But I think it was the way the various branches swerved and swiveled to specific points that gave it almost a Japanese feel and made it so unique. R. told me also in *The Daily Variety*, they had left Chad a gift from them. It was a full-page ad that read, "We Love you, Chad, and we'll miss you! Love your Friends from Carolco."

It is a great honour to be held in esteem by those colleagues with whom you work daily, 50 weeks a year: building, creating, doing battle, laughing, and being a part of your own community. If Chad could lift the visor of each person, see and touch their soul for just a few moments, recognize it, say a few choice words, pen a personal missive, exchange genuine energy from the heart's place, maybe that is enough to last a lifetime, to make a difference in a Life. –The trade paper, *Daily Variety*, is a publication major studios use to promote their most important and expensive films and film stars. —And here was a full-page tribute to my Son, Chad, my 1st little boy, with the bright eyes and unfailing smile and overly curious nature. He had befriended a Court of loving, creative people who reciprocated with their own Love – during his very first step of adulthood. I could never be prouder of you, my Son, and these dear new Friends who had come to love you in their own way and were helping me and your Family say goodbye to you…

Here – at this moment to come - is where the steps were always leading. In your half-real state of mind, you are probably not consciously aware that the human body is a miraculous entity of protective mechanisms. In its most critical moments, it can go into a state of shock and not be fully aware of the pain that would kill it. Looking back, I can say, it was the living of my entire Life that prepared me for this moment: A spiritual quest and subsequent growth of the soul for the past 20 years. Trauma and survival in one's own Life from childhood on, as many of us face. Watching the First Lady of our country enduring the loss of her husband, our President, as she faced the nation holding the hands of her two small children with such grace and dignity -even as a schoolgirl, I could not understand how she could do this.

Any more than I could understand what my former mother-in-law was saying to me a few days before, as she had taken a gentle but firm hold of both of my arms. And holding me at arms-length, she said, "You must be very strong. – This is going to take a *long* time for you to get over…" I was looking at her directly in the eyes. I heard what she was saying, but that day I felt like I was five years old and was not fully comprehending her words. – And in a very real sense, I was five, because she had already gone very far into that journey and then some. She had lost her young husband from polio at the very same age she was now burying her 1st grandson. She knew exactly what those words meant… I was just a fledgling taking the first step.

I wasn't sure I was going to- going to be able to view my Son, and no one would say a word to me one way or the other. It was my Son, Curt, whose words convinced me. We were now standing in front of the edifice; many people were around, most people I had never met. Curt had a fever and was getting sick. He was going back home. I remember as a boy, he often might get a fever when he was upset, or there was an excitable incident; it seems that was his body's way of coping. This night, he said, "Mom, [it's okay] Chad looks like he's sleeping…" It was those words from his brother and my middle Son that gave me the courage to say goodbye to my Son, Chad.

–And he was right, it was as if Chad were sleeping; the look on his face, so peaceful. It's as if you had looked in on your child, and a smile would come to your lips as you quietly brought the door to, not wanting to disturb. The things you remember: his long lashes that touched his cheeks and that glorious, dark flowing hair, and the pristine baseball uniform that he would go to Heaven in. He loved baseball best of all. Dimaggio and Mickey Mantle were on his wall at Carolco… maybe just waiting to see him, kinda like *Field of Dreams*. One of his friends at Carolco had asked me to pin a little angel to Chad's shirt, which I did, with my own. I was also going to put inside the casket a picture of Chad and his two brothers sitting on a hill in Wheaton, Illinois. I had written on it. (I thought I would have a chance the next day… I wouldn't. The casket would be closed. I guess I was meant to keep this picture… However, I learned later that one of Chad's friends wanted to put a particular ball in with Chad. – The funeral director made sure that was possible.)

A few months later, one of Chad's best friends and I were talking on the phone, and he made mention that he thought I would have been more upset [crying]. I had been in shock, a protective shield I had learned to have a long time ago, and tears were not a part of its fabric. But I think myself also knew deep within, the inklings of what my mother-in-law was trying to tell me, I would have an entire lifetime to deal with this; there was no hurrying the process… My soul knew I would have the rest of my Life to mourn.

However, the state of shock does strange things to you. I remember I was greeting everyone and thanking them for coming. Whenever I saw a guest kneeling in the pews who was apparently upset, I brought him or her a rose from Chad. One young man broke down when I gave it to him. – There was nothing I could do to comfort him. When I looked around, besides our relatives and longtime friends of Chad, whom I knew, there were so many more of every age, heritage, and orientation that I didn't know. Chad had always loved *all* people – and they were *all* coming this day to pay their respects.

Chad's youngest brother, Collin, stood like a centurion at his brother's casket all night. Dressed in his double-breasted suit, he reminded me of a young Tom Cruise. All of my Sons took me to see my 1st Cruise movie, and we shared many after that. That's what we did: films in LA – theatre in NY. How was this going to work now, with one missing? … This was going to be a very long road.

Every culture has its traditions, its rituals. What I know with Chad, as sensitive and empathetic as he was, there was a reserve and dignity that I know we all respected. His brother, Curt, had a dream once that he was next to his bedside, and he was crying, and he looked up, and Chad was awake, "You're crying??? Go over there and sit! No crying." - So even in the peaceful place he now sleeps, he gives us the courage to be strong.

CHAPTER 5

Son/Sun

...And so finally we made it across the long, formidable bridge. We endured the tempests that paralyzed us; were eased by the kindness of strangers who welcomed us along the way, and, now, we arrived at the place we had avoided since the moment it happened. It was The Sun that stood tall that day and greeted us with an exceedingly beautiful California day. So high and bright was it that it lit the entire sky - a cerulean blue which lay a path for the gods to welcome their young warrior home.

As our car made its way to St. Charles Borromeo Church, I remember passing the last apartment I lived in L.A. It was on Moorpark Street- just blocks away from the church where Chad would last be remembered. Chad had helped me assemble my 4 poster bed in that apartment. – Every street would now hold a memory as the tires touched its pavement carrying us through a thoroughfare that had been a daily artery of our lives. This was also the church where Chad had stood on these very same steps as Best Man…at Louis and Veronica's wedding. Then I recollect the faint sounds of the bagpipes assailing my senses as we neared the church. The sounds increasing as we drew closer as if he, the Bagpiper, knew – step up the pipes, the 'Family' is drawing near.

I remembered at some point on the plane suddenly turning to Carl and asking him if we could have a Bagpiper, and we could, as evidenced by this man standing as a guardian at the entrance of the

Church. He was attired in his traditional plaid kilt and playing this wonderfully unique instrument to announce to all the reverence and honour of this occasion. I had never forgotten that lone piper that greeted us at the funeral of Carl's Uncle Pete in Detroit. He stood at the iron-gate to welcome us, dressed in full regalia befitting a Scotsman coming home. But it was the haunting melody of his tunes filling the air that heralded his presence long before we saw him. I felt the same seeing and hearing his kinsman this day. The Bagpiper is said to have a military origin and his instrument- not that of a king but of an ordinary man. And Chad sharing a Scots-Irish heritage, it should be this countryman at the gate to welcome and receive him. Now, I felt a huge sense of relief; I knew we could begin. The Gatesman was at his post.

As we waited in the entry of the church, Carl had asked if I had my remarks in readiness… and though try as I might the last few days, I could not find the words I wanted to say, and so I deferred to the Father this privilege. It would take another month for me to collect and organize, and write those words I was unable to say that day but so wanted to. I wanted to especially thank Chad's Friends and Colleagues from Carolco for all they had given me in sharing their private words and keepsakes from Chad, and, in June, I would send them a smaller version of what I write here. –It was titled, *The Chad Book – the Younger Years*, so they could also come to know the Chad they never got to meet – young Chad.

That day, as I looked back from the front pew where the Family sat, I saw every seat filled, and the boys' Uncle Eric would tell me later, he had looked at the sign on the wall and the church was filled to its 600 seat capacity. And when we left the church, it was overflowing with additional guests waiting outside all the way to the street. St. Charles Borromeo Catholic Church in North Hollywood had been filled to capacity, just as the Wake had been inundated with flowers right to the back door. I would learn later that for all intents and purposes, Carolco had closed the studio that day because everyone wanted to attend Chad's service.

Chad's Aunt Lisa, with a lovely voice, sang the service from the church balcony. She told me afterward that at one point, the organ player had leaned over and whispered to her, "Who was he—a Senator?" I, his Mother, answered that query silently, "Yes, a young 'informal' Senator" (I told him he would make a great Politician...) -who wore not a suit but a baseball and football uniform. He Loved Life, and cared about People—all people: Black, White, Yellow, Red, 'cool,' 'nerds,' Presidents, janitors, young, old, Native American, or recent immigrant, 1-month-old or 100."

His Father gave a fine speech befitting the Life of his first-born child. He always was an eloquent speaker and had taken JFK's speech, "Ask not..." to the regional finals in Michigan. –It should be his rightful place to give the eulogy to those who were paying tribute to his Son. One thing I remember was the humour – when he regaled how Chad had once turned his house (which was up for sale in Toluca Lake) into a "Wiffle ball stadium," as evidenced by the hundreds of ball marks on the ceiling. That brought the levity needed as everyone seemed to know Chad's all-consuming passion for sports, and one could hear a genuine gust of laughter crescendo throughout the church.

As the service ended, the pall of the inevitable began to suffuse the spirit of all, even as the sun continued to shine gloriously. But it was the image of Chad's brothers, Curt and Collin, his Uncle Eric, and his best friends, Louis, Sean, Kevin, and Robbie carrying their brother, friend, warrior, and sportsman down the aisle that will always remain in my heart's vision. It would eventually find its way to Chad's website in a classic poem:

To An Athlete Dying Young

The time you won your town the race
We chaired you through the market-place;
Man and boy stood cheering by,
And home we brought you shoulder-high.

Today, the road all runners come,
Shoulder-high we bring you home,
And set you at your threshold down,
Townsman of a stiller town.

-A.E. Houseman 1896

The moment was at hand… the blur began. I cannot remember the trip, and although the conveyor belt remained invisible, its motion was felt with every revolution the tires made. I remember someone telling me later there were so many cars waiting to go the cemetery that the CHP (California Highway Patrol) actually had to stop traffic on the Ventura Freeway to allow all the vehicles to gain access through the down ramp.

After a small measure of time, this indistinct haze gained immediate clarity as my foot stepped onto the ground of the cemetery, the sky boundless blue without a cloud. The sun reigning so high, it was not easily seen; only its presence felt everywhere—quiet, perfect, and non-assaultive. The sound, too, changed appreciably; it was as if my foot hit some unseen lever as it made contact with the pavement. For as the car door shuts, one is aware of nothing but the ubiquitous stillness of peace. There is nothing like it. Even the chirping of the birds and all the sonance of nature seem more reverent in this environment.

It was something in my peripheral vision that instantly caused my head to turn. –It was a small chapel across from the gravesite with a spiring steeple that looked like the Minutemen Church in Boston. How Chad would love this, especially with his knowledge and zeal for History. Curt and his then-girlfriend had been on a Sunday drive a few weeks prior and found themselves meandering the winding, gently rising roads of this very cemetery. He noted this very landmark and the one above which housed a historical mosaic of grand proportions recounting the American Revolution. Both edifices were nestled at the foot of the Hollywood Hills, and so when this sudden tragedy struck, Curt would approach his Father and ask if Chad could be buried here. – He had found the perfect final resting place for his brother, never realizing what he was looking at that day, and it just so happened that that particular place still had plots remaining. A Sunday Drive in the cemetery was something they had never done before.

I must say with an apology, I do not remember the words spoken by the kind clergyman who officiated the ceremony that day. In all fairness, he would have needed some voice enhancing instrument to be heard by all. For on that beautiful 28th day of April day, anno 1994, perhaps close to 300 steadfast Friends and Family gathered on this very plot of Earth to pay tribute to young Chad Alan Butrum. I have not attended many funerals in my Life, but always remember it was a small gathering of friends and Family, 20 to 30 people huddled near the gravesite. Here, for this moment, it looked as if we had taken over a good portion of the cemetery. A bountiful, mass of guests, 7, 8, 10 deep, perhaps a quarter size of a football field came to say their goodbyes. –And yet it looked so natural. It was truly a Circle of Love that no one wanted to leave, even after the priest had completed the ceremony.

Finally, Sharen suggested to Collin to distribute some of the baskets of flowers to friends and Family throughout the circle, and maybe that would be a signal that the service had ended. But for another long while, people did not especially receive that message and continued to linger, not wanting to end this moment... The enormous Love felt for their Friend that emanated from that gathering was like a bond of unity no one wanted to break. There were no photos taken; it was not spoken about, but for everyone who attended, they had their own camera's eye that will make this an unforgettable, personal moment of Love, Respect, and saying Goodbye.

Perhaps because all knew there would be one more stop to gather and talk and reminisce, the gentle unweaving of the circle eventually began. Many began making their ways to cars parked a long distance off. Most would find their way to the Reception following, hosted by our dear Family Cousins, Mike, and Donna, in their copious home in Northridge. Their home even housed several out of town guests: – My stepfather had flown in from Michigan; all the boys loved Grandpa

Payne. He was the funny grandpa who never forgot their birthdays, and who taught them all how to fish (including their mother); Chad's Grandma Edlund who also told me later she was so glad to have Chad spend some time with her one-on-one, and Mr. B. B., Carl's 1st boss, who had met our boys when they were 3, 4 and 5. When Chad's Foundation was up and running, Mr. B. B. never missed a year for his gift donation until he left us a few years ago. It is special people like these in your Life that will help get you through the tsunamis that rage unexpectedly- without season; it is they who become your lifeline.

Then, it was as if an instant Fade out and Fade in took place - as if we never left Chad's final resting place. The sun disappeared and reappeared again. And somewhere in between the blank spaces of the transition, it was if time and place stopped and only our clothes had been replaced. There was a strange, beautiful coda to this journey… which was not ending yet … and perhaps it never would. –Today it was Chad's birthday, one day after his funeral – much too tender a moment not to acknowledge… in some fashion. In fact, Chad had prepared all of his co-workers for his special day, and had written in his Superior's computer calendar:

> *"Friday, April 29th*
> *REALLY BIG AND MOMENTOUS OCCASION FOR TODAY IS THE DAY CHAD ALAN BUTRUM WAS BORN IN GROSSE POINTE FARMS COTTAGE HOSPITAL, 12:30 PM. TREMENDOUS GARGANTUAN CELEBRATORY FESTIVAL OF FOOD COLOSSAL FEAST AT VIVA LAS VEGAS YOUR ENTIRE ENTOURAGE TO ACCOMPANY"*

It ended up that all of Chad's friends at Carolco kept that birthday luncheon date, and I'm sure they had the best time they could muster because that would have made Chad happy.

Our birthday party assembled at the gargantuan garden of flowers, now covering Chad's gravesite. –Why it was nearly as big as my studio apt. in NY, 18 x 14 feet! It was indeed more beautiful than a typical garden because amongst the array of flowers of every colour and kind, were interspersed huge red ribbon bows, looking so natural as if they too were growing freely in this mini-conservatory. Gardens have spaces in between the flowers; this garden had no spaces, only flowers. Think of a florist shop in its entirety dropped from the sky onto this plot; now, you have a picture.

It took all of us a few minutes to absorb the sheer size and breadth of the site. Then one of us saw someone had beat us there and left a present. It was planted right in the middle of the garden: Chad's favourite – a carton of milk and green grapes (that habit started very early!) It was as if that visitor had gone to a florist shop and said, "Yes and the centerpiece will be a brand new half-gallon carton of milk… because that's all that Chad drank. And then work in a pound of grapes in a creative fashion …. because those were his favourite. Add plenty of fresh-cut flowers… he loved those, too. It's for his birthday." That was a well-thought-out gift… and left by a special Friend who knew Chad very well. Thank you for that birthday present; I know that made Chad happy, and I still have the picture I took of it.

To those who knew Chad, they would not be surprised he still had sway over us, wherever he might be. – And after all, it was his birthday, so to celebrate one of the brothers brought a baby nerf football and, well, we just wanted to play a small tribute game on our knees… And it was a part of the cemetery with just green grass and not many plots yet. So brothers Curt and Collin, Maria, myself, Lissa, (a longtime family friend from the sons' high school years who had flown all the way from Connecticut) Louis, who often called Chad the brother he never had, and young Uncle Eric took to our knees for a few quiet spirals and catches. - But the 'win one for the Gipper' game was short-lived for a groundskeeper we didn't see but who saw us came over and told us we shouldn't really be doing this.

One of the brothers apologized and told him about the special birthday celebration. – Musta sounded kind of lame… this was a cemetery... And boy was I glad I looked like one of them, dressed in one of my Son's sweatpants (have no idea how they were being held up), one of Chad's flannels, and his "A" ballcap. We all apologized profusely and got off our knees. Then something very strange happened: the faraway lilts of a Bagpiper could be heard as though coming from the distant hills. –We all looked at each other at first... Are the heavens opening and Chad sending us music for his birthday?? Or are we just hallucinating... There wasn't another funeral taking place within the eye's sight. Uncle Eric, the tall, blonde Nordic-Scot, led the charge to follow the sounds of the music, and some of the fellows went off to accompany him on the search.

Meanwhile, another guest had arrived, and she was standing on the rise a few feet away from Chad's grave, having her own private moment. With the towering Hollywood Hills behind her and another brilliant azure sky painting the day, it was quite a picture: she holding a single red flower, and her face reflecting some heart-felt memory she would cherish forever. She shared that singular, precious moment with us. She had written Chad a letter once in high school, and the letter she took from her wallet that day was the same letter Chad had written to her in response. Incredibly, he had written it on April 29th, his birthday, maybe 8 years earlier. Amazingly, she still carried it in her wallet...

As we were reflecting, another visitor approached us, tentatively. She had been visiting another gravesite, but she just had to ask about this incredible bed of flowers that were nearly two feet deep! "Was it a whole family who had perished? Or a celebrity?" "No," I answered, "It was my son, a young athlete who died suddenly while playing football." Then she told me something surprising pointing to a rise on the hill nearby. "There was a young football player that attended a college in the Midwest, and something similar happened to him. His grave is up there, he was 21 or so... I think his Father was a Dr. at some university here." I thanked her and told her, "Please, take as many flowers as you like..." She did depart with a few baskets of flowers on her arms, once again offering her sympathies.

We ambled up the rise and found the young man's grave, so very sad... Somehow it brought comfort to know he would now have a big brother right down the hill. ... I would try and contact that Father after I returned to New York. Our sons seemed to have suffered a similar fate, and for the moment, I had not a concrete reason why.

I saw another Lady looking at all the flowers and bid her take some if she'd like, as many as she wanted. I could not count how many flowers made up that garden. We, each of us at one time or another, found ourselves comforted by this coverlet of flora that transported Chad to Heaven as we lay or sat upon it.

Then, if there were not enough surprises– on the horizon, cometh Uncle Eric and our entourage accompanied by the BAGPIPER who was dressed in full regalia. They had found him yonder (a Chad word) in the hills playing for another person's funeral. But when our search party told him about young Chad and it being his birthday, the fine gentleman didn't think twice but accompanied our party over several small hills and dales. He wanted to pay homage to the young man by playing, especially for him. And he did - 3 lovely, brilliant songs just for Chad. He, in the attire of the Highlands Scot: a kilt of brown and blue tartan pattern, with black weskit and unique hat, a sporran pouch decorated in fur, replete with knee-high white socks, and the traditional ghillie shoes with long laces that wrap around the ankles. And we, dressed in our California nerf playing attire, stood at enrapt attention as the extraordinary sounds of the bagpipe filled the air and the neighboring hills, paying tribute to our Son, our Brother, our Partner, our Friend, our Athlete. There could not have been a more beautiful celebration for Chad's birthday. That day we did take remembrance pictures, and as the Bagpiper played his soulful melodies, we see behind him the exact replica of the Old Church in Boston with its single white spire and brick edifice. This symbol heralded the birth of a country in Paul Revere's famous ride. Chad so loved the History of our country; it was meant to be that this would be his final resting place on Earth.

And as my Family and I took deep umbrage in this blanket of flora that all of you weaved together for us, we also took comfort in each other, and I remember one time Maria was laying utterly prostrate, face down on all the flowers. – There was ample room for all of us, and I have a picture with my hand laying gently on her back.

…And as I lay flat on my back upon the vast carpet of garlands and bouquets that was for the moment my Son's private garden, I was completely at peace. I was feeling a tremendous warmth and essence of Chad beating down on my face, filling my being through the sunbeams that day –April 29th, 1994, his birthday: And I felt another "birth" taking place... As I had birthed my fair Son to Earth 26 years ago, I was now, as I lay with him filling my being, birthing my great, fair Son to Heaven 26 years later - to the Home from where he first came and must return. The Home from where we all came… and must return. On his birthday, April 29th, Chad's "Circle of Life" was complete…and that glorious golden cord of Life that was made in and led to Heaven returned Home, and can never be broken.

I have been blessed by two beautiful Sons to remain on Earth with me while their Big Brother does God's work in Heaven. And I/ We have the Love and Comfort and Prayers and Friendship from all of you, who Loved my Son whom he Loved. As we saw each other last … 300 of his Friends who gathered to see him off … in a grand "Circle of Love" – it will always be- with Chad, as the Heart at the center. – A Heart so grand, it belonged in and to Heaven!

"To My Son, Chad's Dear Friends: who gave/shared so much of yourselves, your Love with me and my Family these past weeks; who shared your intimate moments, and private letters and cards, and beautiful tributes, thank you. It was the most precious gift to a Mother and a Father – to know their Son in the later years by the people he Lived, Loved, and Played with on a daily basis. And because one of his best friends who was with Chad to the very last, thanked me for sharing 'the young Chad' with him–the Chad he never knew… And because Chad so Loved to hear *the younger stories* – "Mom, tell 'em how I _____," I thought I might share Chad with you in the following chapters as a small token of my Love and Appreciation, the Chad you never knew. They are a Mother's private, precious moments…for I knew his Soul as my own—and once that extraordinary bond was fused, it is forevermore - "Chad, A Celebration of Life…"

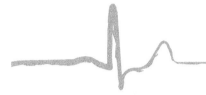

CHAPTER 6

The Early Years –
Detroit, Michigan

It was a sunny, spring day in April, the 29th to be exact, which heralded the day that Chad Alan Butrum would make his debut into the world. He came a few weeks early, and it was a long labour. – Well, what did I know at 18 years old, you're like the- no you are the 'fool or jester,' just diving in, not knowing what to expect. But knowing you are in the hands of a good family doctor who delivered the rest of your husband's siblings, it gives you confidence that you and your baby will also be fine. Where Chad was born was a lovely, old 'cottage setting': The Cottage Hospital, in Grosse Pointe Farms, Michigan, not far from the St. Clair River and all the old manors from the Ford Estate and the like. They lay hidden well ensconced by great gates of foliage on the riverfront. Chad would like that, especially with his love for ancestry and tradition, which would walk with him all the days of his Life.

There were some minor complications, however, and Chad's Father wouldn't be able to hold his first-born son for 10 days. He was a bit concerned too about his son's very flat forehead - but you see, there is a reason why it is so malleable. It has to get through sometimes very narrow canals before reaching its final destination. I also wondered why, as the youngest mother in the ward, I was shuffling like a stooped-over elderly person every time my husband and I walked to the nursery window to see our baby. It may come as no surprise to many of you that Chad made his entrance into the world with a "big bang," pioneering and paving the way for his brothers, Curt and Collin...soon to follow. Or as Chad would unabashedly announce later in Life, "Tell 'em how I broke your tailbone, Mom..." He was quite proud of that feat- and so am I, for I was breaking ground for an exceptionally unique human being.

Our first environs were modest, depending on how you look at it. We rented the 3rd floor of my in-laws very large, stately home in a beautiful, quaint place called Indian Village. It was a historical placemark in the city of Detroit, just bordering the Grosse Pointes. Here, back in the day, the most prominent elite of the city lived there, such as Edsel Ford. The grand homes were complete with maids' quarters, the butler's pantry, and doors opening to formal dining rooms and separate libraries. Today, however, Indian Village is the home of artists and artisans, discerning professionals and entrepreneurs that restore and maintain the dignity and character of each home's particular beauty. The residents have made it a unique oasis skirted by an otherwise not so desirable part of town. Their house had a stucco façade with a sloping roof that reminded me so of the hue and allure of the Cotswolds in the English countryside. I had always had a great fascination for that historic land beyond the pond, and it would filter through to my children during the years, especially Chad.

But that April day, when baby Chad and I made it up to the 3rd floor, we were greeted by such a celebratory sight. Chad's Father had taken such care in streaming crepe paper in blue and white all over the ceilings, and he had hung a special sign that said, "Welcome Home Chad!" It was here in these tiny accommodations, where I cooked in the alcove on a dual electric hotplate and washed the dishes in the bathroom sink, which was quite accommodating being the original porcelain sink. In fact, it was quite large with separate spigots for the hot and cold water. It was here I nursed my first-born child and learned to be a Mother while Father worked at GM (General Motors) during the day and studied pre-law at night at Wayne State University. His father, Carl, Sr., had been on his way to becoming an up-and-coming attorney when polio struck him at the young age of 26 years and took his Life – the same age that this baby I held in my arms would join the grandfather he never had the chance to meet. Chad's father was only 4 when his father died, but he always wore his father's ring with pride, which had the same initials, C. A. B. That ring was meant to go to Chad, the first-born son, who now bore these initials as would his brothers.

I had worked very long into my pregnancy as an Executive Assistant to the president of a Graphic Arts company so we could save for our own little bungalow. Think Clint Eastwood's movie, *Gran Torino,* well come to think of it, I think that film was shot in Detroit.

Yup, Clint got it just right – traditional Detroit bungalow: brick façade; 5 stairs leading to a railed front porch; and a narrow driveway leading to a one-car garage with a backyard, the size of a footprint of the house.

Asking price, $12,500, huh? You couldn't buy a car for that today. Factor in the upstairs dormer and separate entrance for a bachelor renter at $124 a month, and you just got a great deal–mortgage payment $44.00. Boy, would we need it considering our family would blossom into 5 members within 3 years.

But it was here at the Evanston house that Chad was sole King and had the run o' the castle for a whole 18 months... and they were memorable. He showed his hand quickly. He came into the world, 'athletic,' and could be seen doing pushups on all fours at the age of 3 months old. Really, I still have the picture.

And Chad's omnipresent creative ingenuity became evident not too long after that – about 8 months old. He would rock his crib back and forth (on all 4's), inching across the wooden floor until it reached the other side of the room where his dresser was. Then he would ceremoniously open all the drawers, pull out all his clothes, and throw them on the floor... He was very goal-oriented at an early age. This became a daily part of his regimen when he awoke from his nap.

A neighbor might be visiting, sitting in the living room, enjoying her coffee and cake (home-baked... I did that back then), when all of a sudden, a steady creaking noise would make itself known, and it did not abate. As after all, I was quite used to it, I made no reference to it. However, as it went on for several minutes, the neighbor was forced to say, "What is that??" "Oh, just Chad…" I said, smiling matter-of-factly. "He's just making his way across the room. - Would you like to see"? The neighbor, quite curious now, followed me to Chad's room, and as we slowly opened the door, Chad is revealed in his determined glory.

He has reached his destination on all fours, and now has pulled himself up to the corner of his crib, opened each of the top dresser drawers, pulled all the clothes out, and thrown them on the floor, completing his ritual post-nap workout. Following the eyewitness account, the neighbor's eyes fell to my belly bump, and I could see by her look, she was certainly glad she wasn't me.

First-time mother, scary. Poor first-child, why I was going to teach him to read at 8 months old. I had found a program that said it was possible– use big pieces of paper sporting words like 'daddy,' 'mommy,' 'car,' and 'apple' on them. Show one word to the child many times. Why, he was a genius, got them all right. The only problem is your child is visualizing that particular configuration of squiggly letters as the word.

However, when your child gets to school and starts learning to read, it's taught phonetically. The sounds of each letter comprise the word. Chad had a terrible time learning to read, and, of course, I blame it on my super enthusiasm to have a super child. Chad's brothers were spared the confusion.

He also had a discerning palate as a tot and once from his high-chair handed his plate to his Father, "Here, Carl, you eat this." But in the main, he was a very healthy, happy eater. This trait would follow Chad and his brothers to their own households later in Life as they would need the most particular ingredients or condiments to make their best-liked foods, often traditional family favourites. When I introduced Chad to lamb chops, he asked me where they came from. I answered a lamb. He looked at his plate again and said, "Thank you, little lamb…" I never looked at lamb again without thinking about that.

Chad also loved music. From quite an early age, he could be heard breaking into song, full-throated, crib-side, "CELIA, YOU'RE BREAKING MY HEART!" Often, this was meant to serenade other surprised guests, who thought he'd been asleep for hours. It's almost as if he were waiting for a particular lull in the conversation before he would insert his musical talent, so as not to interfere with adult conversation…just enhance it, fill in the pauses. He was always a polite child.

I thought, too, for a few moments… make that many moments, I might have a baby Picasso on my hands. One morning I ventured into the living room to bring his orange juice when I encountered him painting his little Mexican straw chair with oatmeal, using his spoon as a paintbrush. And then, looking at the TV, I realized why, there was Mr. Rogers, as in Mr. Rogers Neighborhood painting on a canvas propped on an easel.

His choice of mediums grew as did he, becoming quite interesting, to say the least. Something else was growing, too, the baby bump! And soon after, I could be seen spiffing up the room for the new baby to come and had been putting a fresh coat of something on the floor to make it shiny. - Several days later, I came in after Chad's nap, and he wasn't in his crib. I spied him on his chubby little knees creatively applying *Vaseline* all over the floor with his industrious little hand while sporting his signature sparkling smile. Now 16 months old and exuberant with his accomplishment, he announces, "Chiney, mama."

Ay! Just not what a pregnant woman wants to be cleaning up on her hands and knees.

But the coup de grace of the budding Da Vinci came on a day very close to the next baby brother's arrival into the world. Chad, still enmeshed in the nuances of potty training, was taking a bit too long for fatigued mama, and so I said, "Darling, just do your business in there (a la portable potty). Then hop up on mama's bed when you're finished; mama has to go lie down on the couch."

Ah, yes, and after that refreshing nap, the renewed young mother, about-to-be mother of two, cheerily opens the bedroom door, only to find a new Chad 'masterpiece' awaiting her in their 'master bedroom.' The medium was breathtaking... literally. It came from what was readily at hand- in the pot, which the baby artist helped produce himself. – And not a mere small painting was it, but a full-on 'Installation Art.' Not only was it all over the walls from whence, a 17-month old arm could reach, but also decorating the furniture. And of course, a baby tricycle had to be in the room, and we just had to try some of this new material inside the handlebars...

I must have slept a loong time, for this was a 'major project.' I shut the door quietly and quickly; and, it took everything I had to clean up the baby artist and not become, you know, ill over the adult size potty. This was, indeed, the "Time" for the call to Father, "Father, this is what your son did." When Father arrived home, suit and tie clad, he opened the bedroom door. And after one long, all-encompassing look- just like mine had been, soon closed it.

And without words, we could hear his footsteps assertively going down each step to the basement. He returned several moments later, bucket and mop in hand, but in the other was a book which he handed me, without hesitation. On the front cover, the title read *Child Psychology*. "Here," he said, "Find out what's the matter with your son," and into the room he advanced, and did not re-appear for at least an hour. It was very quiet at the Butrum house that night, and the emerging baby Picasso realized by the demeanor of his parents he best try a different medium and a different canvas for his next creations.

Enter baby brother, Curt Adam, 18 months after Chad, and 14 months after that baby baby brother, Collin Aaron. Yes, a baby factory, 3 under 3 years old...what were we thinking...or not thinking. But to 21-month old big brother, Chad, this was just what he had been waiting for - 'Human Art!' Curt was his first model- funny, Curt later became a model and even Collin. Now that I think of it, all three of them did some modeling in Chicago and St. Louis; perhaps Chad was being a toddler make-up artist for their trade to come. In any event, the white sticky dots on 3-month old baby Curt's face were placed quite strategically, in a symmetrical pattern. It was quite impressive as one little chubby hand can fit just so far through the bars of a crib. And where was the burgeoning artist? Hiding in the corner, with the culprit tube of the diaper rash ointment hidden in his hand but clearly visible through his legs. Really, Chad, the 'ostrich head-in-the-sand' isn't cutting it.

But it was baby baby brother, Collin, who got the full treatment. Chad was ready now, experienced and skilled, and it happened on a night when I was exhausted, not just exhausted but mightily so. Ah, the saintliness of Motherhood, cooking and cleaning and diapering and laundering and feeding, ad infinitum, but tonight, tonight I could go to the mall and buy make-up—real girl-makeup just for me. Because Dad was studying at home tonight, not at the library or in class, meant I could take a long hot bath. Yea!! But, Dad was so concentrated in his studies and I so immersed in my bath–enjoying the privacy of bubbles, sans children, we did not notice, there was one child afoot.

The only sound to be heard was me, this time singing full-throated to myself. I emerged so relaxed from that heavenly spa sanctuary (lodged in the *Gran Torino* type home), I can happily check in on the children and then off to the waiting luxury of bed! I opened the door, a smile warming my entire face, which quickly turned to horror. For in the dark, lit only by a sliver of hall light, the baby's sheet was covered in dark liquid. I thought he was bleeding profusely!! The light-switch couldn't flick on quicker, and then I saw my new three-month-old baby had a very tan face. My cherished, long-awaited make-up was now on my baby's face, his bedclothes, and his sheets.

Yes, Chad had snuck into the bathroom as I bathed and serenaded myself. He climbed atop the toilet seat, reached to the shelf where sat the shiny new make-up (can he see through walls??), and scoffed it up like a baby vulture, to apply with great ardor on his baby baby brother's face. – I must admit it was a progression from the white spots on his other baby brother's face.

57

Okay, it was pretty good coverage, but he forgot one thing, which 3-year olds in the dark might be apt to do, to put the cap back on the bottle. I never understood why these baby baby brothers never made a sound during their make-up lessons. – Why, they were probably as amazed at this baby person as their mother and father were. Thank God he got that painting period out of his system for that was his last foray into the art of make-up design, well for the moment… and it was time to explore other avenues of ingenuity.

Let's say mechanical engineering… It happened one Sunday morning when Mother and Father are especially appreciative of a few extra minutes of sleep. However, this morning they realize there were too many additional minutes of sleep, as both their heads rise simultaneously to acknowledge… just before the great BANG!! It's kinda like CSI. One has to discern from the crime scene initially because the perpetrator's not quite 3, and he's not talking. And the witnesses can't speak yet, one-word maybe, full sentences at least 6 months away. It turns out the new baby baby brother, Collin, couldn't climb out of the crib to play with Chad and his other baby brother, Curt, so undaunted, the big brother climbed into the new baby's crib and with a dime- who knows?? He did have a piggy bank in his room, unscrewed one side of the crib, so one side would fall down… And the baby could fall out and play with them? What goes on in a 3-year-old's cranium?? The behaviour would manifest itself later in Life to bigger and more complex challenges. His buddies would often say, "Chad made me do things I never thought I'd do – no way." "C'mon, you can do it!" he was relentless. Later his friends would tell me, "And we'd do it … and it would work!" But first, he practiced on his baby brothers.

And it also became apparent Chad was indeed a born leader from about the age of 3 years on. I shall always remember a beautiful picture of Chad leading the way on a family outing in Chandler Park, Detroit.

We, as proud, young parents watched in wonderment, not realizing these moments would sustain us a lifetime. Little man, Chad, would forge on using a 4-foot walking stick—all 3 1/2 years of him, and Curt, not quite 2, following his every movement, his every step carrying a 3-foot walking stick. He, too, questing for new ventures, fighting off invisible foes behind the trees and yonder. It was a real-Life "baby version" of – "I'll be your Don Quixote if you'll be my Sancho Panza…" Another time at the open market, big brother is watching little brother in the stroller, while Mom and Dad venture quickly into the spice store, one eye on the stroller. Big brother is looking very responsible, yet we are not seeing what the other hand is doing- feeding one grape to the baby, one grape to himself. By the time we return, there are 10 grapes left out of 2 lbs., at least he was a sharer.

And Chad got to experience the Christmas tree of all Christmas trees just before his 2nd brother arrived. We the 'family of traditions,' thought how wonderful it would be to show little Chad how we go into the woods and cut down our own Christmas tree. So off we drive with my stepbrother and his wife (she and I being very pregnant) to the wilderness Christmas tree farm an hour or so away. It was soo cold; the owners finally took pity on chattering little Chad and took him into their warm house. Meanwhile, we Bravehearts went Christmas tree hunting. Quick to complete the task, we dragged whatever trees we could find, tied them to the car rooftops the best we could, and made a quick path for home. When the tree made it up in the living room, even 31-month old Chad knew as he peeked precariously at the backside, this tree needed major help with so many branches missing. And so the decision was made, Father this time would drive 8 blocks to the Christmas tree stand and buy the most massive tree he could find. A quick call to the brother and yup, their tree was all scraggly, too; he was on his way to buy another.

This time the tree that Father bought was sooo big and beautiful- why a mini-Rockefeller Center spawn, and we adorned it with abundant decorations because of its many full branches. It was still fanning out by the end of January, and we didn't have the heart …or time to take it down. I'm so happy Chad wasn't in school then for his show and tell might sound something like this: "Well, we spent Valentine's Day with our Christmas tree because it grew so big it took up half the living room, and our doors weren't big enough to take it out, so my Daddy had to bring in sawing machines…" Okay, so this was a De-troit city folk story of cutting down their first Christmas tree.

Sometime after all the babies were born, I decided to take a little break from babies and went to a Shiseido Cosmetics luncheon meeting with our cousin, Eileen, at the J. L. Hudson Company-the Macy's of Detroit then. Well, that particular outing eventually launched a career in what else? Make-up and skincare! Why Chad was just preparing me for it, and I soon took a two-day position at Hudson's, which brought a whole new dynamic of two parents working. One of those days worked was Saturday, which became Daddy and Sons day; however, I know how hard it is to wake up a very tired father as we actually missed a friend's wedding one night because of one such long nap.

Well, this day, as I arrived home from the bus and reached my driveway, I came upon a strange sight: our Chevy car door was open on the driver's side, with the back-seat pushed forward. And in the back of the car stood our wine bucket filled with grapes–those grapes again.

However, as I ventured inside the house, there was no big brother, no little brother, and baby baby brother was in the crib crying, not a happy sight. Holding one's breath again, I not too gently shake Father on the couch, "Where are the boys??" "What??" said he, eyes and ears adjusting quickly to the jarring words of a wife looming over him.

He is up instantly bounding out of the house, with a quick pause to check out the curious picnic scenario happening in the back-seat of the car as he makes his way down the driveway. He didn't get too far when he hears the sound of continual banging on a piano which is coming from our next-door neighbor's house, where two very nice elderly ladies reside. Quickly, Father approaches the door and sees our little boys, and the little girl from down the street banging on the piano, whilst the dear matron is sputtering unable to make them stop. Now in all fairness, Chad was the leader of the little brother, but the girl at 4 ½ was clearly the precocious leader of the pack and had been forbidden to play with our boys without adult supervision. She was clearly the alpha dog here; Chad was just preparing a picnic... and got waylaid by the vixen and the sound of music.

And as we moved to the stage of verbal communication, things became more interesting. Once as I was in the hall, I heard a 3-year old Chad exhort, "Mamma's too lazy, she makes me do all the work," as he carried the baby's diaper to the pail as I'd asked him to do. The toddler to toddler conversation was the best. As I left their room one day, pulling the door to for a 'time-out,' I heard Chad now near 4, say, "I think Mama is quite upset," to which his equally very vocal 2- year-old brother Curt responds, "I think I'm pretty upset, Chad." He was always looking out for Curt, like when he came to tell me, "Curt needs Draino; his nose won't stop running!"

In all his years, I never saw my Son take even a sip of alcohol, a puff of a cigarette, certainly not a drug, and never utter vulgar words. Well, there was one itsy bitsy time when he was 3 1/2, and he really didn't know what he was saying. It was Mother's Day at the Dixie Restaurant, where now we have progressed to talking children, at 3 1/2 and 2, and Collin is the silent partner. As we entered the parking lot, his Father said, "There's a hell of a line, we'll drive around until we find a place." Curt responds, "Aren't we going into the restaurant?" Chad, very matter-of-factly answers, "No, Curt, there's a hell of a line." (I was always writing down what the boys said for posterity sake. Little did I know how precious these little pieces of paper would become.)

And, of course, it was a big day when the 'pigskin' was introduced. Chad may have been 18 months old. I remember the first time his Father threw the ball to him, and the first time he got hit by it because he didn't catch it. I remember the day–playing with Chad at the park, his Father fell on something and gashed his thigh, and then drove home. He handed Chad to me from the car window through the storm door, whose glass Chad had broken a few months earlier. —It was the precise way two little hands hit the glass. Chad sustained not a scratch....those Angels again. And then there was the most precious picture when all three of the brothers are in their 1st football stance: Chad and Curt, ready to go, baby Collin, can't quite do the stance yet but he is in the line. This famous picture would be reproduced again many years later as young adults, this time with their stepbrother, Nicholas, in the picture. And later, in New York, they would be playing football with their Father on 3rd Avenue in midtown Manhattan. I'm glad it was the weekend. I'm sure the drivers were just thrilled with the spontaneity of 'the game.' A caveat, not something I would recommend duplicating.

And once before baby #3 came along, we dropped toddler, Chad, to stay with my foster Mom, Auntie Fay, and baby #2 to Carl's parents, and took a quick weekend trip to Montreal. -What a charming, graceful city on the St. Lawrence Seaway it was, with the old-world complexion of Europe. It was a few days of alone time that were much appreciated before '4' became a family of '5.'

Through many, many moments, our young Family grew in all ways- physically, mentally, emotionally, socially, and the weekend finally came when all three brothers could be left with their best-loved babysitter, Mary, 'with the buckle shoes.' Chad had fashioned that moniker…for the obvious reasons. She was the oldest of 11 children; all loved her, and she was most mature for her age. She was just a call away from her Mom and the boys' Grandma Edlund, and so we were off to a weekend of skiing in the high hills of Michigan. It was unfamiliar being in the big car, sans babies, but we finally were able to adjust and were elated at the getaway weekend. I remember when my husband took my hand and said, "Ready for the slopes?" I answered excitely, "Can't wait!" but then other thoughts started to wash over my mind. Looking back, it was one of those defining moments in Life when you begin to realize your Life matters. Other people are relying on you now… Life will never be quite the same. This is what I was thinking, but what I said out loud was, "I have to be careful now."

Soon after, the winds of change were upon us. The time had come. The burgeoning, young family was about to pick up stakes. It was time for a new state… not because of Chad. Well, it's true, he was already moving his horizons to the neighbors' house next door, but an opportunity of a lifetime had presented itself. Carl was offered a job at a radio advertising firm, but it meant we had to move to Chicago. This was a significant career move to an entirely different field…and the beginning of leaving home and seeing the world. – Looking back, I think there are two kinds of us: one, the ones that need to stay home and keep the farm, and two, those that need to see what's beyond the farm. Our little Family belonged to the latter.

CHAPTER 7

The Windy City, Chicago, Illinois
The Hamlet of Wheaton

Wheaton, Illinois, is a small suburban hamlet, 25 miles or so west of Chicago. – Perfect for a family and perfect for commuting, it was just a short hop to the train station. Here in this slow-paced, friendly community, we found a two-story, white, clapboard house directly across from Wheaton College, Billy Graham's alma mater. Just two doors down from us lived The Reverend and his kind Mrs., gentlefolk, not the least bit obtrusive, they invited our boys to attend some of the summer bible school classes. It didn't matter that our boys had been baptized Roman Catholic; God is God. Collin, having just turned 3, thought he actually saw Jesus walking down the street one day. He was clad in sandals and modern-day shorts; he even had long brown hair. Collin would ask me later if I thought Jesus wore green on St. Patrick's Day, an interesting question… Collin and I would spend much of our days together, as he was the youngest. Curt, being the middle child, got squished in-between, the middle child syndrome. Yet, he and Chad seemed inseparable for many years.

As school started that Fall, I remember it as clearly as yesterday. It was adorable as Collin, and I watched his big brothers, 4 and 5, walking hand in hand to school, wearing matching denim jackets and waving back at us. - Different times then. I think today, I would be following right behind them in my car.

Then, it was a new day for us all: dropping Father at the train station, going for modeling go-sees in the big city of Chicago, having 12 sets of friends and family up on the weekends to explore the sites of the windy city when we were only there for 11 months. We also became quite athletic and ran around the Wheaton track as a family at least a few times a week. We had a big mulberry tree in our backyard, and we would lay a sheet under the tree, and after we shook the tree, I would have bountiful berries to make a homemade mulberry sauce for pancakes. Chad rarely got sick and never complained, but one day, he had an awful stomach ache, so bad I even had to carry him to the car. It was so appreciated when the doctor called the house that evening to inquire how Chad was. How nice to know that that kind of small-town personal attention still existed.

With autumn came the smell of freshly-pressed apple cider and the tantalizing aroma of fresh-cooked doughnuts in the cider mills of Michigan. Here in Chi-town, we also found the local apple orchards, and hand-picked bushels of apples to take home with us. However, back at the little white house where we resided, it looked a bit antebellum as *I* was the one in the enclosed back porch doing all the coring and peeling and making the fresh applesauce. Where were those daughters??

We even ventured to Wisconsin one summer weekend with friends, but Curt, now 4, got bit or ate something and had a horrible allergic reaction. His poor, little mouth swelled up like Howdy Doody until he couldn't talk. In fog as thick as soup, our hostess drove us in the middle of the night, to a small, country hospital. Thank the Lord for Benadryl and whatever shot that emergency room doctor gave to Curt, for the swelling which was now spreading down to his groin, began to diminish immediately. It was a scary moment which he still remembers–a small child not understanding what's happening to him.

Here, the boys had an ample backyard in which to play all day long, within the confines of nature. And, amazingly, when they were told they could not go anywhere near the train tracks which were way in the back of the property, ungated, they listened....even Mister curious Chad. Collin got nipped by a squirrel, so that was our first trip to the emergency room. Another time he fell off his bike, and we had to get a butterfly bandage in the same hospital but never, thank the Lord, did we have any broken bones or stitches…. those Angels again.

One Christmas, I even cooked a traditional *English* Christmas dinner: with roasted goose, Yorkshire pudding, and fresh-from-scratch Plum pudding, which we set aflame with rum. I can still see Chad and his brothers' eyes lit up in the backdrop of the fiery glow. We had birthday parties with special Civil War cakes, which I decorated with cannons and soldiers. Life was pretty happy and carefree–except for one big whopper Chad orchestrated.

By then, at 5, his powers of 'persuasion' were in full swing as he got his brother Curt, now 4, to climb to the top of the 6-foot storage shed in the backyard, and of course, the query is *how does one get down…* As I pulled into the driveway returning from a go-see in Chicago, my portfolio dropped to the ground, as Chad's voice rang out, "C'mon, Curt, jump. – You can do it!" As my high heels took off groveling in the gravel, I saw in my periphery, the neighbor lady running from her garage with a ladder. Why Chad had even pulled over an 'empty' swimming pool to *help* his brother. – Curt jumped (with Angels on his side) and thus began a Lifelong edict. How could any of us say "no" to Chad? His brothers were his 1st candidates… and then pretty much the world. – Chad had coined a new word, "Chadisma."

Recently, a friend gave me a gift that I hung in my New York apartment. It was a picture of the young Beatles taken by a famous photographer. Paul had on a dusty pink suit and Ringo, a denim one. Unposed and candid, they had that look of awe and promise of the world in their eyes, much like the picture of my sons, which hangs below it. Ages 3, 4 and 5, Chad with his arm around Collin, Curt next to him, they sit smiling and happy on the sloping grassy hill that fronts Wheaton College. It's one of my favourite pictures of my boys whose young eyes shone with the joy and the wonderment of Life. It occurred to me the other reason I hung the Beatles' picture above theirs is that it reminded me that Chad had also master-minded a concert one night. They were The Beatles: one had a child's guitar, one an empty cardboard toilet roll holder, aka 'mike,' and the 3rd a broomstick (guitar). They even had those 70s type haircuts, mini-Beatles. The Superman bathrobes were their funky attire. It was a memorable concert… sure wish I would have taped it.

It is here in the windy city where Chad's veritable rainbow lens also revealed itself. Here and, later in St. Louis, for whenever he brought his playdates home, it was always a delightful surprise: Willie, Sydney, and Cindi could be yellow, brown, white or black, Christian or Jewish or none of the above. He never saw the colour of your skin, only you. This trait would characterize his true nature all the days of his Life.

And as motherhood goes on, you begin to realize it's just as important how you nourish the inner as the outer. What was beautiful to watch was Chad's own moral compass come to be. In all his years, I only saw that strong, calm leader openly cry 'once.' Chad, now 5, runs into the house, trying to hold back tears which refuse to be held back; his little chest is heaving. His brothers now 4 and 3, run in after him, quite concerned because they have never seen their big brother so upset. "What happened??" said I, seeing the ruckus. Chad, still too upset to speak- his chest stifling sobs, turns to his brother Curt, "Did you see Eddie break that bat?" "No," answers Curt. Chad finally unable to contain himself, shouts, louder than the tears, "Eddie broke my bat, and he LIED ABOUT IT!!!" Then still fighting back those cries, he belts out, "I know, I'm gonna ask Jesus, he'll know. When I die, I'm going to ask Jesus!!!" – All I can say is, "Eddie D., you're in Big Trouble now!"

And that looked like the exit cue for another new state, for Carl was being transferred to St. Louis, Missouri, this time to manage his own office. It was only 11 months in Wheaton, Illinois, but it seemed like another lifetime. I will always be grateful for being able to raise the boys in the Midwest. There is a steadiness in that part of the country. Things are not torn down so fast or rebuilt so quickly. The middle country is linked to the out-of-doors. That is the room where they are to play and explore. But most of all, I am so glad they had each other, for the transitions are difficult– changing from one school to another so quickly, making friends for a short time, not getting to use to *anything* before it's time to move again. But one thing would never change – their centerpiece- they always had each other.

CHAPTER 8

St. Louis, Missouri, Gateway to the West

In the sprawling lawns and rolling green terrain of St. Louis, Missouri, our journey continued. Our first home was a quad-level modern brick dwelling on Olivaire Lane in Ladue. -That was always one of my primary criterion- to find the best school district. In the more pastoral, neighborly environs of Wheaton, we experienced the tight-knit community and friendliness of small-town America. St. Louis, with its towering Arch and diverse topography, led to more expansive ventures for us to reconnoiter: the Mississippi River, the stalactites and stalagmites in the caverns where it is said, Mark Twain, himself traversed, and paddlewheel boats which took us back to another era.

Sans internet, there were still so many places I could find for our family outings, be it looking for edible mushrooms or persimmons. (I felt like Marco Polo discovering a new fruit which I could now make into persimmon bread!) And their Father turned into an agrarian Stanley coming upon Livingstone. Only his eureka was, "Polydor frondosis!" when he came upon a particular configuration of mushrooms attached to a large tree. And something I started doing during our vacation days, was planning an outing with just Dad and each son, so they were not only seen as a threesome but each separate and *so* individual. He would always return home with a memorable story of each to tell again and again after such expeditions.

In the inclement weather, the three built-in playmates could always create plenty to do and have plenty of places to do them in, in this spacious multi-level home. There was the time, laundry basket in hand, when I happened upon an eerie sight, and had to back-track my steps to witness more fully what I was seeing and hearing. - All three of them were playing Dr. Frankenstein at the basement level. Curt, now 5, was the monster laid out on the tool bench, while Chad, 6, was *the mad scientist* adroitly working on him. All the while, he would be giving serious instruction to his 4-year old assistant, brother Collin. –Oh, to have had the touch *Video icon* that moment…

It was here in St. Louis in my continued note-taking that I begin to see their value systems take hold, their questions of Life arise, and their unique personalities start to reveal themselves. As always, there are the funny things kids say. Once, as they watched *Gone With the Wind*, Chad asked, "Dad, what is that she's putting on her face?" "Toilette water, Chad." "Why do Ladies use toilet water, Dad?"

It's funny too how their concerns arise with each passing year; I came across a note I'd written as Chad sat on the Dr.'s table waiting to be examined. "Are we still going to be living with you when you're *real* old?" he mused. "Well, Chad, in different cultures, people always keep their parents or grandparents with them until they die." "Why don't we do that here?" "Because," I answered, "every country has different cultures, and some respect the old more than we do." "Can we live at home until you die?" "Sure, but when you get older, I'm sure you'll want to get married." "No," he brightened. "We could all stick together like the *Three Musketeers*– we don't need to get married. Then we can all live together as a family 'til you die." I continued writing in that note, "Chad at this age is very conscious of doing everything with his brothers. He wants to wait until all three of them are old enough to partake before he does things like go mountain climbing, camp or join the Cub Scouts."

However, there were times when the brothers found their voices. We could also see the other facets of Chad, as reminded by one note I wrote about what Collin said at age 5. "It's not nice to make fun of Black people, or White people, or old people, or any of us. Cause we'll hurt their feelings like when Chad hurts mine and makes me cry." ...Big brothers are far from perfect.

But the ultimate Kodak moment of that extraordinary bond that brotherhood forges came after a long day of a family hike in the forest. It was amidst the gentle background of nature as the tiny threesome tries to make the last trek homeward: Chad and Curt, now 6 and 5, are holding up their 4-year-old brother, Collin, with their arms around him. He is sandwiched between them; so tired is he, he is hardly able to take the last weary steps out of the forest, which leads to car and home. That picture has been laser-imbedded in my mind. – I actually made a video of *The Young Years,* using the aforementioned as a featured picture accompanied by the background music of George Winston's piano solos from *Winter.* But sadly, it has been lost to the many moves of many people. However, if anyone should come across that carousel of slides or that video, it is to this Mother it belongs, and there is a reward... for that picture, no earthly belonging could compete.

Athletics has always been a part of Chad's Life, starting with his baby push-ups. In these early years, we had a bit of the Kennedy–esque thing prevalent in our lives. Their Father was of Scotch-Irish, English, and German stock; and had even done the Kennedy "Ask not..." speech in the Michigan regionals. And in our whirlwind moving days for his job, family activities were very important. We might be seen doing football plays in the St. Louis backyard, or taking turns from the top of the hill, skating down the long, curved, sloping driveway on skateboards, or running around the track as a family as we did in Wheaton, IL.

Once Chad was pretty winded from running, but even as a young boy of 6 or 7, he didn't like to give up. It was only when we arrived home, did we feel awful because the doctor had called, and the X-ray Chad had taken the day before showed pneumonia. Thus began bouts of asthma, and a relationship with long, hot showers. Initially, I would join him and read to him until the room was warm and steamy. Then as he got older and even on his own, they became a calming, soothing way of relieving his wheezing and a comforting drawback to childhood.

Living in the suburb, Ladue, in St. Louis, was a beautiful thing. When the owner decided to sell his quad-level home where we enjoyed living for a year and a half, we then found a 3 and a half-acre property in the same area. This property would have been prohibitive in Chicago and impossible in L.A. It was a one-story ranch style home of considerable length that sat on a hill with a vast rolling front lawn that spread out before it. Collin at 4, would industriously make snowballs larger than himself on this lawn. Incredibly, he would shovel that large sloping driveway, that some folks out for a drive thought was an access lane and drove up the wooded path, not realizing it was our driveway.

The new residence even had a private creek with a promontory and a rope tied to a grandfather tree. Here you could bravely hold on, jump and swing across the creek and hopefully back again. Some of their Dad's clients passed on trying it, but eventually, all 3 of the boys made the swing, again with angels on their side.

Collin would soon be starting preschool, and Chad and Curt were in 3rd and 2nd grades, respectively. And Mother was so excited to receive a 4-year scholarship to Washington University in St. Louis, majoring in Psychology (I wonder if Chad's painting incident was a factor....) In any event, I would become a psychologist! I had taken some courses at Wayne State University in Detroit, but the babies took precedence then. Now that they were older, what a wonderful thing, and I was also doing commercials for a Hawaiian bank. - Go figure, the only Hawaiian-looking person in the city of St. Louis, maybe all of Missouri. It was about to be a very busy year, so a tight ship was to be run: Laundry piling up, clients' dinner parties for 10 or 20, father out-of-town, more laundry, finals, Father tripping over laundry basket which hasn't been put away, homework, papers, soccer practice.... Oh, and that occasional trip to Calgary or Montreal, Canada for Shiseido; can we clone me??

One day, returning from my classes, I just heard the phone ringing as I was leaving. Tardy already, I almost didn't answer it but did so on the last ring. The tight schedule would be disrupted today; it was Chad's school calling. There were only two times I can remember he got in trouble; today would be one of them, in St. Louis, Missouri. He was 6, and his friend(?) dared him to take the little hammer and break the school fire alarm. ...He took the dare, fire alarms went off everywhere; the whole school was evacuated, and fire engines showed up quickly. I think Chad was asked to go home that day to think things over. (I think he was thinking, 'What happens when you hit the glass with the hammer.....?' He did get his answer.) Hmm, and did I not recall another incident, perhaps a precursor, when we were on a family outing at a Chicago museum, and we were always going back for Chad. For even at 5, he would be looking at historical markers for hours, and we would always be back-tracking to find him. Only this time, the exit door alarm went off with a blaring announcement, and all we needed to do was follow the sound to 5-year-old Chad, who had *read* the sign and pushed the door open. (... wonder what happens when it says, "Do Not Open," on the door....)

In school, though he may have had some challenges with his reading, his teacher told me at a parent-teacher conference, Chad is a very polite boy... I often hear him saying to his classmates- at 6, "Don't call her *'she,'* that's your Mother." Those words he would remember from his Father. This always boggles my mind because it begs the question, "What if we had fed them the *wrong words??* It is said that Hitler said something akin to give me the child, and by 5, he belongs to me... I would impart those words to Chad at the appropriate time. And amazingly, he would reiterate a version of those same words years later in a card to his friend and coworker at Carolco Pictures who was about to have their first child.

But for the moment, he was *imparting* teachings to his brothers and also becoming their 1st teacher of the "Birds and Bees" at 7. While I was readying myself for university one morning, the boys were watching T.V., and suddenly I heard tittering... a lot of tittering, and I poked my head in, curious. "What's so funny?" Curt answers, unabashedly, "Chad says, sometimes when you look at a pretty girl, you feel funny inside..." "Well," says I unfazed, "It's only natural, as you grow older that the opposite sex is attracted to the other, and you have these special feelings"— Chad, suddenly breaking in, "Mom, can you tell me when I'm 9?" "Why, sure…" - Shut me up.

Once I recall a spectacular Fall day when the boys and I went walking. The air was crisp and clear: the kind that tickles your nostrils and pockets your hands. We made our way up Olivaire Lane, a sumptuous blue sky bidding us hello with a few cumulous clouds joining the parade. Surrounded by the glory of autumnal leaves of every richness and hue, it was a feast for the eyes and senses. Suddenly church bells rang out in the near distance. I think it was Curt who said, on one of the most glorious days of our lives, "It's like being in England, Mama!" And it was. Chad and his brothers would often pick up that book on the coffee table, which was my favourite *This England*, and we would go through it page by page. Interestingly, I would have the privilege of taking a class with a British professor from Oxford and Cambridge that very Fall, on "Tudor and Stuart England." That is one of the things I will always miss… not having Chad here to travel with us so we could explore the countries we only dreamt about.

But that slight chill in the air was also precipitating something else. This would be our 2nd and last season in St. Louis and my final year at Washington University, host to the World Fair in the early 1900's, whose architecture of Collegiate Gothic quadrangles were actually reminiscent of Oxford and Cambridge. Soon, the winds of change would be upon us again; this time, Big Change – Los Angeles, California. Carl would assume a very significant position there. It was if the looming stainless steel edifice–the St. Louis Arch or "Ouch," as Collin called it, was beckoning us through as we looked out its futuristic windows at its pinnacle. As its moniker implies, "Gateway to the West," we were looking into our own future in Los Angeles, California.

My sons would tell me years later that I scared them to death by asking them, "What are you going to do if someone comes up and offers you drugs on the playground?" What did I know… a young mother, born and bred in the Midwest suburbs of Centerline and

Warren, Michigan, where underage alcohol was about the worst drug you could find. So my stereotypical view of L.A. came from all the Hollywood movies I saw... Still, it was like setting foot in the modern-day covered-wagon of the day, a jetliner, and discovering a whole new land, you'd only heard about, seen pictures of, and had defined through a small or big screen.

As we said goodbye to St. Louis, it was in a way saying goodbye to our childhood and our original roots, and venturing further on to parts unknown to us. We faced growing up and on, the future still veiled with all its attendant challenges. But this place, beckoning on the horizon, was "The City of Angels," where Chad would choose to be, and we would share, explore, and experience many fine years with him that we would cherish forever.

CHAPTER 9

L.A.
City of Angels and Sunshine

The first thing that defines the City of Angels when you debark the plane at LAX is the superabundance of sunshine that greets you and is ever-present. Chad loved it because it meant 'always a great day to play a game,' and his brothers followed suit. Our first introduction to L.A. was the landmark beach cities of Santa Monica and Venice Beach. We were able to stay seaside for a few weeks as our home in Agoura wasn't ready for us yet. But Father's job was in readiness, so we were lucky puppies during this time and could enjoy the sand and surf, and the fairly deserted beaches. My sister, Liza, was up from Michigan, and she joined us, enjoying the playfulness of her nephews in the California sunshine.

One day on Chad's exploratory ventures, he came running back to our beach blanket, reaching for my hand to show me something—"Mom, come and see Arnold Schwarzenegger. He's working out at Muscle Beach." "Okay," said I with my brood 8, 9, and 7 in tow, not quite sure I knew too much about Arnold but was sure Chad would enlighten me. Mr. Arnold was a very nice man and, yes, the musculature of all was quite impressive. Arnold even came over to say hello to all my Boys. Years later, this very nice man, with great responsibility as Governor of the State of California, would send us a letter of support for the work of *The Chad Foundation for Athletes and Artists*. And at a subsequent time, CHAD, amazingly, would be screening 16 countries of homeless athletes participating in the *"1ˢᵗ Homeless Streetsoccer World Cup,"* in Mr. Schwarzenegger's hometown of Graz, Austria. It is said there are no coincidences…

Another marvelous intro into the "Entertainment Capital of the World" came with an invitation to our country's "Bicentennial Celebration," at the venerable Lakeside Golf Club in Toluca Lake. It was known as Bob Hope's country club. As Carl's boss and family would be going on vacation, we got to be their guests here at this once-in-a-lifetime affair. I sat there surrounded by movie star celebrities. The Gordon McRaes were on one side, Patrick Wayne behind me, Don Knotts greeting me at the buffet table, Abby Dalton smiling and floating about, while my children played in the pool with all the other celeb children.—They were the only untanned children in the pool… That would change; they would be soon be California-tanned forevermore.

My visage may have appeared not to be affected, but it was a nice act, for I was very affected. What were *we*- from Centerline/ Warren, Michigan–very small-town USA doing here? Not being born of money or entitlement, or possessing any exceptional talent or notoriety, here we sat amongst these very wealthy, famous people who most Americans don't get to see in person, much less in the relaxed environs of their own private country club. Here they do not perform but are entertained by other artists– talented, but without face or name, you might readily know.

It is here in this milieu, amidst the cool California nights and private fireworks display that lit the entire sky before us and beyond, that we celebrated our country's 200ᵗʰ anniversary. Die-hard patriot that I am, I thought, I should have done something extraordinary for this extraordinary occasion. That night, I began to see, we, in fact, were—for we personified in our own individual way, the meaning of the "American Dream" come true. We raised our horizons further, accepting the opportunity afforded us, leaving all that was familiar behind, and marched across the country to meet and make new dreams come true.

If that future timeline had revealed itself in the night skies that evening, between the shout and glow of red, white, and blue stars of every size and shape, it would show a tall, handsome Chad, grown now. He would be attending his best friend, Louis Milito's wedding reception, as the Best Man, in this very spot. And, a few years beyond that, unbelievably, we would hold in the same place, the first six *"Annual Chad Foundation Volleyball Tournaments benefiting Children's Hospital Los Angeles Heart Institute."* They would be attended by Louis and many of the same young men in his wedding party. This time Chad is the guest of honour and always would be, but he would always be somewhere else now. There is a reason why the veil does not reveal the future ahead of time, for how many of us could even begin the journey, knowing where it would end.

And so with the knowledge of our future well-protected and out-of-sight, we were free to explore the new world of Agoura, California, beginning with its dirt hills... – Well, if we're going to move clear across country, you had to have mountains...even if they were just high hills interspersed with trees. We did have one reasonably tall, verdant mountain, right across the Ventura Freeway: "Ladyface Mountain" named so for the peaks and valleys of her profile which from a distance resembled a lady's visage. It had to be one of the hottest days of the year when Father led the first assault. We may not have made it all the way to her summit that day, but there would be many more climbs, and each of the sons, beginning with Chad, would take their girlfriends up the pike. It was to become a family tradition.

One of our first family road trips was to a desert air show. Our good friend, Mike G., was in from Michigan, and it was a perfect outing, experiencing the various climates and diverse terrain in California. As we settled in to watch these mammoth machines taking off and performing miraculous moves as they vaulted and twisted and turned at a moment's notice, Chad suddenly, and without warning took off across the field where the long grasses waved and pressed down in the wake of the jets. He ran like Forrest Gump as fast as his legs would carry him as all our voices shouted, in collective unison,"CHAAAAD!!!!! However, they were completely drowned out by the mighty roar of the engines as they lifted their bodies to the sky. It was as if his spontaneous, unrestrained spirit took charge that moment... and there was NOTHING we could do stop him, but watch him run halfway across the field, holding our breaths, hoping that he would be all right. The pure, unadulterated spirit of Chad came out in full force that day.

Now I may have grown up on a gravelly, semi-rural street where sometimes the greenish tint of oncoming tornadoes could be prevalent in the summer skies. But even with an unpaved road fronting our house, we didn't have things like slithery reptiles with patterns, shading in our gardens. Oh, how can you boys pick up those things?? How do you know they are not poisonous? The neighbor boy next door told us... Hmm, and what else is this neighbor boy telling you... And this is the moment that imperceptibly comes to every mother: where her brood is no longer underfoot and under her watchful eye every moment; and, you must loosen the strings and let them take dirt bikes out to the hills and pray the angels and wisdom are with them. And there are times when you are compelled to ask those Higher than you, did I temporarily lose my sanity when Chad wanted a pet snake for his birthday? Complete with a terrarium, and I agreed?? That must have been an excellent report card. It's a good thing he didn't ask for a chimpanzee.

And thus it went: acclimating to 80 degrees in November, buying Christmas trees in shorts, and reaching for a dress in your closet only to find a baby lizard in camouflage taking umbrage. So the boys explored the barren hills and the different species of *non*-poisonous snakes and reptilians, which made it to the 21st century as the fauna of the region. Mother learned about horticulture as the new home had to be in readiness quickly for clients may be in town at any time.

This house was in the California Tuscan-style, and we filled it with diverse species from the coastal plant kingdom: A Tahitian

Bridal veil hung cheerily in the kitchen window. A Staghorn fern peeked out from its sturdy platform on the living room wall. A bright, dracaena flowering cactus beckoned you to enter the sun-filled family room. And, lastly, the tall green Ficus Benjamina framing the patio doors, bid you view the outdoor garden at will. All of which Mother learned was like having very temperamental children: all requiring different watering times, methods, and quantities of food and water… and nary a brown leaf. Her boys were sturdy, outdoors boys who played from dawn to dusk in the land of no computers. They had no seeming interest in participating in the domestic or culinary arts, only admiring and enjoying them.

When they came home from school on the school bus and headed down Green Grass Court to the cul de sac, it would often be to the sounds of Diana Ross… 'you know where you're going to?' wafting from the L-shaped abode at the street's end. And as I sanded and stained, Father attended to his many corporate and client responsibilities, then he had a *very long* commute home. Carl's boss and his Mrs. were our first dinner guests, and I had prepared my specialty, *soupe a l'oignon-gratinee,* and a killer *Mousse au Chocolat.*

In those days, all my creative energy went into home and children… and I'm so glad it did, for they were paying attention. Oh, you wouldn't think it mattered as they ran in and out and in and out, but as they would grow, the importance of their own homes having style and being aesthetically pleasing- no undue mess and clutter, yet warmth everywhere, was like osmosis and informed each of their homes and their individual palettes …as well as palates. For introducing them to distinct, new foods at an early age, being as simple as fresh-picked mulberries and persimmons, to later smoked clams or escargots opened up worlds to them, they are still expanding upon. I remember getting Gram Edlund's family recipe handed down from her Grandmother Nixon in Scotland to make authentic Scottish shortbread. I was thrilled. Chad loved those cookies; he was the first to sample.

Our little Family's Holiday desserts have now been passed down to girlfriends and wives as they call asking for Collin's favourite. Oh yes, the "Cranberry Almond Refrigerator Cake," or Curt's, the "Frozen Champagne Custard Mold with fresh Strawberry Sauce," which was served as we opened our Christmas presents. Mom was wearing a Juliet type gown with black velvet bodice and Renaissance sleeves. Wow, someone was surely intent on trying to make a perfect Christmas… maybe a little overkill?? Chad loved it all, taking from everything, but I think what he savoured most was Mom's homemade mashed potatoes… that would become his crowning glory.

As for school, I had been accepted to USC, but my scholarship from Washington University wasn't transferable, so I decided to take some classes at UCLA. I had never been entirely comfortable looking directly at the camera and talking in those St. Louis commercials. Why not take an acting class? Enter Professor Arthur Friedman and a "Moment of Truth." How can a simple improv exercise change the course of your Life? But it did. In the scene we were given, I was to ask my milk-toast husband to go to the window and tell the person not to play his music so loud. After 3 times of asking him and the response is non 'action,' I go to the window myself and shout to the guy to shut up!! – When we did the scene in class, and I went to the window, I screamed so loud, I scared myself, the professor, and the students sitting in the amphitheater setting. But for me, it was like an epiphany—like looking inside yourself and seeing for the first time an artist waiting to be born, and you could never deny it again… It was transformational.

But that part of the birth of my very own Life would have to lie warm and dormant for a long while for another massive upheaval was taking place, so cataclysmic that the metaphor was like viewing a new landmass of your own formed when the blast of gusts diminished. But there remained one constant – the unabated Love for our Children.

When the unexpected tempests rear up in Life, you can only hope that every moment of care and love you've built into the foundation will sustain and nourish your brood until they are creating, forging, and building their own Lives.

That season of Fall was upon us again, and with it, a major transformative change the family would face and endure. We felt it should be preceded by a glorious, once-in-a-lifetime adventure that we would always remember, and we made it thus: our Family trip to Sequoia National Forest. This giant forest is home to 5 of the most massive trees in the world, one of them being The General Sherman tree, who some claim is the largest living organism in the world at 274.9 feet in height. To view the highest, best, and strongest was a superlative end to a new beginning. Driving to Sequoia National Forest and ascending the beautiful mountains on its switchback roads, meandering hither and thither, we were suddenly met by a double rainbow, a most fortuitous omen of the sites to come.

One cannot appreciate the enormity of these majestic creations until you stand beneath these leviathans of nature, and feel like Alice in Wonderland did when she fell down a hole into some magical land and found herself Lilliputian size. As the park was vast and silent, we roamed freely, nary running into another soul the entire day. And if we saw another traveler in the distance, we waved– more in collusion of bearing witness to the prodigious sites before us. As there was not an excess of historical markers about, we did not lose Chad easily. He, for once, seemed in awed silence. Every clearing led to more magnificent trees and flora, and I remember halfway through the day, Curt took my hand and said, "Mom, this is one of the best days of my Life." Yes, it was. Family and God's untouched creations, what could be more sacred. It would also inspire the line in my first, off-Broadway play, *All About Sneakers*, which I wrote for the co-lead, Danny, "It's like being in a cathedral in the forest, their bark is like velvet." These moments in time that we create/experience are given as enormous Gifts that buoy us through Life. They are written in our souls, a spiritual bank we can always draw from, without fee or depletion.

CHAPTER 10

Malibu – OP'S, Quicksilvers and the Halcyon Days

It was the dawning of a new day, a new Life, and I applied the same principles to navigate the land of the new as I had used to navigate the old. But Life has a way of laying a path for you when you don't even know you're taking the steps. All those years of setting up cosmetic promotions and developing clientele in Montreal, Calgary, Chicago and the like, developed a skillset which the executive search firm saw immediately. Soon I was offered a position in Beverly Hills as a Showroom Manager for a wholesale manufacturer of textiles, used commercially and residentially. Here, I met the top designers and architects in L.A. Within a year, I was offered another position as the first woman Account Executive at an international wall covering company. My position entailed calling on top clients such as Walt Disney and Hotel Equipment, the buying arm of Hilton Hotels, and included a company car, travel, and expense account. This time I would be entertaining clientele as well. It was another 'Angel's Gift'– a proper job for a single parent who hadn't completed her college degree.

Next,- and I call this a most fortuitous gift from the universe/ God- the two terms are synonymous for me, we found a proper home. As mentioned earlier, the school district was always a number one priority, and I wanted Santa Monica; however, did Santa Monica want us? Every Family apartment I applied to turned us down. "Three?

Young? Boys, you say? Ah, that would never work." We were on the brink of laws that would consider this practice discriminatory, but we were a tad too early. So one day, as the time for starting school was closing in, I picked up the Malibu Surfside News, saw a condominium for rent in Malibu, made an appointment with the 'owner'– *not* the apartment manager, brought my credit report, and was signed for a 4-year lease on the spot. Divine Providence.

It was a lovely gated community, and our home was a 3 bedroom, 2½ bath condo with a 2-car garage. The inner private courtyard rose to the levels of the upper bedrooms. It was landscaped quite pleasantly with the natural flora of the region, which received direct sunlight from the open space that led right to the sky. A pebble floor of concrete was perfect for barbecuing as the outside L-shaped patio doors led to both the dining area and the kitchen. The interior had very appealing architectural appointments: high-beamed ceilings and a raised dining room, and it was affordable by standards then. Today? I'm just thankful we got the gift then.

It even had a cozy fireplace, which we found we would often use in the brisk, cool nights of southern California, especially living near the ocean. And, every Christmas morning-even in Malibu, Santa made his way down the customary chimney to make his unannounced visit. –Why one Christmas morning, Collin even found a piece of Santa's beard attached to the fireplace. And like so many young ones were even more delighted to see only crumbs left on Santa's plate of cookies. Big brothers, Chad and Curt, never leaked the 'Santa secret' to their little brother… They were such sweet boys; did I mention that already? And Collin carried that Christmas spirit with him a long time, to this day, in fact. His wife told me for years, it was like pulling teeth not to get him to put the Christmas decorations up *and start the Christmas music* so early or, God forbid, take everything down too soon! (Baby baby brother must have been in Heaven looking down at Chad and the giant Sequoia Christmas tree in the Detroit living room, and couldn't wait to come down and cut his own tree.) And so we did- even in sunny California. My companion, V., packed us all up in his yellow van and drove up a few

Malibu mountains, not large ones, lovely rising ones (mountains, as you may remember, were a requirement for living in California). We found the Christmas tree farm, cut down our own tree, and carried it home in the van to its eagerly awaited space by the fireplace. There is something to be said for Christmas tree hunting in California vs. the icy tundra and freezing temperatures of Michigan; however, on the flip side, who wants to bake a Christmas dinner in 80-degree weather in your swimsuit attire?

Halloween was another fun event in the Villas. The boys would go out trick or treating, and I would be making the traditional fresh pumpkin pie from the pumpkin they carved the night before, sans can. Once you've had the real thing, there's nothing like it! And we'd also offer, right from the oven, freshly-roasted pumpkin seeds from our pumpkin to the scary tykes and toads. Chad always liked the aromas and the traditions. He would have a very memorable Halloween with Maria in years to come, carving his own pumpkin. (a reality pumpkin, complete with his 'birthmark.') In our new environs, I think for all of us, something was comforting about hearing the doorbell ring, and the enthusiastic sound of young voices, calling out "Trick or Treat!" Even in Malibu, California, 2,000 miles from whence we came, nothing really changes, only the scenery! Although, on that note, it was an ultra-big change of scenery.

The front of our condo faced the Pacific Coast Highway- PCH to the natives. It was located right across from Paradise Cove, the famed location where James Garner's old series, *The Rockford Files* was shot, and where we would spend many a weekend. No A.C. needed here because the sea breezes kept it comparatively cool. And all you had to do most times of the year was to follow the scent of those sea breezes, traverse the steep hill on which the Villas sat, meander through the unique tunnel that burrows under the PCH, and you were soon on the private white sandy beach at Paradise Cove. A place we all especially loved, and where I wrote my first screenplay, *Welcome Home Kelly!* I carved out a patch in the white sand on the left side of the pier away from the beachgoers, played Frisbee, ran along the beach, and watched my boys cavort in the wide, blue ocean.—We had all come a long way, and for a moment in time, these were the Halcyon Days. Walking one day, I met Dick Clark and his wife and chatted like old neighbors. A few years later, Chad would drop his resume off to Dick Clark Productions. In many ways, his charm walked through the door before him and never left. He would eventually come to work for Merv Griffin.

We figured out the schools: Pointe Dume Elementary and Juan Cabrillo, and later for Chad, Malibu Park Jr. High. The school buses were grand because I could just head straight off to work. One must remember everything in L.A. is a commute, at least an hour. –But really how can one complain if upon returning home with your sunroof open to the sky, serenaded by Streisand and Steve Perry, and accompanied by the Pacific Ocean sailing you home to greet the sunrise or sunset, you are always in the state of Paradise!

You better be dressed for it, too. For this, I take complete responsibility for the Midwest attire, which followed us from Detroit, Chicago, and St. Louis, but needed to be lost in the environs of the beach cities, especially Malibu, which I found had its own dress code. My boys were the best and truly never whined and complained that they didn't have this or that … but strangely, when I began to see holes in their shirts, where logos used to be, I kind of figured, their shirts did not have the appropriate logos. Now I know you may be thinking of the iconic line in *Rainman*, but no, we didn't shop *there… not quite...* but would be shopping somewhere else we've never shopped (but not that frequently…). –So, as the old saying goes, if you want to bring your children to 'Rome,' then you must do as the 'Romans do.' - Here that meant Polo shirts as in Ralph and O.P.'s and Quicksilvers, which, for the uninitiated, as I was, are boys' corduroy shorts, which are the standard uniform of the day, all year round. Who wears shorts all year round? Where are we?

A very wondrous, fortunate place where I could sign my son, Chad's permission slip for a day trip- where? To go Whale Watching in the Pacific Ocean. I saw a film recently called *Blackfish*, about the abhorrent treatment these magnificent creatures endure, captured and enslaved in small tanks to do tricks for the benefit of our entertainment. Mother and child are often separated, bringing extreme trauma. My first thought after seeing it was I'm sure glad Chad never saw this film; he would have been so very upset. I'm delighted he had the real pleasure of seeing these great beings delight you with their own wondrous tricks in the vast oceans of their own natural environs.

Malibu was also a place where Family reigned supreme. Every year, PCH was closed down for the "Annual Little League Parade," and all the young players would be riding atop firetrucks waving to their friends and Family. It's true, you might be talking to a famous film star standing right next to you about her next movie, but you could see the pride in her eyes as her own child's team came by, and she was smiling and cheering him on. We were all just parents enjoying the heck out of our children, and just being parents. Hollywood gets a bad rap sometimes, but there in Malibu, it was a community made up of regular people, some of whom were famous, but somehow it didn't matter there. They, too, came to raise their Family with fresh air, and normal schools, and regular activities, out of the glare of paparazzi and spotlights.

It had excellent community spirit, which I don't think I ever had the pleasure of experiencing before: coaches were always kind enough to drop my sons off after practice, as I was often still on the road. Friends would take my son skiing with their son and even opened their home to our youngest during a difficult transition period. During the wildfires, everyone was pitching in, bringing water from a local well down the street, alerting each other as to where the fire was heading. Once, we were told to pack one bag and get ready to evacuate if the Firefighters gave us the word. Little did we know, the Firemen couldn't give us any word because they couldn't get to us. The fire was headed straight for our condos; in fact, it singed the back row before the wind turned abruptly, headed across the Pacific Coast Highway and toward Paradise Cove, destroying some trailer homes.

It was like being in a semi-pioneer state sometimes. When they closed PCH because of torrential rain and mudslides, one had to maneuver over the canyons and through the woods to the Valley, and traverse back again. I would tell my boys, "Hold the Fort, I'll be back with the bacon!" Once, the powers that be decided to extract a 2-ton boulder from the side of the hill fronting PCH. Well, for years after that, all the rocks that had been blocked by the 2-tonner rained down rockslides. Never understood the logic…

It was also a grand time for baseball in our family times 3. Before it was a bird sanctuary, the tract of land near Cross Creek Road was the Little League field and held two diamonds, which often kept me busy running back and forth between innings to see which son was up to bat. Curt struck out Chastity Bono once, and Collin with his ambidexterity was starting to be scouted at 11 for his pitching. Chad was learning to perfect his batting stance, and well when he graduated to the Pony League, *Field of Dreams*-California style, I experienced one of the most beautiful vistas I had ever witnessed.

As I sat in the bleacher seats, perched on a rolling green, graduated hill, my view led down to a 180-degree panorama of the Pacific Ocean. The soft oceanic blues barely rippled, and gradually coupled with the skyline of the same colour that went on forever. One-story, California style buildings found themselves sprawled out on the hill- laid out like a college campus… This was Junior High?? And then letting my eyes drift slowly to the right – a completely different landscape emerged. In the not too far distance, one could see a few horse riders gently galloping through the higher bluffs, their manes blowing in the wind as did the free, majestic animals that conveyed them. …And this was where my son, Chad, was playing a ballgame, and I, his mother, watching him! …I'm not sure who won or lost…

Chad loved his environs, and he loved baseball. There was a notable family of actors that live on the Pointe, who also had sons that played baseball. One was older than Chad, and Chad could be seen *more than* once in awhile walking through their door, and feeling quite at home as he greeted the Mrs. politely (he better). …And well, *they* had a batting cage in their backyard, and *we* had a concrete driveway in ours. But I'm told the Family was always kind and welcoming to Chad. I also still have the ribbons Chad won in athletic competitions: a red 2nd place ribbon from Malibu Park Jr. High, and a white 3rd place from Westlake Athletic Association's Junior Olympics for the 50-yard dash.

It was also fun ferrying the boys back and forth on PCH to the local cinema and pizza parlor and school dances, pre-licenses. You never knew who you had in the back seat. Always buckled up, of course, that was a family rule that has been carried on by all the boys to men. Curt and his friend, Chad Lowe, could often be found cutting up back there, and actually, they were quite amusing... Who knew that these young men would grow into a model and a very fine actor. Collin, too, was just beginning to dabble in acting. We worked together on his first extra role in, *Star 80,* and his first audition for a movie about Pele; that was great fun.

Like Agoura, the hills were alive with the sound of music when they returned from school. Only, Mother had changed her tune from Motown's Diana Ross to Streisand in Malibu. I think the boys on their riding excursions came upon her home once and stood for a moment in reverence. Perhaps they thought the mellifluous sounds that emanated from their windows when they came home from school might arise from the house whose voice originated it... Wouldn't that have been something? In that case, I should have bought a dirt-bike and joined them.

Here, too, I discovered Chad's love for his "shoes." – Well, my 'nose did' as I opened his closet one day and found a mountain of shoes... probably some carried as far back as Chicago and St. Louis! He said he loved his shoes and reminded me that I always told him, "Good shoes, (and good food) always gave you a good start in Life." –I replied, yes, he was precisely right... but due to hygiene, which is also of utmost importance, he couldn't keep them forever. He could select 4 or 5 of his favourite pairs of old shoes to save. I never knew if he found another hiding place, assuming not since my nose would have detected it, but he always continued to love his shoes and the 'feet' that went in them. You had to have perfect toes, or Chad would quiz you, "What's a matter with your toes?" (ask his friends) ...If they were hanging over your sandals or going this way or that, he would give them the 'Chad scrutiny'– like we all didn't have perfect toes like he did, or thought he did.

And once in a blue moon, we and Chad's toes and feet, and shoes ventured out of the Kingdom of Paradise. Once, over hill and valley, we traveled in search of Frank Lloyd Wright houses to experience and explore. The sons (and their friends) were introduced to the Father of Modern Architecture through the *Architectural Digests* that often went missing from our home; even the neighborhood kids were in awe of the designs. I had brought them graph paper so they could design their own floor-plans and layouts. Though we couldn't visit the Ennis House as it was a residence, we could view it from the street. Perched on a hill, it was a striking example of Wright's Mayan architecture. On another jaunt, we drove all the way to Griffith Park in search of his Hollyhock House. Bummer, it was closed temporarily… but like curious children, we ran all around its perimeters, trying to catch a peek of the magnificent work within. There is nothing like a Frank Lloyd Wright House, the most sublime of architecture, and yet it's a home you want to live in. The hollyhock flower detail and distinctive mannered design of the Hollyhock House just begged for the doors to open. Oh, well sonnies for another day…

However, the most memorable of all our trips outside Paradise came when I was working as the Account Executive. I took the sons on one of my road trips, for my territory was quite large- from San Diego to San Luis Obispo. My girlfriend, Susan Rene, tagged along to keep an eye on the young charges. Little did she realize the young charges were always charged up, and she got far more than she bargained for. It was going to be a long road trip.

First stop Solvang, a charming city in the Santa Ynez Valley, which was founded over a hundred years ago by Danish settlers. It was like stepping into a quaint European village with traditional wooden windmills and pointy, colourful thatched roofs, depicting typical Danish architecture of the 1600s. We got to experience authentic Danish pancakes, which were round like apples. Next, we visited the pretty Seaport of Morro Bay. The massive promontory rock that can be seen for miles seems to anchor the coast to the sea. (sorry boys, as enticing as it was, no climbing...)

But I think it was Hearst Castle and Madonna Inn that were the highlights of the trip. The thing about California is that you can drive an hour in any direction and be in an entirely different climate, place, and space of time. As you climb the mountain to the Castle, the trolley slowly winds its way up the hill, and it suddenly becomes one of the quietest and most peaceful places you've ever experienced... like ascending to the heavens. I watched my boys' eyes as the guide told us about all the exotic animals that once populated these grounds making it the most abundant natural zoo in the world at one time. They seemed to be seeing each animal come to Life as its name was spoken. The castles and there are a few, if mini- versions of the main, were incredulous. We thought we lost Chad once, but he was just checking out the heirlooms, which were bountiful and breathtaking; I can't blame him for wanting to see as many as he could. We're still a young and green country– a 'teenager' as my new Brit friend called us, but this is America's Castle and the journey to see the grandeur of what one mega baron can build in the wilderness is worth the trip. This has become another one of our best-loved excursions and has been affectionately shared with girlfriends and wives. They are our simple pleasures and treasures of Life, like Yamashiro's in the Hollywood Hills. It was the setting of the film, *Teahouse of the August Moon*, starring Marlon Brando. And Huntington Gardens in Pasadena, an all-time haunt of ours, which we watched grow in stature and beauty just as my sons have, since their 1st visit, 25 years ago.

Madonna Inn, in San Luis Obispo, is a different sort of Castle with a different kind of appeal... a Queen of whimsy and kitsch castle with turrets and a candy pink dining salon, and waterfalls in the men's bathroom. Every room is decorated in its separate style and theme from The Caveman's Room, to the American Beauty Room to the Safari Room. We stayed in a room with a horse theme, and I think I remember blue ribbons embedded in the shower glass door. It was dressed like a tack room. In the morning, Chad led the brigade, made friends with the maids (he wasn't of dating age yet), and he and his brothers got to see many of the rooms that were being cleaned. It was like falling inside *Alice and Wonderland's* world. And they all seemed like kids in a candy store, checking out the décor and pulling in one another to see another cool room. That was a trip we will always look back on with fondness. They have all made that trip back a few times with the Loves of their Lives.

For me, a heartfelt remembrance that took place in the Malibu days was on "Mother's Day" as we went bike riding on the Santa Monica bike path near the pier. Lots of folks just sat on the wall, people-watching as riders leisurely cycled by. That day each of the boys had a tee-shirt on with their favourite pics of Mom on the front of it. Chad may have led the pack, and I came up the rear; and, by the time my bike reached the point where they each had passed, all at once people started cheering and clapping. I looked around me to see what they were cheering at and realized the people recognized me from the pictures, worn by my Sons – and were paying tribute to a Mom. Wow, what a special Mother's Day that was—one of the best ever. Some days should just be emblazoned in the sky!

Malibu was that mid-mark in the Heavens… the time on Earth where you can just discover, grow, and be. They are the moments I hold closest and are dearest to my Heart because we were all together – these were the Halcyon Days of Our Lives.

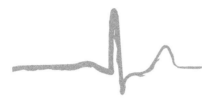

CHAPTER 11

Just Chad and Mom
Toluca Lake, CA

I think we'd always known with Father's job New York might be the last stop on the Butrum Express. The years had flown by so quickly: Detroit, Chicago, St. Louis, Los Angeles, and finally, "The Big Apple." The two younger brothers, now teens, were drawn to the lights of the Big City...possibly modeling for Curt and Collin had discovered break dancing. Where better to experience the dance of the day and all things related to art and music than New York City? But Chad loved Los Angeles—where the sun held court and it was always a great day to play a game. Also, of far-more reaching importance, he was graduating high school this year from North Hollywood High, so I would stay behind and graduate my 1st Son from high school, and his brothers would head East to the City Lights with Carl and Sharen.

This was the most difficult transition of all. – We had all lived in the same city, even in the later teen years with our blended family, where we traded weekends and switched households, like so many of our modern families learned to do. But east coast – west coast was a 3,000-mile separation. This would be a challenging time in our lives, but like so much of Life, all the years and moments we *did* spend together, every day, helped us get through the days and moments we could not.

I found an apartment for Chad and me in Toluca Lake, the same beige-pink stucco California signature- a 2 Bedroom, 2 Bath. And Chad decided to make his entire room the 'sports closet' along with everything else and opted to sleep in the living room. Below us lived a very nice older couple, and I must say they were very tolerant of Chad playing his heavy metal music at a hair-raising decibel when I was off to the makeup artist job. - What else? Yes, the makeup story continues, but it took on a more 'observant' tone this time in regards to Chad, rather than participatory. After all, Chad was the Quarterback of his football team, so the 'arts' were taking a secondary seat… somewhat.

Once, he showed up at Robinson's (Department Store) with two of his *girl*friends in tow (as opposed to 'girlfriend'), which he also had. I was working as a freelance artist for Chanel, the prestige colour, and skincare line. The trio watched very quietly, wholly engrossed in the process as I first applied the essential skincare, which precedes any makeup application as it lays the appropriate foundation. Its real purpose is to keep the skin perfectly cleansed, hydrated, soft, and supple. This was another step that did not escape my first-born, and he would edify his friends, both male, and female, as we shall see…

But today, he watched closely with a precision eye, even more astutely than he had at 18 months old when he had viewed his young Mom dabble in makeup artistry the best she could. Today she was the professional artist applying makeup for a client: using a special brush for each particular step, personalizing colours, showing which eye shadow goes where, how to blend, and the finishing touch - a face chart. This map of sorts showed where each colour I had used on the client was strategically placed so the customer would be able to duplicate each step at home. Chad just had to draw closer to have a better look at it. Naturally, I could tell he had his eye on that Impressionistic chart. This time he did not win; the customer won. She wasn't about to go home without it.

From that moment, I had a steady stream of candidates to '*make up*.' Willingly or not, he would lead them to whatever store I might be working, "My Mom is a makeup artist, she'll do your makeup."

Not a question, but an imperative, and they all came – at the business establishment or our home. (One of those lovely young ladies had approached me years later on a much different occasion where she had taken out a letter from her wallet. Chad had written it to her on his birthday. And as I mentioned in Chapter 4, she shared it with us at the gravesite, and then turned to me and said, "I don't know if you remember, but you did my sister's and my makeup... Chad took us there." (- The wonder of Life and the priceless interludes we have. I don't think any of us will ever forget the makeup lessons we had or gave, or the person responsible for them.)

And his football mates were no different... I kid you not. – One day I came home from work and was greeted with an uncanny site: four football players, still dressed in their uniforms– minus the helmets, were sitting propped against the far wall. Their faces were covered entirely with the Borghese mud mask. –Uh, huh... "How ya doing Boys?" said I, oblivious to the thick layer of goo on their upturned faces, as if I saw this every day of the week. "How you doin' Mrs. B.?" And I thought as I passed them, 'NO ONE IN THE WORLD EXCEPT CHAD' could have gotten these big galunkas who crash into each other like refrigerators to put a mud mask on their faces. Well, it wouldn't be in vain, I thought, they *would* like how their faces felt– so clean, especially after practice. But I'm sure the one and only had edified them with these benefits...

He also had this thing about his uniforms – they had to be continuously washed. I was later informed by his friend, Lou, that during the intense summer football practices, they would come home at the break and wash their uniforms at the apartment. When we lived in Malibu, Chad started doing his own laundry—*his own clothes,* that is. No one else's laundry could go in with his. A bachelor-in-training, I thought... good luck to the girlfriends.

Friday night football was a standard fare even if your Son wasn't the Quarterback. Here is where I learned a stellar quality about Chad – his absolute positive attitude and his tenacious perseverance... against all odds. Just like in the *Rocky* movie when the hero is getting pummeled and thrashed and looks up and gestures for more. - He's not quitting; this was Chad. It wasn't the greatest season by far as wins went, but Chad just kept at it trying to inspire his team. Once, I remember turning to the gentleman behind me on the bleachers and proudly pointing, "That's my Son, the quarterback." "I'm sorry," he said, not maliciously; no offense taken. His Aunt Liza (on my side of the family) was living in California then, and she would come to a few of Chad's games. At one particular tough loss, she told me she was preparing herself before she went to talk to Chad on the sidelines. She expected him to be quite sad. On the contrary, he greeted her with a big smile and said, "We did better than last week!" Afterward, she found me in the stands and said, "He is the most positive person I have ever met."

The art of film continued, undiminished, and I remember he and Lisa, his 'girlfriend,' coming home one night after having just seen the movie *Cocoon*. Chad was so excited, did we know any older people we could tell to go see this movie because they would love it. (He was one of the few young people I have ever known who genuinely cared about the feelings and interests of older people as well…and, of course, their 'history.')

On this note, his Grandpa Luzod and step-Grandma Juanita from Michigan came to visit us in our Toluca Lake digs. With his inimitable, out-of-left-field zingers, bright, smiling Chad offers, "So Grandma Juanita (who was born in the Philippines), "If Asian people's eyes are going this way- (complete with demonstration, pulling the eyes more lateral) what nationality are they? – Or what about if the eyes are slanted upward?" (again the appropriate demonstration, while we, the half-sibling brother and sisters, are standing open-mouthed, thinking we just entered "Scotty, beam me up Land…") And then, to our utter amazement, *the grandmother* starts to answer him with the same demonstration of eyelids, tweaking them up, then lateral, then down!! "Well, I think if they are this way, they are Japanese" "or maybe it's the other way." Liza, Lonnie, and I burst out hysterically laughing. The two of them were actually having this conversation – in all seriousness, replete with the gestural demonstration. Call in the Anthropologist! -It was the day of "The Epicanthal fold and its

Variation of Eye Slanting Positions" query by Mr. Curiosity, who else... You had to be there...

But one of the fondest, most enduring memories was a Sunday morning when Chad dragged me out of bed, literally, to come and see this charming, old-fashioned movie he was watching. It was a movie about a producer who becomes a bum and travels on the train with the vagabonds so he can do some real-life research. I later found out the actors were John Garfield and Veronica Lake. How gratifying to discover both with my own Son! And it wasn't until the very end with the credits rolling that it dawned on me, "Chad, it was a beautiful love story! And they never even kissed..." He, too, respected the traditional mores. I think I was living with a very old soul. He was a classic soul who, despite his heavy metal proclivities, also listened to classical music at pool-side. He looked forward to growing old together and planning a life. He even started thinking of names for his children. He even wore classic penny loafers. They weren't even made in his lifetime... or so I thought. (I now have his with me.)

I remember, too, it was Chad who introduced me to Bono and u2. I think his album, *Joshua Tree,* had just come out, and I found earphones (the big ones) being placed on my head. I had to listen to the entire album. Needless to say, the moment was priceless... We never think about how precious each moment is...because after all, there will always be more to follow. Life is young... How I wish I had paid more attention to that moment, listened more intently to the lyrics, and had more times my Son, Chad, would have placed his earphones on my head – as both his brothers have continued to do during the years.

We share music new and old together when we are driving down the streets and freeways of L.A. This is one of my most cherished things on Earth now— listening to music, all kinds of music with my sons, Curt and Collin. Curt, introducing me to the old radio plays that entertained before either of us were born (complete with the sound effects!) or discovering Iggy Azalea, thanks to niece Anya, or singing along with Collin to the many Bon Jovi anthems, or listening to the great Chester Bennington and Linkin Park. I enjoy it immensely– never checking out, never missing a beat. I think that is a great Gift Chad has left all of us – to Live every moment of Life with laser precision.

As far as another subject, Creative Writing went, I saw an inkling of what would someday pour out profusely in his very unique 'Carolco Chronicles' days. One Saturday, Chad's girlfriend, Lisa (yes, popular name back then), and I were standing over Chad's shoulder watching him type. Girls are funny creatures, too; they think it's so cute that his big hands are finding all the keys. And after oohing and aahing, I think Chad shooed us away. However, later, when I would read what he was typing, I would see a very coherent, engaging story about the Boston Minutemen. I thought he was copying it from a newspaper but, I found out he had actually written the story himself. Another time, I remember reading a poem he had written for one of his English class assignments, titled:

"She Lives in the Shadowy Past"

Hollywood is only a shadow of what she once used to be
It's a place of yesteryear and now transients roam free
Producers use you, and you chase your dreams
But lost souls are all you see
True it once was the place to go
But now it has gone down so low
Hollywood thrives on its past
And she lived a little too fast

What it comes down to is she burned herself out
Yet after all these years the Old Lady still carries some clout
Hollywood is where you can make it real fast
Or fall on your face and come in Dead last
She is still respectable, and you got to like her
All that happens to her causes quite a stir

The Old Lady of the West will always be bright
And in my mind will always be a shining light

No, the poem did not receive high marks, but what I saw within it was the irrefutable optimism that was Chad's core – the ability to always find something good within everything. –And, too, when I think of his own little pharaonic resting place, isn't it perfect that he should have around him the replica of the Chapel of the Boston Minutemen, which he often alluded to and the mosaics of the American Revolutionary that meant so much to him. And on the other side of the mountain from where he lies is the iconic Hollywood sign. This is the City of Angels he loved, felt most comfortable in, and never really wanted to leave.

During the year we were together, Chad's step Great Grandpa Gil passed. He was a fascinating gentleman. Born in India and a Sikh, he had been a very respected engineer in Detroit and personally had known a few astronauts of the time. They were a very striking couple: Carl's grandmother, brilliant blue eyes and platinum hair and her husband, dark-complexioned, poised, and quite affable. I know it meant a lot to Grandma Gil to have her great-grandson Chad attend the funeral and vice versa.

But I also got to learn a few more things about my Son from his solo journey to San Diego. He told me while he was in the airport, he saw a man continually berating a Hispanic janitor. Finally, Chad got up, all 17 years of him and went over to the man and told him he shouldn't be doing that. The janitor was only trying to do his job, and where he came from had nothing to do with anything. I was so proud of Chad, he always had this sense of justice about him- ever since he was 5 and had gotten so upset that little Eddie D. broke his bat and lied about it.

And the other thing I learned is how much Chad cared about his Mom and wanted her to be happy and have a partner, too. - Now, who hasn't seen the film *Sleepless in Seattle*? Well, it turns out I had an older version of the young boy in the movie by about 10 years. As soon as Chad was unpacking from the trip he had made to honour his great grandfather Gil, he presented me with a business card. "What's this?" He answered, "I sat next to this nice businessman. - He's very successful, nice-looking, you should call him." "OMG," I said silently, how am I going to get out of this…

Can you just picture this scenario? Chad, checking out his unwitting seat mate's shoes because after all, according to *The Book of Chad* –you must have good shoes. Briefcase- that's good, too. Attractive, intelligent, sense of humour… good candidate. The guy has no idea he's being scouted… by a son. How he got the man's business card, I didn't ask. 'The card' sat next to the phone for two straight weeks. Chad is relentless; every day, when he gets home from school, he asks, "Did you call him, Mom?" He is never going to let this go, so to get him off *my back*, I pick up the phone and call the stranger. Of course, Chad doesn't leave the room. No, he moves closer so he can hear me speak better! "Uh, hello, sir, you don't know me, but my son sat next to you on the plane when you were coming from San Diego to Los Angeles about two weeks ago …. (silence) And well he thought I should give you a call…."

Can you imagine the guy on the other end of the phone??? I can assure you he will be wary of amiable, unassuming, inquisitive young men sitting next to him on planes and not be giving his business cards out to strangers, especially if they are 17! I was so happy the all-important prom, and graduation dates were nearing, and Chad would now have more pressing things on his mind than his mother's 'matchmaking.'

However, as the world would turn, Chad would have to scurry to do some matchmaking of his own, for as we all know, fighting will always be a part of the landscape of the high school couple and not always 'great timing.' - Let's say just two weeks before prom, the couple, C and L, are not speaking. And how do I always get thrown into the mix, "Mom, if I can't find a date, you're going…" Of course, he was kidding, and of course, he found a date. (There are just so many things a mother can do for her child… I mean, really.)

Lovely girl, the new prom date, though I did miss Lisa – after all, we hung out a whole year together; she even called me Mom! Fabulous limo, the couples all rented, well the parents all rented… but aren't we glad we did? (That picture with Chad leaning on the limo in his tux jacket will be used for a long time and for very specific reasons, more in Part II.)

Graduations are one of the main events of Life, and I remember that day. I was working at a private colour clinic for Chanel at Bullock's Wilshire. The store was one of the most elegant stores of the day, reminiscent of the specialty doors of the '40s when white-gloved elevator attendants brought you to your floor. In this event, clients had been booked for months in advance, but I had to beg out an hour early so I could make the ceremony. "My son is graduating at 7 PM." This supervisor, who did not know me well, said, "Graduating? From what, kindergarten?" (Well, I did look young then... because I was! That's what happens when you have your babies when you're in your teens. They are suddenly teens and graduating before you know it.) It helped that I had an outstanding day at the store. I had 4 clients that bought nearly every item I put on them. Typically, one does not/cannot leave an event early, that's what you're booked for, the whole affair.

I did make it just in time; however, Father couldn't make it because of a business trip. But Sharen flew in from back east, and she and I were there to see the memorable moment of Chad in his cap and gown, and then surrounded by his great friends, Louis Milito, and Sean Smith. (Though it may sound very glamorous working as a freelancer for prestige companies, the pay is often 1-2 months in coming; and well, Chad ate for 3—there must have been an extra person in there. Sean's parents belonged to the country club where Chad often was – eating! To this day, Sean's Mom is the first to send her gift to "The CHAD Foundation Annual Benefit." Can I tell you how fortunate we are to have these wonderful lifelong friends? Chad brought us together and keeps us together.)

In my time with just Chad and I, we shared some of the dearest moments of my Life. I wish I could have been able to get Chad his high school letter jacket, I wish we could have taken that trip to Europe together... but for me to give acknowledgment to these thoughts is to diminish the magnificent moments that did happen. I have also, through circumstance, had the time to spend a year with just Collin in Malibu, and Curt in New York, post 9-11. Each child is so unique, and I am thankful for that gift of being able to spend individual time with each of them and get to know the persons they have and are becoming.

As our year together came to a close, I accompanied him to his first community college orientation as I had in kindergarten. As every parent knows, that is a heart-tugging passage. I also sanctioned his first roommate living situation. CB was a musician living in the Valley, no drugs or seemingly wild lifestyle, and several years older than Chad. The one thing I was also grateful for was Chad was a big, strapping young man and could take care of himself, and Chad was not easily influenced; he was 'the influencer.' Plus, mothers often have this gut instinct and a good sniffer. So with the musician, Mr. C., it seemed a good place to leave my grown-up boy. You know we always think of our boys as boys regardless if they're shaving! One day I was on a date (yes, I was capable of finding my own, too!), and as it was getting late, I said I have to get home to feed my child. "Oh," said the nice fellow, "how old is your child?" "Eighteen," said I without blinking. When he picked himself off the floor, he said, unabashedly, "Is it a man or a woman?" Great line, funny guy!

Chad, too, was a funny guy and one of the most free-spirited individuals I have ever met; I never knew what was coming next or when. When I first encountered his new roommate, he directed him, "Carl, show my mom your studio and play some of your music." Without delay, Carl led us to his studio with keyboard synthesizers and started playing his music. All of a sudden, Chad grabs my hand and starts dancing and swinging me around all during the song. Carl never knew what was going on behind him; he was into playing his music. Chad was into his dancing. It was the most extraordinary dance to remember always... so dance with your Sons, Mothers, and Sons with your Mothers and Fathers with your Daughters. Chad taught me you never need a special occasion to dance – you make every dance a special occasion.

He also had this amazing, unexpected thing he'd do when he was 5, 16, or 25. He would be talking to a friend (or me) on the phone and suddenly would hand the phone to us: "Here _____, talk to my Mom," or "Here, Mom, talk to _____." And there we were... two strangers talking to each other. We didn't know each other, or well, but we would talk to each other, thanks to and because of Chad. I never really entirely understood it, but when I think about it, it was quite lovely, wasn't it? To have your Son want his friends to know his Mom and his Mom to know his friends is pretty special - some of whom remain friends to this very day.

But the tide was changing again, and the East Coast and Chad's younger brothers were calling. Now that big brother was graduated on the West Coast, it was time to think about moving East but not before a quick trip to Michigan to see my foster-parents. They were beautiful people, salt of the earth, who raised me from 3 months to 6 years old. Something was drawing me there for a visit, and within 3 months, my dad had a stroke. It had been so lovely to get to spend time with him and get to know things about him that I'd never known. For instance, he actually had a visit to the White House and met President Roosevelt. And it was a Gift to be with my Mom Fay, who was the single most important person in my Life. She taught and gave me the most essential Gift of All – Love - which is the single most significant Gift I could give to my children. Talk about a legacy...

I stayed with my parents an additional 3 months to raise the monies to move to New York by doing what else, working as a makeup artist at the J.L. Hudson stores for Shiseido cosmetics. I guess I had come full circle, but the oldest cosmetic company in the world would again serve as a stepping-stone. And thanks to them, I would have a job working for them at the largest department store in the world, "Macy's, Herald Square."

I guess you might say we were *stretchers*. All born in the breadbasket of our country, we took our family the farthest West we could then the farthest East: – I took it literally, settling on the white sands of the Pacific Ocean in Malibu, where I could go no further, then to the Atlantic Ocean on the East Coast. The Seaport was my first home in New York and the place where many of our ancestors first stepped on to this land.

Chad stayed in his City of Angels, eventually moving in with his best high school friend, Lou Milito, in Los Angeles. Lou often referred to Chad as the brother he never had, and Lou's parents opened their house and their hearts to our Son. We have been blessed by so many real-life Angels in our Life. The Milito's became Chad's West Coast Family for many years as Mom headed East, bracing herself for the Big Apple to be near her youngest brood.

CHAPTER 12

Chad in New York
The Best Christmas Ever

The moment my foot first stepped down on the soil of Los Angeles, I knew I would not be there forever. I remember thinking this as my Family, and I stepped on to the escalator to retrieve our luggage, and looking up, a sign, "Welcome to L.A.," greeted us. I didn't know how long it would be, but I knew I was only a visitor in this, the City of the Sun. However, this day when I pulled back the curtain 3,000 miles away and stepped into the symphony of brilliant noise that New York City is, it was like coming home... and I knew I would never leave. Only two days there, scouting out an apartment, and tourists were coming up to me asking for directions. That's pretty funny since I had only been there a few times: the first being when I was just 16 and was accompanying my Drama High School Club to the Genesian Festival in N.Y.C., and the second being a special weekend trip with Chad in my tummy. (I'm sure he remembers... He remembers everything).

His Father and I figured how many weekend trips could we expect *post*-baby, so we made this trip to New York a special one. We visited Central Park, and- I still remember what I was wearing. It was a turquoise wool suit, with a delicate bronze line forming somewhat of a plaid. Chad, quite content within, could not be detected from the picture which his Father snapped. I sat comfortably on a mound of granite rock, which serves as a piece of furniture we recline and rest upon throughout Central Park. It is an antique remnant from the ice ages.

When we visited Greenwich Village, it was a strange and wondrous place, with great music pouring out of the venues. Many were tucked behind the doors of basement-level brownstones. Tenants would be sitting on the steps (their outdoor furniture) chatting up the day or flourishing the sidewalks with abundant accents, and laughter punctuating the music like a coda. They were all just part of the fixtures that made this place so magical.

In midtown, I remember I was very tentative as I ventured from the safety of the door that led to the observation deck of Rockefeller Center, high above the City. I could say it was probably because I was pregnant, but in reality, it was just plain scary and windy. At that time, as I recall, there were not high barriers around the perimeter wall. As we peeked down from the heights, who knew that the Father would be working at "The Rock," one day eventually becoming President of his company, or me, a fledgling actor, would be writing and performing in off-Broadway plays... Life is hidden away as a mystery, pulled forth by each step we take.

So this New York gene couldn't help but penetrate our children by osmosis. They certainly heard their Mother calling forth N.Y. often enough during their L.A. sojourn. But you know that old saying, "Beware of what you ask for because it just might come true" - even when you're not so ready for it. But the Universal Teacher is no-nonsense and wisely throws you straight into the pool of Life, whether you think you're ready or not: – "Sink or swim." And I'm too afraid (and stubborn) to sink so, like many of us, you learn to swim... quickly.

But there is that added incentive that overrides all – this extraordinary bond I've spoken about that exists between parent and child. I was watching *Planet Earth* recently, and I saw this phenomenon again and again. It goes all the way back to the beginning of time! Watch a mother bear or elephant protecting their young—to the death if necessary. Observe the father penguin protecting the egg at all costs, in subzero weather, often going without food for as long as 3 to 4 months. Witness a parent give up their life savings, their house, their jobs to save their sick child. So it isn't really a choice when your children are in need of you, but nature just continuing the inextricable tie that perpetuates Life through the 21st century, ad infinitum.

And so I came to be near my youngest and my dream place, New York, but it wasn't so dreamy the first year. When Chad came to visit that Christmas, my year was planted all over my face in the form of adult acne, something my son was not used to seeing. He took a long time in my studio bathroom writing my Christmas card, a card I will treasure until the end of time – because it was my son now giving back to his Mother:

> *"Dear Mom,*
>
> *Merry Christmas! I know that you've been through some tough times, but they are no tougher than before. As you always told me without the bad times how can you appreciate the good times? Well with your hard work and dedication things in the end will all work out.*
> *I miss you mom but when your better and rich you'll have two homes one in N.Y. and one in L.A. In the future we'll see each other more often. Merry Christmas mom!*
>
> *Love*
> *Chad"*

My son, Chad, the soul of positivity, was right. Things eventually got better, and the sun did come out in New York as well, and sometimes often. The Butrums had arrived and survived. And Chad's brothers had the best of both worlds in Connecticut and New York. Carl and Sharen had a beautiful house in Stamford, country English-style, with a pond in the front yard. And I would often be invited for Thanksgiving dinner, and it was only an hour's train ride away. Mom had a studio in a 4th floor walk-up on the upper east side where the brothers, friends of the brothers, and girlfriends of the brothers would come and hang out. On the weekends, after clubbing, they would sleep sprawled all over the hardwood floor. I have no idea how we all fit, but we did – and memorably.

When Chad came at Christmas time, my Christmas present to all the boys were orchestra tickets to a Broadway show. Notables were: *Cats*, *Our Town*, starring Penelope Ann Miller, and Eric Stoltz, which they enjoyed immensely because these were contemporary actors of their time. We also saw one Christmas *Taking Sides* starring Ed Harris, who gave a powerful performance along with British actor, Daniel Massey. Ed Harris, who is one of our all-time finest film actors from *Apollo 11* et al., showed us that his heart and his talent also belong on the boards where so many great actors began their careers.

Curt was very fortunate and started his modeling career while still in high school. His first ad was for *Commes des Garcon* and then Calvin Klein; youngest brother Collin did a Levis commercial ad and started studying acting lessons at the Neighborhood Playhouse Theatre. My good actor friend, M.C.R., told me that it was the best place for young actors to go. He was right – the luminaries that went there are astounding: Robert Duvall (who was on Chad's Hall of Fame wall at Carolco), Gregory Peck, Diane Keaton, and Tony Randall to name a few.

While Curt was doing one of his European campaigns, Chad came to town, and Mom did her traditional Thanksgiving spread. (I burnt my arm a bit as it touched the outer rim of the upper oven. I had a tiny scar for years, and I was glad I had it because it always reminded me of our Thanksgiving with Chad.)

While the turkey was in the oven, we all headed down to see the annual "Macy's Thanksgiving Parade" but got waylaid for 45 minutes by an awe-inspiring group of break-dancers who were performing nearby. That was the incredulous thing about New York. You have the most astonishing talent in the halls and corridors of N.Y. streets and subways. Professionals and students alike serenade commuters, denizens, and tourists with voice, household objects, grained-wood violins, and taps on shoes. Debark the subway at Times Square and be assailed by the sounds of brass and horns, and trumpets and sax.

Follow your senses through the crowd that surrounds a Swing Band comprised of young musicians of every heritage pumping out tunes from the '40s.

Chad would have loved the performances they're doing today – *were* doing in the subway cars because it's been outlawed, but it sure was impressive. Performers would be hanging from bars, doing intricate moves and backflips down the subway aisles, while never losing a beat.—All the while, dancing and singing to rap, yet they would never touch a passenger by accident with their maneuvers. Well, at least not in the performances I saw. Chad would have loved the music and the athleticism. He would have been watching them for hours just as he did the break-dancers on our Thanksgiving holiday together. The Macy's parade was over by the time we got there, but we were together with Chad living a moment of Life in New York that will never come again, and that's all that mattered.

Chad came to live in Connecticut for a year and went to school and made the Dean's list. I was so proud of him. We all missed him, and I think it was difficult for him. He was still young, lost in L.A. without his family, although he loved being there. Sharen and Carl invited me up for Easter dinner at the restaurant Chad was working at. Here was Chad dressed from top to bottom in the Easter Bunny costume – a rather tall bunny. But all the children loved him, and they were hanging on mightily to his hands and legs. Chad loved it all and was beaming with that effervescent smile we all knew so well. He was soo good with children; they adored him. (His former high-school girlfriend, L., told me at the Wake, Chad had come to meet her son one day, and found his room untidy. So Chad had suggested to him, "Let's go and straighten up your room; that way, you can find things." Hmm, methinks I've heard those words before. (Me also thinks if there was a theme song for this book, it would be the beautiful one sung by Barbra Streisand, *Children Will Listen*... an appropriate choice)

Chad was always so polite, even in New York City. Once he was right behind me as we boarded a city bus; however, when I looked back, I couldn't see him. He was still at the door, letting 10 people board ahead of him.

He was going back to L.A. after that year, and we spent the last day together in Battery Park. I have come to love that area, not only because it was once the cradle of our country and our country's capital, but also because it was one of the last times Chad and I got to spend the entire day together all by ourselves. - Now he is there with me always. I've lived in Battery Park City twice and spent much time on the promenade, whether it be writing a play or rehearsing for *Days of Wine and Roses*. I've always felt Chad there with me. For all my sons, it has become such a memorable part of us.

We had planned to visit the Statue of Liberty later, but by the time we got there, futzing around all day long, the last ferry had left, and so our plans were thwarted. (This wouldn't be the last time…) And so we spent hours looking at names engraved on "The World War II East Coast Memorial" located in historic Battery Park. The memorial was comprised of tall, oblique, monoliths of Gray granite, rising like an honour guard paying tribute to servicemen of many forces: airmen, merchant marines, coast guard, soldiers, and sailors who gave their Lives in WW II. They had made the ultimate sacrifice on this, the western side of the Atlantic. Here were the names of 4,611 heroes.

…I have never met anyone who spent more time looking at just one name. Was he envisioning what this serviceman looked like, what his heritage was, what state he hailed from, how old he was, when he died, his rank, his force, what it must have been like, who were his cronies, or how it was to die at sea? There came a time when, after I saw all I could see with my limited sight that I just observed my son. – Maybe I could learn to recognize every soul more closely as he was doing if I could just learn to see what he was seeing.

The Human Being is an incredible repository. There is just so much to access: what someone else is thinking, doing, saying, and feeling. The sight within is limitless. My Son was lucky to have it. – Most of us just wondered at its mystery, its untold beauty; he actually saw it. I spent his Life watching him wherever he went. — It was as if he was accumulating volumes and volumes of unwritten knowledge to carry with him, a library in his soul that he could carry with him for all times. I think he was not saying goodbye to our City, which I often call the "microcosm of the world," but he was celebrating and memorizing it for all time.

The Best Christmas Ever

…What could possibly be better than Christmas in New York – except that it would be the very Best Christmas of our Lives! Chad was bringing his Maria to N.Y.C., his partner for almost 4 years. She had never been to New York before, and she had never seen snow. We were about to show her both in a style that was exclusive to the Big Apple! Carl and Sharen had moved to the City and had a 3-story townhouse on E. 48th Street. I lived 10 blocks up on E. 58th St. so we were easily able to share the happy couple. I was working for a European company, Lancaster, a few days a week at New York's fashion emporium, Bloomingdales. (Bloomies to the natives) Finally, after hearing so much about my 3 sons, my colleagues were able to meet all three in person at the same time, and my 'neighbors' from nearby counters talked about these affable young men for months to come. I still have pictures in front of the Lancaster counter with Chad and Maria. At least he had grown out of experimenting with *my* makeup and had his own lady to experiment with.

We explored many of the cornucopias of eateries in N.Y.C., but it was the fun of the 5 of us being together: holding hands in the cold, sliding on the snow which the good witch of the north was kind enough to supply plentifully. Maria was appropriately introduced to the joy of intricate snowflakes alighting on her hat and eyelashes. I have an excellent illustration of this as Maria stands in front of a stately wooden double-door, framed in its entirety with boughs of evergreen branches. There was a myriad of snowflakes that were captured through the lens; some were almost half the size of her face! And of course, my traditionalist son couldn't come to New York during Christmas without taking his lovely on a horse-drawn carriage ride through Central Park with its magical stone gateways and forests. I'm sure when the colossal Christmas tree at Rockefeller Center filled their vision, it reminded one of them of a Christmas tree that once filled half his living room in the Midwest. And it couldn't make it out the front door!

Our journey continued with faces upturned like children taking in the majestic holiday windows at Saks and Bergdorf Goodman's. Our walking tour was accompanied by the aroma of street vendors roasting chestnuts. They consumed your senses at every corner, enticing passing parties to stop and partake. Subway rides were packed with numerous packages attached to happy people from everywhere you could imagine. Kitsch? Nah! Just a New York Christmas that the whole world comes to celebrate.

But the most memorable trip we took that week began at the corner of W. 53rd St. and Lexington Avenue. Full of Christmas cheer and merriment, we bundled into two cabs and headed down to The Statue of Liberty. The only problem is one cab went to Battery Park *City* where when I resided there, we all used to look out at The Statue Liberty from the promenade. The other cab went to Battery *Park*, where you actually buy the tickets to board the ferry that goes to the Statue of Liberty. It was icy cold, and by the time our party finally found each other, a bit of our cheer had been stretched, and time once again foiled our plans to go see Miss Liberty – the last boat had just sailed.

Undaunted, the party sallied forth, Sons and Mother, and Girlfriend deciding on another most famous landmark, The World Trade Center…. and aren't we glad we did. Fortuitously for us, considering the season, the lines to World Trade Center's Observatories were very light. It was maybe a half-hour wait at most. Though being a Manhattanite for several years now, I had been to the fine eating establishment in the heavens called "Windows on the World," but never to the World Trade Center's Observatories, which were located in the South Tower. I have a marvelous picture of Maria with her arm around me sitting in Santa's sleigh, which lay nestled in the corner of the indoor observatory on the 107th Floor. A big wreath with the customary red bow above it completes the picture.

But the single-most spectacular image that has been engraved in my mind and heart, and framed in the heavens – is the boy we have watched since the age of 5 reading historical markers. For hours on end, brothers, Father, and Mother were always going back to retrieve him. And here, today, I watched my son at 26, reading deep beneath the marker for the quintessential core of its soul, which held untold information about The City we loved above all. As Chad looked down from that high glass, as from a Cathedral window 1,310 feet above the Earth, I knew he was seeing profound depths into the heart and flesh of this City, which he would take with him forever.

Mom's Christmas Eve Dinner was the 'Mother of All Dinners' that year. Chad ate for 3 straight hours. His brother finally had to remove the plate from his lap. Well, *plates* as he had one just for Mom's freshly-made mashed potatoes, which yes, were his undisputed fave. It was accompanied by the fresh giblet gravy made from the fresh turkey (as opposed to frozen) that we always ordered special for Thanksgiving. Chad loved the family rituals. – Each son had their faves: from the traditional bread stuffing to the yam banana pudding, to the Cranberry, almond whipped crème tri-layer dessert which was Collin's 'always asked for.' I had cooked for days, and my roommate, John, said he saw the maternal bear instinct apparent in his refrigerator which was packed for weeks.

The sons were most helpful in cleaning up the kitchen after big dinners. This was a kind and appreciated custom which was passed down to them from their Father, who inherited the convention from his Swedish stepfather, dear H. E. The kitchen was soon spanking clean, and we retired– all fat like turkeys to watch a Christmas film. Someone, maybe Chad, chose Sylvester Stallone's *Cliffhanger*. (I now, gratefully have the *Cliffhanger* cap, bequeathed from Chad.) –And so Mother Bear and her 3 Sons settled in with tummies overflowing. Even the lean Chad bear had unbuckled his belt… to see a Christmas movie: entertained by '*Rocky*' in The Big Apple. It was the most special of all Christmas's because We Were All Together.

My gifts from Chad and Maria were also treasures and would reflect that classic, distinguished style that he is so known for. One gift was an elegant, forest-green, crushed velvet scarf, in the antique-style with long silk fringes of the same colour; and the other, a delicate, crystal perfume decanter. Both have followed me to my various abodes, and always grace the Christmas season.

For the crowning glory, their Father and Sharen had invited the sons and Maria to join them at their annual New Year's Eve celebration at the renowned Rainbow Room at the top of Rockefeller Center. I love the pictures of Chad and Maria, and brothers surrounded by a bevy of their beautiful friends in full gala trappings in celebration of the New Year. In another, Chad and Maria are sitting barside, he, handsome in a sports coat, and she glamorous in a black dress. Atop her red locks sits a New Year's crown adorned with fluffy white feathers. His wine goblet is filled with orange juice, his signature drink, and hers with champagne.

There is a picture that adorns my New York apartment wall. It is the happiest picture of my Life: Taken on Maria's first trip to N.Y., my Sons, Maria and I are standing in front of the antique grandfather clock, which is set to midnight. And the mirrored wall next to us is filled with the Holiday cheer of Christmas cards. It is a snapshot immortalized in time – a Mother, with a smile that could fill all of New York because she is surrounded by her 3 Sons at Christmas. It was the Best Christmas of my Life, and I am so thankful for it. Today happens to be Thanksgiving Day as I write these words. I think the words were waiting for this special day to be written.

CHAPTER 13

Coming Home

Coming Home is the sharper side of the double-edged sword Life has dealt you because its penetration is permanent. One finds that the shock that has cushioned your body from this trauma for many weeks is beginning to wear off... and in its stead, comes the realization that a significant accouterment of your body/your Life is no longer there—missing forever. But like the heroic counterparts of war who return home with their literal limbs and other essential components torn from their body, one begins the process of learning to heal and walk again. Step by step, one learns to live without that invisible missing limb because Life is the most powerful, relentless force on Earth. It bids us live, despite the most rigorous and excruciating challenges. It is a miraculous force that drives every cell of our being forward.

...And, indeed, rigorous this journey can be... In what I call the early, raw days, I remember one of the hardest things to encounter was coming home to an empty room, and finding myself turning round and round, looking for some*one*/some *thing* to hug. – I would find myself putting on Chad's flannel, which I had brought with me along with his brothers' flannels, which I had also brought, and learning to embrace myself surrounded by the essence of my Sons. This was my own private war- every parent's war, who is now without their child. I knew it would take every cell of my being to get through this, but I also knew if I could get through this, I could get through anything in Life. Things might have looked pretty strange had the 4th wall been broken, and one could see into the privacy of my cave: big round brushes in my hair and wrapped in Chad's green plaid flannel. And stepping into his classic penny loafers while watching my most special Chad video where he comes running onto the baseball field with his super smile that lit up the diamond, the dance floor, the workplace, wherever he was. - I remember touching the T.V., as would a child who wants to reach in and touch the character inside. Only as an adult you now realize, this is the only way to touch your Son now… a sobering moment Life teaches us is part of loss.

It was here I began to know that I had to develop and exercise my spiritual muscles so I could transcend this space and place and time to learn to be with, to see, to communicate with Chad differently. I remember my good friend, Dave, from Canada, telling me once: "Remember, Arista, you are a spirit having an experience in a body, not the other way around." Chad's best friend, Keven Simmons, was playing football with Chad when he collapsed and was the last to speak to him. He said at his interview at one of The Chad Volleyball Benefits in Hermosa Beach, CA, "…He's here, you just can't see him…"

The greatest lessons in Life sometimes come because of the great tragedies and traumas of Life– you are forever changed. You are forced to grow in ways you never imagined. Your values and priorities are turned on their head or at least re-examined. In the ancient Tarot card deck, there is a card called The Tower, which can mean sudden and complete destruction, the sweeping away of all the illusions with the intention of re-birth; the phoenix always rises. That was the way my world was beginning to look.

One thing I learned early on is that I could never again lose anything that would be greater than what I just lost. Once I was at a casting audition at ABC-TV, and I left my portfolio. The casting director came running after me to give it to me, but then, I lost it again on the bus. It was expensive. I had saved many months before I could buy it: All leather from a prestigious Italian company, Cantelmo, I think. It had my name embossed on the cover and many

11 x 14 colour pictures within. I called the "M.T.A.'s Lost and Found Department"; no one ever found it or turned it in. –Who would want or could use a portfolio with pictures of me and my name on the cover?? But I learned it didn't really matter, did it… It was a 'thing.' Things could be replaced; people cannot. One sees a family whose entire house is burnt to the ground. Yes, they are sad to the core, but they will tell you to the camera, "We are all safe, that's the most important thing."

Loss at a young age also affects the young and causes them to reassess their lives. Louis, one of Chad's closest friends, said in his interview at the Chad Zuma Beach Tourney in Malibu, that this deeply impacted him and his wife. (She, too, had lost a dear brother shortly after Chad). They decided to start their family earlier than they had initially planned so that they could begin to replenish some of these holes their leaving left in the Universe.

Replenishment, resourcefulness, and revelation have been my steadfast guides and centurions that give me sustenance and hope in this most important "rest of the journey." Replenishment of the heart, soul, and body– whatever it takes, in whatever form, however long… and that may be a lifetime. For me, the journey began a long time ago, questing for meaning and for answers with an open mind and an open soul, and it led to my core spirit within which led to my own personal connection with my Godhead. – Without that rock, I would not have survived… or well. It was with one hand always reaching inward, and one hand outstretched – for we all need each other. We are Human Beings. I remember I was recently standing on a crowded bus, and a woman came aboard and found her place next to me. You could tell she was a bit frazzled, and she began to tell me she had been in the hospital for the past 20 hours in the emergency room. Her friend/relative—it was unexpected. And just by talking, she was getting relief. It seemed at that moment she was bonding, not with a stranger, but with a like member of her species who was capable of understanding, even though she had never laid eyes on her before. That's all she needed. A moment of human connection. She was "replenished" from the heart. She could move on.

"Resourcefulness," I think, comes from how we are hard-wired as a species and have learned through our evolutionary process how to survive at all costs. Whenever I find myself in a pity party state, I have one image that sets me straight– our heroic Veterans. Some have come home with half of what they left with. And yet somehow they learn to triumph and be the strongest of us all, with a smile on their face and an iron will to live and make the Best of Life. In our darkest hours, I think there are nuggets of resourcefulness just waiting for us as lifelines when we are ready to reach for them. – Being an Artist was one of mine.

And Angels abound to help us. There was a German movie I saw once about angels coming to Earth. I see them now because I *recognize* them better. – They are just dressed as human beings, and surely I acknowledge them and appreciate them more. One of them was my friend, D., a man of many hats- actor/model/writer/ photographer, and as busy as he was, he was the first one there to take me to dinner not long after I arrived home from that sad journey in LA. D. and I performed in the first play I had written, *All About Sneakers*, at the Shooting Gallery in an off-off-Broadway production. He had almost met Chad one year when he was going home to North Carolina for the holidays. But as Chad flew directly to Asheville to see his grandparents who were living there at the time, and didn't stop in New York, he never had the opportunity.

When I wrote *Sneaker's* a few years before – I log-lined it as an old-fashioned love story between two quirky New Yorkers who want to re-find the long-lost steps of love. It is their partial Cherokee heritage that helps find them by bringing them back to Earth and away from the materialism, promiscuity, and addictions that their world has become. After my son's passing, I thought this would be a perfect indie film project for Chad's Foundation, especially with Chad's love and respect for the Native heritage and his old-fashioned values. I also thought it would be interesting to have a love story co-written by a man and a woman, who just happened to play the roles off-Broadway.

And so D. and I embarked upon this unique adventure, even planning on going to the Cherokee reservation in North Carolina to research the screenplay. Honestly, I also think this was a Godsend, the salve to begin to heal a heart that was still an open wound. (The 'resourcefulness' I allude to that comes in strange packages.) But D. was pretty hooked up to the inspirational Gods himself because he came up with a plot twist one day that I would have never thought of…or would have agreed upon.

I remember the day when he told me–like it was yesterday because it took my breath away for about 10 seconds. I was sitting on the floor in his room, where we took turns creating: his room/my room. His space had modern architectural appointments right in the middle of a photographic studio in Chelsea, and mine had access to an L-shaped terrace that had a view of the East River in Sutton Place. Those were the days… great rooms, but not full apartments; the price of being N.Y. artists. - I could tell he had something he wanted to say but didn't know how to say it. Finally, he just blurted it out, prefacing it in his genuine baritone North Carolinian accent. "Now you don't have to do this if you don't want to - it's up to you… but I think you should. – Cristan [the main character] has lost a child… a younger child… and she's having a hard time going through it. And Danny (the other lead character whom I named long before I chose D. for the part) helps her to get through it.-

I remember I couldn't answer because all I could think of was - how in the world could I play this part? But then when I started breathing again, and my mind began to receive oxygen, my artist took the lead. I knew he was absolutely right. – It was finding the full Circle of Life– Birth/Death/Rebirth through our Cherokee heritage and its connection to nature and the Earth. From that moment on, the story took on a life of its own. We did go to the Cherokee reservation in North Carolina, twice. We met a woman, Myrtle Johnson, who I came to call my adoptive Cherokee Mother. We met her Family and several members of the community, and she procured for us the blessing of the *"Eastern Band of the Cherokee Nation"* for our film project. Myrtle, as our consultant, brought in the traditional ceremonies of purification in the creek waters that would help Cristan's Spirit to heal.

Chad was with us always, and he was helping his real Mother heal through the creation of this story, now called *Earthen,* which calls upon the ancient healing powers of this great tribe who were among the first entrusted caretakers of this Land we now call our "Home." The Universe is a great caregiver. It nourishes us and sustains us daily, and it takes from us daily, but also provides us with the resources to replenish and rebuild our cells and our souls. I learned in Cherokee that the trees do speak to you in gentle whispers, but only when you listen with your heart can you hear the purest part of your Spirit decipher their meaning. (I think Danny said this in one of the lines in the screenplay, *Earthen*.) A Mother found replenishment and restoration through the instrument of Art, which has been with us from the beginning of our species and an indigenous tribe that inhabited our lands first and were in touch with their Spirit, Mother Earth.

"Revelations" are the Gifts that keep on giving. Recently, CHAD provided a heart screening honouring a 16-year-old football player, Miles Kirkland, who died suddenly of Hypertrophic Cardiomyopathy, the leading silent killer of Sudden Cardiac Death in Young Athletes. He was at football practice at Curtis High School in Staten Island, N.Y. In preparing his Story Poster, his mother told me stories of how many of Miles's friends would approach her and tell her what an impact her Son made on their lives. One friend of his had decided to go to nursing school because of him and his encouragement. There was another friend who lacked confidence, but Miles, 'the gentle giant' as he was called, took him under his wing and helped him with his training program. –It is stories, anecdotes, tributes that people give you that are your continuing nourishment for Life. The continuing revelation of your child through other's eyes is the ultimate tribute to your Child's spirit; however long or short, he/she graced our presence. Every second has meaning.

A most cherished gift came through the mail arriving, not intentionally... or so we think...on my birthday a few months after Chad left us. It was from Joan, Maria's Mom. As mentioned, she was a nurse and a world traveler on her holidays. She was scheduled to visit Yugoslavia, but there was a civil war, and her trip was canceled. However, she found a sealed envelope (which she opened to see its contents), and it was *"Chad's Wish List."* He had given it to her to place at the statue of the Blessed Mother for legend had it if you place your wishes there, they would come true. It was written in his hand. I was taken aback to see such wishes...written from a young person. He never expected anyone to see what he had written, but somehow I don't think he'll mind if I share it with you. As you may remember, he was always handing me the phone, "Mom, talk to _____" or "_____, talk to my Mom." ... And as I exercise my spiritual muscles, we will continue this ongoing 'Spiritual dialogue,' for I think Chad never wanted us to feel alone. He always wanted us to have each other...

"Chad's Wish List"

I hope I live an emotionally and physically
satisfying life!
I hope I'm healthy to the end
I hope I'm Lucid in mind and soul
That I reach all of my untapped potential
I hope I bring happiness to others
I hope I leave my mark on this
world and will be remembered
as a solid contributing citizen
With honor and honesty and dignity
I hope I leave a rich legacy to my family

Chad Alan Butrum

It was one of the most profound and beautiful birthday presents of my Life. I was truly honoured and humbled to be the Mother of such a special, caring Human Being, and after reading my Son's *"Wish List,"* it became apparent Chad didn't need the statue after all. - All of his wishes had come true.

Maria and I continued in close contact. I can't imagine the pain she was going through. Her Mom told me she would cry for hours, and there was nothing I could do so far away, but at least the brothers were there to look after her. They moved her into a new apartment, which helped her to begin the painful start of a new journey. Once, she and Curt were riding together in the car on the freeway and coming upon the cemetery. Maria started to get upset, and Curt grabbed her hand and told her not to look – "He's not there anymore.…" And once she and Collin were walking in the hills and they talked about God and Heaven, and what Chad might be doing.

She would send me lovely gifts like "heart pillows" made in her feminine, Victorian style. She would reminisce how Chad would spend hours in a Retro store trying to find the mate for a particular pump he wanted for her. He was a throwback to some elegant era. He could have stepped into the ambiance of *Gatsby* as quickly as take the dancefloor as a cool dancer in the coolest club in L.A.

She laughed when she remembered a story about the animal rescue shelter where they went to volunteer. One time it was Chad's duty to bathe the birds. Maria was doing her thing, and later when she turned around, she did a doubletake.– There stood each bird freshly bathed with a paper towel wrapped around it like an Emperor Penguin's cloak, and they were standing all in a row. Chad had lined up each bird on the counter. Even the birds didn't move and listened to him – it was that "Chadisma" – his own particular form of charisma that informed everything he touched. Maria thought that was the sweetest thing she'd ever seen. And other moments may arise instantaneously. … While Chad was playing his last game on Earth, Maria was at the movies seeing of all titles, *Four Weddings and a Funeral*. The costar, Hugh Grant, and Chad, almost resembled one another with a cursory glance.

One night, Louis, (Chad's best friend, who often said Chad was like the brother he never had,) worked together with both of Chad's brothers, Curt and Collin, on the movie *Infinity*. The set was located on the other side of the hill from Chad's final resting place. They even threw the pigskin around. I know that was a tough night for all of them, yet I know Chad was pleased they were all together.

Chad saw and made and found magic in the most mundane moments. He loved Life with a fanaticism and made us all sit and enjoy it with him. "Come watch this- Come listen to this" …and we all did (often watching our own clock ticking in the background) –but aren't we glad we did. Louis would say, the only thing Chad asked of you was *your time*.

These were the days of the New Journey, where your ship is missing a Mate, a Mate you thought would always be with you – a Son, a Brother or Sister, a Friend, a Partner, a stalwart pillar you could always call upon. - Now everyone is just trying to rudder their ship in their own way. There is a painting on my bedroom wall loaned from an artist in my building, which illustrates it so well: Dark golden, billowing clouds, fringed with golden gilt contrast with a navy sky, heavy but always moving forward. They ride above the charcoal storm clouds that rake the horizon. Streaks of sunlight filter through them as they guide the shadowy ship through the murky sunbeam…

…More Revelations

The mail, the phone, the computer were like beacons of lighthouses that helped us move forward. Someone's friend knew of a baseball team, called the "Blackball Team." And when they found out about Chad, they wanted to do something memorable for him. I have the team picture they sent me, showing how they had Chad's name printed on the back of each of their shirts along with their player numbers. They made it all the way to the playoffs that year, and the Team Captain had written me that they were having some trouble in the last games. But then they all got into a huddle and prayed and said, "This one is for Chad!" They took the field, chanting his name. As I recall, they won not only that game but the final playoff game! That would have made Chad very happy; he loved baseball so. A beautiful gift from strangers I never had the pleasure of meeting, but the story of a young sportsman touched their hearts, and we will never be strangers again. A few years later, Maria and I spoke, and it was the year baseball went on strike. We both agreed, in this instance, we were glad Chad wasn't here; he would have been exceptionally distressed.

As for Chad's intellectual curiosity, it began at a very early age. "I'm reading, I don't know what…but just wait till I get old enough to ask QUESTIONS!!!" I found a gem in his yearbook, "…No more questions, Chad! –I don't know!!" And his Australian granny would say after hours of his *inquiring,* "Anything, Chad, just leave me alone." Granted, some of his questions were pretty bizarre and came out of nowhere, such as "How much does a head weigh?" Well, we never heard that one again until the 5-year-old kid in *Jerry Maguire* asked the same question. We were all peering inside that kid's head, "Chad, are you in there??"

In regards to "Friendship," I think Chad took that word to its highest meaning. Coming home, I began to sift through the pages of his Life, and I began to see a singular thread woven into all the stories, cards, and tributes. When Chad saw *you*, he saw only *you*, talked only to *you,* and cared about only *you*. He looked deep within and saw your unique potential and encouraged it… In his high school yearbooks, I found the words of two Friends I'd like to share with you:

> *"Dear Chad,*
>
> *I just want you to know that you've been my hero for the past three years. I can't understand why you even talked to me, I was a freak. You helped me get self-confidence and overcome my super shyness… And thank you for your ragging powers.- I*

never knew how to handle myself when it comes to a fight with words, now I can hang with the best of them.

(Mister D.)"

And from a young lady schoolmate-

"Dearest Chad,

You're definitely one of a kind and your definitely not like the other guys in our society. I think people don't know the meaning of friends until they have you.

(Miss S.)"

I think that's just who Chad was, someone who had compassion and understanding for all peoples, including the underdogs. He was born with a birthmark on his cheek, slightly darker than his complexion. Later in life, he tried laser therapy but was allergic to it. In nursery school, he would come home and ask me at 3 years old why kids were so cruel and would call him names. I think this was when he began to form his own code and how he would protect those who other people picked on because of whatever difference they might have or be. I remember once when we were living together in Toluca Lake, I came home, and he was still in his football uniform but icing his face. He had gotten into a fight, but he told me he realized there had to be a better way of dealing with people like this: he didn't want to look like a monster. Guess he got it figured out. That year his classmates at North Hollywood High voted Chad and L., the best-looking boy and girl in the Senior Class.

Some Friends saw Chad's *own* potential like Jake Downey, who went on to pursue a professional career in broadcast and media. He thought Chad would be a natural and offered to teach him all he could about the profession. Chad even came to stay with him awhile on one of Jake's 1st intern jobs in the west, might have been Montana or Wyoming. He even put Chad on camera as an anchor.

Chad wrote the copy for the teleprompter. One of the stories he was reporting was the sad story of rising young actor, River Phoenix, who had met his demise at the Viper Room on Sunset Blvd. (The irony of Life– when this young 'newscaster Chad,' reporting the story of River, would himself collapse and meet his own demise a few months later. Only his would happen on a football field in Van Nuys. And now, Jake would be shooting interviews and footage years hence about his friend Chad's Foundation.) In these news anchor tapes, it was fun to watch Chad, take after take, having a time with the teleprompter, and him staring it down with the *Chad look* as we called it… *'What are you doing??'* You had to know Chad, never his fault… it had to be the teleprompter! (Thank you, Jake, for these never-to-be-forgotten tapes which kind of give us a peek at what Chad might have been…).

Later that year would come the dedication of his stone ceremony. Carl had called me, and the choice was at once agreed upon, a quote from Shakespeare's *Romeo and Juliet* as the young Juliet regales her Romeo:

Chad Alan Butrum

> *… and when he shall die*
> *Take him and cut him out in little stars*
> *And he will make the face of heaven so fine*
> *That all the world will be in love with night*
> *And pay no worship to the garish sun."*

William Shakespeare
("Romeo and Juliet")

His father surprised me by putting a small, engraved baseball player figure before the poem. Only later did I realize how perfect it was – because the name of our Son's foundation *is "The Chad Foundation for Athletes and Artists."*

Prior to the ceremony, it was Maria who called me and made the suggestion that I read from one of my writings, as I hadn't been able to give a eulogy at Chad's church service. And so one immediately came to mind that I had written in the Malibu days when we all lived together. At the time, I would not know that I would also be writing this poem for my Son, Chad, several years into the future:

There, They Wait

...And laugh did I hear them
At my earthly demise
The Gods were in focus
In gentle disguise.

John, Robert, his brother,
King and Monroe
Stood there all laughing
Four Gods in a row.

"Look, papers she shuffles
And acting's her game
If only she knew that it's
Here where's the gain."

And off they went chuckling
Amused by their play
"When she's ready she'll come
Then we'll take off the day."

And then said I to John,
Robert, King, and Monroe,
"I'm coming to join you, and
We'll be five Gods in a row."

"Okay," they all answered
In mock-serious tones.
"We'll look for your Spirit
And save your sweet bones."

"But careful," they warned
The journey's one track

And once you ascend it
There's no turning back.

"So take care of Earth duties
And clean out your mind
And leave them your treasures
And moments to find.

Take care of your business
And kiss them goodbye
For your real work's in Heaven
That's where you must fly.

"We can't say any more
The rest's up to you
To ponder and sift through
And wonder anew."

"So good luck dear daughter.. (and Son)
We bid you adieu
Til the sky sees your limit
And gives us to you."

Malibu, California
Paradise Cove
by Arista

Dear Son,

I/We have much to do "til the sky sees our limit... and brings
us to you"...But I, We, shall look forward to that day with all
of our Lives-

Love Eternally,
I Love You, Mom &
All your Friends on Earth

The first year ended at the memorable place Chad had brought Maria for New Years' Eve, just one year before– the venerated "Rainbow Room." This year I too was invited to join the annual Butrum festivities, and Sharen's Mom was in from Australia and would join us. We had an incredible time dancing. We *all* loved to dance. However, as the stroke of midnight arrived, it found Granny and I blending our tears as we soulfully embraced cheeks, our foreheads touching the floor-to-ceiling windows that looked down upon our grand City. As we gazed outward, I remembered my 1st born son as he looked upon this city from a different vantage point only one year earlier, The World Trade Center, and she remembered her grandson who asked so many questions. Hers was a double loss as her dear husband of many years had also passed that year.

Chad had also given me an exceptional Gift upon his leaving –his life insurance policy. I remember how kind the H.R. Director was, for she, too, had recently sustained a painful loss. And I remember the day when that envelope arrived, and I just held it for a long time… Could I just give this back to you, and can I have my Son back? No, that's not the way it works - accept this extraordinary Gift, Mother, from your Son, Chad. And so I did and shared a Gift with his two brothers and his dear Maria, which I know Chad would want, and then I gave myself a healing gift. My friend could not get away, so I went alone to the healing waters of the Caribbean for several days in Montego Bay, Jamaica. Here, like no place else, the cerulean sky paints an unending backdrop for the azure seas. And the brilliant sun beats down on you like God's own heart, warming the seawater so you can bask all day long in this glorious bathtub of the universe. It is a place where you can find solace for your own heart and soul amidst the crystalline clarity of the sea. It allows the beauty of its teeming life to greet you from several feet below, offering the silent comfort of nature…

Undoubtedly, the staff wondered why I sat for hours in the middle of the sea. – You could do that in those waters; the shore was shallow for a long while at Half Moon Bay. It was the sun and the sea I was drawing into my being in vast amounts so healing could commence.

And it did, surrounded by my Maker and my Son, I needed nothing else. He had given his Mom the greatest gift – the Gift of Rebirth.

Little did I know that Chad had also given me a *long-enduring gift*, for as life had it, another traverse of mountains was in-store. It happened a few years later when the squalls had started to settle, and it was much smoother sailing. –One day, you're rehearsing for a role in *Cleopatra*, and the next day you bend down at work, and you can't get up. You work out daily and never had a knee problem; then, suddenly, you're being wheeled out of Bloomies on a gurney, geez. Who knew that hyper-flexibility you had all these years could put wear and tear on your knees... especially if your tibias are misaligned? Only one of the best surgeons in New York, Dr. D. Rose, surgeon to the ballet dancers of New York City. And so with expert care, 8 surgical procedures, and nearly 3 years later, I made it through with the help of Chad's gift. There is a Chinese character for crisis, which has two parts: one is "danger," - the other is "opportunity." The 2nd part—"opportunity," I took the ball and ran with it... metaphorically speaking, for I was pretty sedentary during this period. But in fact, it gave me the time to refine my computer and Word skills and put together the infrastructure of our fledgling foundation, legally and otherwise. This was new ground for me, creating and running a nonprofit charity. I've often used that analogy, Chad threw the ball to me. "You've got to run with it now, Mom," but what a Team he left with me to do it as you will see in Part II.

In my Son Chad's passing, I learned two of the most significant lessons in Life: One, there is an awesome, humbling Power that can create an exquisitely unique being as Chad... and I guess only the Power capable of creating it can/has the right to take it back...no questions asked. And two, it is not the personal accolades/titles/status in Life or the possessions one accumulates, but how many people you touch while you are on Earth—what goodness you can do. That's the

Gift that counts … It is not how many years you Live, but what you do with the Years you are given.

What I have learned from writing the 1st half of this book is that I am one of the most fortunate Women and Mothers on Earth to have experienced/been given so many extraordinary moments of Life, times 3 Sons. This is the story of only one Life. Every single Life on this planet is of great importance and has its own indelible story filled with the possibility of millions of precious moments to be Lived. If then we can safeguard and protect Life, we must. -This is why the 2nd half of this book exists: because "Life is the Greatest Gift" we are given and must be safeguarded, protected, and cherished at all costs.

L., Chad's laughing smile and bright eyes
became a signature throughout his Life.

R., His 'curiosity' began early.
Questions, questions…

Above, Chad was very industrious helping
Dad wash the car. Detroit, Michigan

Bot. R., Chad, and Dad, Carl

Their 1st football stance-Curt, Chad, and Collin. Detroit, Michigan

Chad, Collin, and Curt on the lawn of Billy Graham College, Wheaton, Illinois – our 1st step in the journey away from home.

Mom & Chad, Collin & Curt
Annual Applepicking, Rochester, Michigan

L. Chad's 1st Birthday
Detroit, Michigan.

R. Apple picking in the fall, a family
tradition— Romeo, Michigan.
Mom, Chad, Collin, and Curt.

Bot. L., 1st day of school Curt,
and Chad Wheaton, Illinois

Bot. R., Welcome to LA! Venice Beach
Curt, Mom Arista, Chad, and Collin

Top L and Top. R., North Hollywood High School, North Hollywood, California Football, Baseball and Volleyball were Chad's favourite sports. He played with a passion, commitment, and a professional attitude. Every day was a great day for a 'game,' but you better play it *right*.

Bottom Center, Curt, Nicholas (stepbrother big enough to join the stance now)- Chad, and Collin, Stamford, Connecticut

Top L., Chad and Maria's stellar visit to NYC. (Maria's 1st visit; Chad and his orange juice, non-alcoholic libation!) Top. R., Arista and Sharen, Moms, at the Rainbow Room, NYC.

Center L. Chad and Keven S., his best Friend… who was with Chad on his last football game on Earth. Below R., Chad and his Dance Party!

Chad, Curt, Maria (Chad's 4 yr. companion), Mom Arista, and Collin, NYC.
The Best Christmas of our Lives - because we are All Together!!!!!
New York City, The Sovereign

Bottom Center, Chad's Surprise Birthday party – one year before!

Chad's Final Resting Place
The Hollywood Hills, Los Angeles, California

Mom Arista, brother Curt, companion, Maria
"Chad's Garden" of flowers which were your send-off to Heaven

"Bagpiper-Chad's BDay
Forest Lawn"

29th of April 1994
Chad's Birthday
A Special Tribute to Chad
From a kind, Scotsman Piper

PART II
Beyond A Mother's Memories

CHAPTER 14

"The Birth of CHAD"

Raise up your eyes, Enlightened Beings of the Universe! Behold the magnificence of the night sky as the "Lamplighter of the Stars" flits and flurries, sashaying amidst the luminous orbs, seeking one perfect point to dip his wand and set the sky ablaze. – Appearing, disappearing, not here, not there — but HERE! Here the sky turns a brilliant hue of moon-gold at the tiny Castle of Carolco at Easyland and Hollywood where Sir Chad once ventured and became all things at once: Head Squire, Scribe, Poet, Knave, Court Jester, and Knight Errant. And then one spring day while enjoined in a day of sporting events which he loved so much, he is called back quite instantly to the Land where human eyes cannot see, a different mission now at hand. The Court of Carolco, its King and Lords, built Sir Chad's Mother, Arista, a sturdy, foundational vehicle on which she could continue to bring Chad's gifts to All the People He Loved. – As the wand points, the words are emblazoned in the sky: "HEALTHY BODY, MIND, AND SPIRIT."

"Again," says the Lamplighter and flips back just a quick point in time to the "Halcyon Days of Malibu." The wand ignites the star, its beam landing amongst the footlights of a small stage as the young Mother takes her first bow, in her first play, at the Toy Dinner Theater in Los Angeles, *Out of the Frying Pan*. As her head arises from her bow, she sees a handsome, brilliant smiling young man, carrying two dozen red roses standing before her. –It takes her a moment to realize that this beautiful young man is her eldest son, Chad. She has no idea that this is the only play he will ever get to see her take a bow. – That is why he carries *two* dozen red roses for all the years he will miss. She has no idea that something far more important will be sharing center stage with her for the rest of her Life … because of the beautiful young son standing before her– "Chad's Gifts of Heart and Art." Twice, emblazoned in the night's sky!! – "CHAD'S GIFTS OF HEART AND ART."

FADE TO BLACK, but only for an instant, then the inky heavens turn incandescent as the wand tethers another particular point in destiny. It is the footsteps where East meet West: Where a grand Palace of the Eastern persuasion has been placed delicately and perfectly atop and within the Hollywood Hills. It is here the spotlight shines on this Family's most celebratory restaurant, *"Yamashiro's."* Nestled amongst the supreme quiet of traditional Japanese gardens, it was here that report cards were lauded; 1st Loves, and 1st Dates transpired, and many anniversaries and special occasions took place. It is here on these fortuitous steps engaged in the California art of valet parking that the Butrum brothers, Curt and Collin, their Mother, Arista, and Chad's girlfriend, Maria, meet in perfect synchronicity with the feet belonging to Michael Tidik. Michael is Chad's good volleyball mate and Friend.

It is here on these steps that had celebrated so much that serendipity joined in, and Michael came up with the idea of "The CHAD FOUNDATION Annual Volleyball Tournament." Arista concurred and proclaimed it would Benefit CHAD and Children's Hospital Los Angeles Heart Institute." No one knew that moment (except perhaps the 'Starlighter') that this event would morph into an even more stupendous occasion, "The Annual CHAD Preventive Heart Screening Benefit," which would safeguard thousands of athletes' hearts of all ages. Triple Whammy!!! Lights go off like firecrackers—
"CHAD - Preventive Heart Screenings - for Athletes!!!"

And in a grand finale, the Lamplighter makes a vast leap across the map of the U.S.A., stopping at the Emerald Capital, N.Y.C. Then, he heads straight for a corner apartment in midtown Manhattan with a terrace view of the East River. The sky alights with the magnificence of Starship Cyberspace as it delivers a message from Broward County, Florida, to the little Mother's computer: "Broward County doctor provides EKGS due to the recent amount of Sudden Cardiac Deaths in Young Athletes." This would inform the following event to materialize...

Fast forward to the sign which reveals, "4th Annual CHAD Foundation Volleyball Benefit" at the country club in Toluca Lake. PULL BACK TO REVEAL: a grand feast and volleyball tourney in full-swing – the doctors from Children's Hospital Los Angeles Heart Institute eating fabulous burgers grilled expertly by chefs in white hats. PAN TO Arista as she approaches Dr. Michael Silka, the Head of Cardiology, "Dr. Mike, can we do what they did in Broward County– screen young athletes with EKGS?" "Well, if we are screening for H.C.M., hypertrophic cardiomyopathy, [a disease of the heart muscle that is the leading silent killer of Sudden Cardiac Death in young athletes], we would be screening for structural abnormalities, and Echocardiograms are best... That is Pierre's department. CUT TO: Dr. Pierre Wong, Head of Echocardiography, "Dr. P. could we do what they did in Broward County but doing Echocardiograms? Maybe we could have an event at Chad's alma mater, North Hollywood High?" "Well, we will need echocardiogram machines," says he.

Says she, "Do you think those nice manufacturers would lend us their machines for a day?" CLOSE UP on the little Mother. Back to the midnight sky as it flashes the words, "The ASK. – The ANSWER." Blink brilliantly off and on many times. A DUAL PICTURE of the Mother on the phone, doing the "Ask" and the Manufacturer's Account Executive making calls to solicit the "Answer." INTERCUT: a blank computer screen on which appears the words, "P-r-e-s-s R-e-l-e-a-s-e. PULL BACK TO REVEAL the little Mother, typing the words, and then pausing at what to do next. We hear, "How hard can this be.... I'll figure it out..."

Now quickly to the sky where the Star-lighter nimbly makes a pass, highlighting all 4 points: the "Easy land and Holly wood Carolco Castle," "the Toy Dinner Theatre in Los Angeles," "the famed steps of Yamishiro's," and lastly, "Emerald City Cyberspace/Toluca Lake CHAD Volleyball Benefit." Now the entity is ready to take form and flourishing his wand, "Behold!" The entire sky brightens as the light of day to reveal in vivid colour –SFX- FIRECRACKERS AND FIREWORKS.

"The CHAD Foundation for Athletes and Artists"

The Gifts of Heart and Art

CHAPTER 15

The 1st CHAD Foundation Heart Screening North Hollywood High School, North Hollywood, CA & Fountain Valley and Newport Beach, CA

The SOUND of a car door slamming. She looks towards the front steps of the building, tentatively remembering a FLASHBACK as her Son, Chad, kisses his Mom goodbye before leaving the car (a tradition all 3 sons never forgot to do, and never seemed to mind…). She watches him bound up the steps energetically.

Today, however, her foot now holds pause as she walks up the same steps her Son had traversed. This time she carries posters and bags, a look of expectation, not-knowing on her brow—

[The event poster fills the screen]

"The 1st Free Echocardiogram Screening for North Hollywood High Athletes"

Honouring

Chad Alan Butrum

PULL WAY BACK TO REVEAL a very busy but highly organized Principal's office, led by football Coach Ratcliff, who stands behind the main desk, which runs from wall to wall. On a clipboard, he holds the Master List of student appointments, and ticks off their names as the student-athletes enter the office. INTERCUT: Two manufacturer's technicians dressed in khaki pants and 3-button shirts sporting the Agilent logo, [now Philips] pull into the school parking lot. We follow them as they transport two massive hospital 'echocardiogram machines' from the van and down the hallway to the appointed rooms in the Principal's office. RESUMING SCENE, we see two small rooms on the right and left. – Typical nurses' stations for students have now been turned into 'Echocardiogram Screening Rooms.'

PAN TO the examining bench which lies on the far wall and next to it stands the quarter-million-dollar echocardiogram machine. Seated in front of the unit is a cardiac sonographer from *Children's Hospital Los Angeles Heart Institute,* who is trained and experienced in the applications of the state-of-the-art machine. The Echocardiogram is considered the gold standard for detecting structural abnormalities such as H.C.M., hypertrophic cardiomyopathy. H.C.M. is an abnormally enlarged heart muscle, which is the leading killer of Sudden Cardiac Deaths in Young Athletes. As we ZOOM IN closer, we see the technician use a special gel and transducer on the student athlete's chest; echoes of sound waves bounce off parts of the heart and produce a colour image in real-time of the patient's heart on the screen. Students are amazed to witness their hearts beating in real-time.

The echocardiogram screening can cost from $2,500 to $3,500 per athlete if performed in a hospital or clinical laboratory setting. Thanks to the generosity of cardiologists, cardiac sonographer technicians, and medical manufacturers, The CHAD Foundation can provide these preventive screenings free to the student-athletes.

PANNING OVER, you see the technician using the transducer and gel on the student's heart area. The student-athlete will be lying on their side with that area exposed. The test is non-invasive and painless.

PANNING UP, reveals a cardiologist physician from Children's Hospital Los Angeles standing over the shoulder of the technician as he analyzes the screen. The doctor is reading the Echocardiogram and giving the results of the rudimentary screening in real-time.

CLOSEUP on the form the doctor is signing, which contains two options: one, which says the test today falls in the "Normal" range or two, which recommends "Further testing," based on the findings and notes given by the doctor. Each form is signed by the attending cardiologist, thus providing insurance companies and follow-up doctors with the appropriate referral form.

BACK ON the front desk to see an INSERT of the "Chad Foundation Screening Questionnaire/Liability Waiver/Permission form and Family History," which each student hands to the Coach before his examination. We see that the paperwork has been filled out ahead of time, and is signed by the parent or guardian unless the athlete is 18 years of age.

CUT TO: An adjoining room to the Principal's office where Dr. Michael Silka, [then] Head of Cardiology at Children's Hospital Los Angeles Heart Institute, is being interviewed by Chad's friend, Jake Downey, broadcast professional for high school sports teams in Los Angeles. Dr. Silka speaks:

> "The heart problems that cause sudden death in young athletes are not readily detectable by the routine examination- we're talking about subtle abnormalities of the heart muscle or the coronary arteries or the electrical depolarization of the heart, and these are not audible type of findings. These require more sophisticated methods of screening the athlete: uses of the Electrocardiogram for the electrical problems of the heart or an Echocardiogram for the muscle or perhaps coronary artery problems of the heart.
>
> The purpose right now of the screening is to detect any obvious or readily apparent abnormalities. If there is a suspicion of heart disease in a young athlete, these patients clearly should be referred to a cardiologist for further evaluation.

I think right now, screening is very haphazard, disorganized, and frequently addresses the wrong questions. What we need is a collaborative effort of different medical and sports organizations, such as the American Heart Association, The American Academy of Pediatrics, and the American College of Sports Medicine, to come up with a standardized sports screening history and physical examination which will at least address and hopefully triage the most apparent problems as they come along.

(continuing in Voiceover as we SEE the Chad Questionnaire)

I think that's one of the biggest problems we face in screening the young athletes, initially, is that there is no standardized national approach to the evaluation of the young athlete. I think this results in, at least, locally in California, a lot of local high schools developing their own questionnaires. They frequently ask questions which are not really relevant and sometimes fail to ask the most important questions, such as: have the athletes ever passed out before, have they ever been prohibited from prior athletic competition, and some of the specifics of early family histories of heart disease. I think one of the most important things that can be done in this area is the development of some form of standardized national screening for young athletes with a core of five to ten specific questions, and five to ten specific items on physical examination which really should be a mandatory consideration for every athlete."

CUT TO: the next adjoining office where Dr. Pierre Wong, Director of Echocardiography, at Children's Hospital Los Angeles Heart Institute is being interviewed and videotaped for that evening's news coverage on the local ABC-TV station, KTLA.

".. A nice thing about using Echocardiography to screen these patients is that it's a much more sensitive technique. And I think it's helpful that the medical community is aware of this, and if we can get more physicians, technicians and ultrasound companies, like Agilent, [Philips, now] to donate their time and services we can, I think, donate a really good service to the community and all these athletes.

Clearly, there are certain cardio defects that can escape detection by all other means except for Echocardiogram. An Echocardiogram is easy to obtain, the machines are portable, it doesn't take very long. It's easy, it's very reliable, it's very accurate, it's non-invasive, and not painful at all. You do need a technician and cardiologist who have a high level of training, but given that personnel, you can detect a lot of things very easily and very accurately with Echocardiography."

CUT BACK TO: The main office where Arista, herself, is being interviewed by a radio talk host. On the desk, with the Chad brochures, lies her 1st stab at 'Press Releases,' which seems to have worked! PAN TO: Coach Brad Ratcliff, who is also on camera, remaining behind the desk:

"A lot of our players are concerned about, wow, this could happen to me and what it means and everything, so they are real happy to have this done. ... And you can feel the kids being a little apprehensive as they come in, and you can see their relief as they're walking out."

OVER TO the Football Team Captain who is just about to go in for his screening and speaks to camera:

"It means a lot because, after a game, I don't want to be fallin' out because of my heart stoppin' and be dead, so I want to know, you know. Just take the test. – You never know – things can happen."

And the Results of the "1st CHAD Foundation Free Echocardiogram Screening"? Out of 50 student-athletes and coaches screened, there were 10 recommended follow-ups. Two of those minor abnormalities found were a small hole in the heart and very mild thickening of the walls of the left side of the heart. Dr. Pierre Wong, Director of Echocardiography and Transplant Cardiology at Children's Hospital Los Angeles Heart Institute, said the two athletes could still play but recommended to the athletes' parents a follow-up screening by a cardiologist. Remember, besides the H.C.M., Echocardiograms can also detect valve problems, blood flow, and thickness of walls and various other structural issues. This interestingly would become a pretty common statistic in the future CHAD screenings; for every 50 students screened, 10 follow-ups are usually recommended.

A SLOW PANORAMIC VIEW REVEALS what is perhaps the very **"1st Free Echocardiogram Screening for High School Student-Athletes"** in a high school setting in the country in July 2000. It is a pioneering effort by The CHAD Foundation to safeguard young hearts and identify early heart abnormalities, and thus help prevent Sudden Cardiac Death in Young Student-Athletes. It is the little Mother's 1st production. This prototype model is to be the core of the CHAD screenings for the next 20 years and 8,000 persons screened. However, as its screenings grow, so does the "CHAD Preventive Heart Screening Program." In addition to the Echocardiogram, an EKG screening will also be provided to detect electrical abnormalities. And when funding permits, cholesterol, and diabetes screenings are added to identify these early cardiovascular risk factors, which are rising at an alarming rate in children.

But for today, as the little Mother walked back down the same stairs her Son tread daily – though she's not quite sure what just took place, she does know Chad would be proud. – He would want those hearts to be screened so that they could Live… so that each one of them could achieve their full potential and go after their individual dreams.-

CHAPTER 16

California Screenings
Sunny and Welcome

On the 17th of November 1999, in Fountain Valley, California, perhaps another sunny day, 16-year-old Scotty Lang was practicing football drills with his team the Barons from Fountain Valley High School. Tells Mom, Cindy Lang, of her strapping 6'5, 250 lb. son, he was in perfect health and had passed his pre-participation sports physical. But the gentle giant who sported the number "75" on his jersey collapsed that day with his teammates and coaches around him, as paramedics tried to save his Life. He died later at the hospital of undiagnosed H.C.M., hypertrophic cardiomyopathy, the abnormally thickened heart muscle that can cause the heart to pump inadequate amounts of blood when engaged in exercise. Unfortunately, in young people with this heart condition, the first episode can be the last. It is most likely the abnormality would have been detected with an Echocardiogram. CHAD was proud to fiscally sponsor the event for A Heart for Sports later the next year, in which 350 heart screenings were provided to Scotty's football teammates and the community. I'm sure his ever-remembered smile was beaming down on everyone.

It was a grand community affair, hundreds paid homage to a young hero known for his bear hugs and effusive smile. CHAD still carries a picture of Scotty and his story on a poster to many of its heart screening events in many cities. After getting to meet and hug Scotty's lovely Mom and Dad, and blonde sisters, they become part of your own 'Family,' and Scotty becomes an adopted son… He reminds you why you do this work year after year, for a fine strapping boy whose best-loved colour was orange.

In fact, his teammates wore orange socks the whole season to remember their friend, and 2,500 attended his service. So it becomes a no-brainer, "Oh, you mean if kids have this Echocardiogram screening, it could save their lives??" And your Life changes at that moment; there is no second thought. "Well then, I guess, we drag this machine around the country for the rest of our lives… preventing as many losses of these young lives as we can."

At Scotty's event, I also got to meet members of another exceptional family, The Morrells, headed by the handsome, cheeky rogue, Chuck Morrell, former footballer (*Washington Redskins)*, and actor (*Banacek*). Ironically, just like Chad, who was coming out of a huddle when he collapsed face down, Chuck was running for a touchdown as a W.S.U. Cougar, when he, too, collapsed face-down for no apparent reason. – There was no one anywhere near him. But unlike Chad, Chuck got up, having just made the longest run in the Cougar books, 87 yards—fortuitous? Yes, for that moment, a grand record never to be broken, only tied and many years later. We lost Chad, but Chuck Morrell would lose 5 members of his family to this silent killer, H.C.M. Today, we know the H.C.M. gene is found in 1 in 500 births; back then, the awareness of the disease was still under cover of night.

First, Chuck lost his baby sister, Michelle, but 3 years old to this disease; she died in her sleep. Five years later, they would lose their Mom at age 54 to the same heart ailment. Chuck had a twin named Gary, whose son Kyle, would collapse walking home and subsequently died at age 12. Finally, all were tested, and it was found that the twin brothers Chuck and Gary also possessed the lethal gene, as well as Gary's other children, Desiree and Mitchell. Mitchell, only two years older than his brother Kyle would also succumb to the disease just a short while later. Thankfully, the daughter would survive, and I would have the pleasure of meeting her son Tyler at the event. He had just received an internal defibrillator, a device that shocks the heart should it go into an erratic arrhythmia so it can start beating at a normal rhythm again. I would also meet Chuck's pretty daughter, Holly, who would also be diagnosed with H.C.M., and now also has that life-saving I.C.D. implanted within. In honouring her family, Holly founded her organization, "Heartfelt Cardiac Programs," which has been doing community preventive screenings for 15 years. We have held hands at our screening programs and shared the echocardiographic machines thanks to Philips! Holly, too, is part of my grand "Heart Family." Her organization has screened thousands and thousands of hearts. Her Dad is soo proud.

I loved her Dad, Chuck; he always had the cause at 'heart' – to raise awareness of H.C.M. and prevent it from devastating other Families as it did his. He was also a caring, loving human being who minced no words. Once he picked me up at the airport before a Los Angeles heart screening and took me to the Inn where I was staying. Later, he called me and told me to go down to the lobby, there was something there waiting for me. – It was a new set of luggage… explained to me in Chuck's language, "You come in from New York, looking all sophisticated and then this sad excuse for a suitcase follows you down the carousel. – I don't care that is has a designer logo on it. The handle's falling off; it looks like it's been through the war, and I have to put this piece of 'garbage' in my nice car… [only he really didn't say *'garbage'*…more colourful!]

And I still have a few pieces of that luggage left and treasure it; they now carry the cholesterol and diabetes screening machines for the *"Expanded CHAD Foundation Heart Screenings."* Whenever I roll into a screening with them, I know Chuck continues to be with me whatever city I'm in, as does his Morrell Family poster, which I have probably brought to screenings in 5 states. Chuck had a heart transplant in 1995 and always said as he had been given a younger heart, that that's what kept him young. The last time we were together, he was regaling Hollywood tales to Chad's brothers, Curt and Collin, and I at a dark, old famous joint of an oyster bar on Moorpark Blvd. in Studio City. –

He had to say goodbye to his twin, Gary, too, who chose *not* to have a transplant, and; I could tell Chuck never got over that. In 2005, Chuck lost his battle, but it was hard-fought just like the one his daughter Holly would fight when she underwent open-heart surgery recently and survived. I think it's important to pay tribute to the pioneers and pillars of our cause. Chuck was a true athlete and artist from the old school with moxie and colour, and a heart of gold. We all miss him as we continue onward. They are who and what gives us the *heart* to continue the fight when we get tired– the stamina to get up and keep doing. I can see you up there, Buddy, directing the plays from a higher vantage point… And you are here with me in those green suitcases you left me to help make it easier. This gift from your heart I will always carry with me to save future hearts in tribute to you and the other 5 members of your family.

When awareness of consciousness is implanted today, it spreads through society at an unprecedented rate because of media and cyberspace. What did we ever do before? A young man is sitting in a dentist's chair, not on the football field, although he is an athlete. And due to dental surgery, the doctor is monitoring his heart, which shows an abnormal arrhythmia. He recommends further testing as soon as possible; the additional testing results in a diagnosis of possible H.C.M., the deadly #1 silent killer of Sudden Cardiac Death in Young Athletes. This young man, but a junior in high school, finds The CHAD Foundation on the internet. Becoming aware our organization does heart screenings, he has his mother contact me to see if we would come and do a screening at his high school in Newport Beach, California. He wanted to make sure these anomalies were detected and prevent any students from dying from Sudden Cardiac Death. Of course, CHAD would come to Newport Beach and would provide two Heart Screenings for his high school teammates two years in a row. That is the power of cyberspace.

Unfortunately, a few years earlier at this same high school, a freshman water polo player complained of dizziness and collapsed getting out of the pool, and subsequently died of a heart-related ailment. He was a Jr. life-guard from the age of 8. At one of the CHAD screenings, I had the pleasure of meeting his older brother, who became a paramedic because of what happened to his younger brother. – The loss of a sibling at a young age affects every person in the Family for the rest of their lives. This is what the young athlete in the dental chair was trying to prevent.

This California community of Newport Beach, much like Fountain Valley, came out in droves to support and partake in the screenings. Parents and students and coaches were lined up outside the building all day. I remember one dedicated doctor ended the day reading nearly 200 Echocardiograms administered by several ultrasound technicians, and he seemed just as vital and enlivened as he was at the beginning of the event.

Just like raising awareness of Sudden Cardiac Death in Young Athletes and its attendant solution- preventive echocardiographic screenings seed society, I have seen the cause gain momentum on all fronts. Physicians, namely cardiologists in this case, and their cardiac sonographer technicians work hard enough during the week. Yet, they are willing to give up a half-day on a Saturday to work extra hard because they see this is an opportunity to prevent a Sudden Cardiac Death and detect possible lethal risk signs ahead of time. Stipends are rarely given as most of our non-profits are volunteer-based. It then genuinely becomes a Gift from their Hearts to safeguard hearts. Parents in communities who can contribute are glad to give voluntary donations, and some are quite generous, which only helps pass the gift forward to the next high schools.

It is very gratifying to provide preventive screening events in the California sunshine state and see all the successful turnouts. People seem to be more open, aware here- about exercise, health, and practicing healthy lifestyles as a Family. They don't have their heads in the sand like ostriches… 'Oh, I know, I read that this happens, but that happens to *other people's children*, not me or mine,' and they seem in denial of the reality. 'I'm not going to bother to have this $3,000 preventive screening, which is free. My child's too young doesn't need it.' All are given the same statistics to inform and ponder: The C.D.C. says 3,000 – 6,000 young people between the ages of 15 and 34 years of age die annually from Sudden Cardiac Death. The HCM gene is found in 1 in 500 births. It seems in the east, the initial 'sell' is harder- a smaller number of schools or students who will participate in the screenings.

Chad loved the sunny days of California, always a great day for a game. Maybe he found his tribe out here: people who loved exercise on a daily basis, were into sports, chose proper nutrition and treated their bodies like temples.... at least the athletes. That sign that I mentioned in Part I which greeted me at LAX and welcomes you to Los Angeles, I say, "Thank you sunny state of California for always welcoming with open minds and open hearts our preventive heart screenings for your athletes and students. – May you continue to thrive and flourish with "Healthy Body, Mind and Spirit."

CHAPTER 17

Baltimore's Favourite Son, Reggie Lewis and Distinguished Johns Hopkins Hospital

I still remember the moment I first took the call from Peggy Ritch, the Mother of famed young Boston Celtic, Reggie Lewis. I was just stepping down from my terrace at my eastside apartment, so happy we were finally speaking. It was like talking to a famous person of sorts... she even sounded like 'Miss Diana Ross!' I had recently read the book about her Son, entitled *Quiet Grace*, and was still thinking of it with reverence. Even though it was still the early frontier stage of our cause, (felt like I was again donning the bonnet), it was common knowledge that it was Reggie Lewis and Hank Gathers, who brought the awareness of Sudden Cardiac Death in Young Athletes to the light of the nation, perhaps to the world, never to remain hidden again.

Reggie was a rising superstar of the Boston Celtics, and Hank was the promising young basketball sensation from Loyola Marymount University. It is these two young athletes on the brink of enduring superstar careers that brought to bear the undiagnosed heart anomalies such as hypertrophic cardiomyopathy, which could end young lives within moments. And as their passing brought the cause to the consciousness of the nation, we parents whose children followed Reggie and Hank, took up their torch, and continue to shine it as far and wide as we can. We want it to reach as many towns and cities as we can so we can safeguard as many young hearts as we can to preclude Sudden Cardiac Death.

That day as I introduced myself to Peggy, I told her about my Son Chad's foundation and how it had just provided *the "1ˢᵗ Preventive Echocardiogram Heart Screening for Young Athletes"* in the country at his high school in Los Angeles. And we wanted to offer a similar heart screening for high school student-athletes in Baltimore, MD, in Reggie's memory; she was thrilled. A union was formed between us as Mothers and our Sons, Reggie and Chad, that will last forever. I felt better somehow because I knew Chad had a big brother in Heaven, and he wouldn't be alone.

We would provide the screening at Reggie's former high school, Dunbar High, in Baltimore, MD. Due to a serendipitous contact, I was introduced to the Director of Echocardiography at the venerable Johns Hopkins Hospital. It would be the cardiologists and their staff of cardiac sonographers who would administer the Echocardiograms. Agilent Technologies [now Philips] would once again transport the quarter-million dollar echocardiogram machines to the high school, which was very near the hospital.

I arrived in Baltimore on a Thursday evening and was welcomed by Reggie Lewis' Mom, Peggy Inez Ritch. We finally got to give each other the 'Mom Hug,' which we had been waiting for. Later at a well-known restaurant on the Wharf, we were joined by Peggy's sister and an associate from (Johns Hopkins Hospital) who had been my liaison while we were organizing the event. Then, I was introduced to something else –Maryland soft shell crabs. They were amazing and scrumptious, especially coupled with the ambiance of the Baltimore Wharf visited by thousands every year.

That we 'break bread' as a ritual of our species is an interesting connective handshake for Human Beings. – Strangers from different tribes, coming together from distant places, to meet unfamiliar faces and we use as a universal facilitator, the nourishment and joy of Life – the gift of food. –And yet one must admit this was an unusual reason for a dinner party. Two Mothers who had lost their Sons to Sudden Cardiac Death while engaged in sports were partnering with one of the most renowned hospitals in the nation to help screen young hearts to prevent Sudden Cardiac Death. They would do this through a new grassroots program, *"The CHAD Foundation Preventive Heart Screening Program for Young Athletes & Students."* This time it would be in tribute to Baltimore's favourite Son, who had his start playing basketball at the high school next door to Johns Hopkins. — Tomorrow this institution would host an event and provide lifesaving tests with respect for the young man who had made it all the way to the Boston Celtics. Not only had he made his community and Family proud because of his outstanding talents, but with his "quiet grace" gave back to the kids in his neighborhood. Free basketball clinics and a turkey giveaway to families in his community at Thanksgiving, all happened thanks to Reggie.

When I visited Peggy's home, her living room and continuing up the staircase, was like walking into the young Reggie Lewis Museum. Many of his signed jerseys hung in large frames on the walls, and his many accolades, pictures, and articles adorned all the spaces in-between. Yes, all the signs of a Mother and the eternal bond with her Child – the celebration of his Life and all the beautiful moments given to her... for all eternity. That Peggy and her Son grace the foreword of our book is so fitting. Her Son had a lot to do with lighting the torch that would go on for a very long time.

And the next day when I entered the gym where Reggie played ball–he probably always knew he was cutting his teeth for the big leagues, I walked on the very boards that he did. His Mother played on these very planks before him, and his nephews after him. CHAD was so proud to pay tribute to this exceptional young man in his alma mater. I was asked to speak to the Student Body, followed by Reggie's beautiful, tall Mother, Peggy. Then distinguished doctors from Johns Hopkins Cardiology Division told the student body in compelling language how and why the 'Echocardiogram' testing was so important for them. By their reaction and silent attention, we knew the students were listening. Just looking at two mothers without their sons was something that impacted them, even at a young age. They received awareness that day. Their consciousness was raised to the importance of having a healthy heart in the young and living a healthy lifestyle. Then the lifesaving AED (Automatic External Defibrillator) was presented to the school by The CHAD Foundation, thanks to Agilent Technologies [now Philips]. The Student Body spontaneously applauded and cheered when the volunteer member from the Red Cross held up the machine and told them 'they' were the first school in Maryland to have an AED! We all know now that every minute without the intervention of an AED cuts the chance of staying alive by 50%.

WBAL covered the all-day event showing students actually receiving their Echocardiograms in darkened school offices, which we had set up ahead of time to make the reading of the exam possible. There were a few follow-ups recommended that day, and how convenient, the hospital being a neighbor, the students, and their parents would not have far to go.

But there is one story I love to retell about a young man who was present in the student body the day before when we gave our talks. He heard about the special raffle prizes, one being 'a pair of sneakers donated by *Muggsy Bogues*.' Muggsy also played on these same boards at Dunbar, and he and Reggie graduated the same year. Muggsy, though only 5'3," went on to have a 14-year career in the N.B.A. He certainly had a loyal fan that day as the young Dunbar athlete was the first in line to receive his heart test, and therefore the first to receive a qualifying raffle ticket. –He waited <u>all</u> day long there for the raffle drawing with his eyes never far from those sneakers. At the end of the screening when the drawing took place, I think all of us there were silently cheering for him. His name was picked! That was one of the happiest young men I've ever seen, and certainly a "Muggsy Bogues" fan! I think Reggie would have gotten a big kick from the screening in his memory, but most of all, to know that his young teammates coming after him on those Dunbar boards had the benefit of this lifesaving screening. Because of it, they just might have a chance to achieve their most cherished dreams, whatever they may be...even a professional athlete.

A seed of the heart had been sown in Baltimore with the screening in Reggie's memory, and a few years later, when I called the Echocardiography Department at Johns Hopkins to see if we could plan another screening, there was another cardiologist at the helm. He, too, was very interested in our cause of identifying hypertrophic cardiomyopathy early in the young and thus preventing Sudden Cardiac Death. That phone call forged a 4-year partnership-

> Dear Arista:
>
> ...You will recall that our initial conversations almost 3 years ago served as a stimulus for us to launch The Hopkins Heart Hype. Our mission is to influence individual heart health decisions early in Life such that lifestyle changes and medical treatments can be offered in a preventative manner rather than after heart disease has struck. One particular focus is our goal to reduce sudden death in athletes, especially at the high school and college level. We hope to achieve our goals by conducting regular community-based heart health screenings...
>
> We were very pleased to have your support last Year, and thankful for your guidance and thoughts as a member of our Heart Hype Advisory Board.
>
> Yours sincerely,
> Theodore P. Abraham, M.D., F.A.C.C., F.A.S.E.
> Director Hopkins Heart Hype
> Johns Hopkins Medicine
> Division of Cardiology

The outstanding caliber and dedication of our partners are the core of CHAD'S Preventive Heart Program. That is what I meant in Part I when I said, "Chad gave me the ball and said Mom, now, you have to run with it, but what a Team he left me to accomplish that goal." These exceptional Cardiologists and Mentors would be making preventive screenings for young athletes a reality: Dr. Theodore Abraham from The Johns Hopkins Hospital; Dr. Michael Silka, Dr. Pierre Wong, Dr. Alan Lewis and Dr. Masato Takahashi from Children's Hospital Los Angeles Heart Institute; Dr. Michael Willers of The Children's Heart Center in Western MA; the Cardiology Staff from Holyoke Medical Center; Dr. Archie Roberts from the Living Heart; Dr. Benjamin Co in N.J.; Dr. Robert Brown from Lincoln Hospital NY; Dr. A. Farid from N.Y.U. Langone Medical Center; Dr. Jared Lacorte, Dr. S. Duvvri, and Dr. Francesco Rotatori from Staten Island. These cardiologists are the extraordinary Team who have lent their professional expertise, valuable time, and heart to screen and safeguard thousands of hearts with preventive screenings for CHAD time and time again. It is their counsel and experience that helped a layperson navigate the land of the medical field and forge an effective program with best practices as well as innovative Spirit.

Their professional guidance helped a novice to understand why you will encounter resistance and controversy whenever an established, accepted way of thinking or doing things is challenged. –Why should you screen young athletes using expensive equipment and physician's time? You will have a 'low yield.' That means you won't find enough positive results to make it cost-effective. "Low Yield" is the first obstacle I encountered. – "You won't find many H.C.M.'s per the amount of time and service you're expending in screening." –But what about the other things we find? Holes in the heart, Wolff-Parkinson-White syndrome, 10-20% anomaly findings for every 50 participants screened. How many quintuple bypasses might you save if you discover the risk factors when they're young so preventive strategies can be put in place?

I would learn that I/we and I include my compatriots, young frontiersmen, and women, were treading a path like Louis Pasteur. How his peers laughed at him—to think boiling instruments might help to save a life in childbirth or surgery, or that germs and bacteria are responsible for disease. Johns Hopkins was the first to use rubber gloves during surgery. However small our cause may be, this is the same path we must follow to introduce a new practice that is not yet done universally. And, that is providing preventive heart screenings to young athletes *before* they start their season to identify lethal anomalies and help prevent Sudden Cardiac Death. I belong to the school of Dr. Abraham's answer to the query regarding the controversy, "What is the price for a single life?" "We're counting the costs upfront. We're not counting the savings on the downstream end."[2]

The steps of the journey of CHAD were taking me so many places I've never been or expected to be. Here, mounting the stairs of the original portico to this esteemed institution was an awesome feeling. The intricately-designed red and white brick facade befitted the age it was built, 1889 – and that's precisely the era I felt I was entering. Upon the edifice sits a vast green dome and atop that a cupola, where I'm told you can see the Baltimore harbour. It didn't look like any hospital I have ever seen but a drawback to another century. Yet even today, Hopkins is considered by many the highest all-around hospital in the country.

It was here I was invited to speak along with Reggie Lewis's Mother, Peggy Ritch. We were amongst distinguished guest speakers at the kickoff reception for the *"1st Hopkins Heart Hype Screening Program,"* which would take place the following day, hosted at Morgan State University in Baltimore.

As my eyes gazed up at the portraits of prominent people gracing the small elegant hall, I was very humbled to be invited to this hallowed establishment where so many great discoveries of medicine have been birthed to the world. The Johns Hopkins School of Medicine was the first university in the nation to admit women. In the area of the heart alone, the "Blue Baby" paper, which came out in 1945 by a pediatrician and a surgeon, found an operable cure for a heart birth defect saving thousands of babies' lives and ushered in pediatric cardiology.

And I thought our little cause must have importance, too, or we would not have been invited to speak about it. – This stronghold of research and teaching would not be implementing a program and offering its support if our cause, too, did not have significance. A disease that had been under cover of darkness–no one really had any idea how many young people it affected, nor did the medical industry know how to treat it. It, too, was in its infancy stage of awareness. I looked across the room and met the eyes of the tall, lovely Mother of Reggie Lewis, and said silently, "—And your son helped to bring it to light, never to be under the covers again, and my son, represents all the others- thousands who are no longer here but for a test…" "Being here tonight is a one big, solid step toward advancement, Chad." "I know, mom," he replied, "Congratulations!" [accompanied by a huge smile]. The next day would be "Game time," and he would be there, too, with the same big smile welcoming everyone.

Talk about an ideal day and a perfect situation… from our point of view. Morgan State University is humming. Sunny, with a slight breeze, university-size track, bleachers nicely filled. All-day long parents are bringing their teen athletes to participate in the "2012 U.S.A.T.F. National Junior Olympic Track & Field Championships." Even teens who didn't participate could register for a free Echocardiogram, EKG, height, weight, and blood pressure test to detect H.C.M. hypertrophic cardiomyopathy and help prevent Sudden Cardiac Death. Also, the screening could identify early cardiovascular risk factors like hypertension and obesity in teens.

Here was $3,000 worth of Lifesaving preventive screenings free: renowned physicians from your hometown hospital, Johns Hopkins; 100's of volunteers at the ready; state-of-the-art equipment provided by Philips; and Echocardiogram screenings–the gold standard for identifying the #1 silent killer of Sudden Death in Young Athletes. All were set up like a topnotch clinic in two huge, spotless gyms. They were located just up the stairs, in a building just steps away from the field, for the athletes' convenience. A 'No-Brainer,' ya think?? [SFX shrieking wrong answer buzzer] Arista, get your track shoes on (now that's a joke, because everyone knows I'm in lotta shoes, but rarely those.)

However, today the espadrilles were on and in rare form for sprinting; for today, and subsequent events here, I would wear the title of "Coach." I found it would be my job to get that parent and their teen athlete to the other *goal*–"the Saving of the Life Screening Goal," which was up the stairs, before or after their child's event took place. "Hi, there!" " – Please join us for the <u>free</u> heart screenings, just up the stairs, only takes a few minutes!" - "Oh, no, thank you." "Sorry, no time." "Oh, what is this, a heart screening for 'him/her'? Oh no, thank you ... he/she's too young." "Another time..."

– Not to worry, I had the Big Guns... the only ones that mattered. I had brought them by train from New York... I have brought them by car, train, plane, *and* boat (as in Staten Island Ferry). They go wherever CHAD goes. They comprise what has come to be known as the "Stories Table." (Coined by one of the nurses I think who volunteered for our CHAD screening in Massachusetts– the name stuck and is perfect.)

In my most polite, persuasive, non-aggressive voice, I ask, "Could you just step over here, just for one moment? Real quick...I want to show you something." It's a very polite group of people, and although, indeed, they may be headed to their Son or Daughter's meet, they do follow me over. As we step to the "Stories Table," we see, as I mentioned earlier, there is Chad's smiling face and his physique well-toned on an 18 x 24-inch poster to greet them. No holds barred, you have about 1 minute tops for them to listen; the gloves must come off. "Meet my Son, Chad. He was playing football in California, came out of a huddle, dropped suddenly, and his Life was over shortly after that. – He was only 26: he was healthy, never had a heart problem, never drank a drop of alcohol, smoked, or did drugs. -He also never had the advantage of having an "Echocardiogram," and I point like a setter to the building where these lifesaving tests are being held, "Please take a few minutes to have your Son or Daughter screened." Then my hand goes immediately to the "Stories Table," and I say, "Meet Chad's younger brothers and sisters; they, too, were seemingly healthy athletes – and none of them had the benefit of an Echocardiogram.

They go to see the picture posters and stories: 13-year-old David Deuel, a basketball player; 19-year-old Anthony Bates on his way to play football at Kansas State; the entire Morrell family, 3, 13, 14 and 42; the Parent Heartwatch deck of 40 cards, each showing a child victim of Sudden Cardiac Arrest from ages 5 to 26; Andrew Helgeson, 18, an all-star lacrosse player from Silver Spring, MD., who died from Sudden Cardiac Arrest, a week before his high school graduation; and Baltimore's favourite Son, Reggie Lewis, 27, star basketball player for the Boston Celtics, and more and more.

Now they will read the statistics on the postcard I gave them: 1 out of 500 births have the abnormal H.C.M. (hypertrophic cardiomyopathy) gene. The C.D.C. says 3,000-6,000 young people die annually from Sudden Cardiac Arrest between the ages of 15 and 34. More young black men die from H.C.M. than whites (44% vs. 22%). Beware of fainting, dizziness, shortness of breath, blackouts. I could spout out statistics until I was blue in the face, it wouldn't have meant as much to them. *It was my Son and your Son/Daughter and everyone's picture and story on that table that made the difference. They looked just like their own child walking next to them. —Yes, that's what this is all about; we don't want your child's picture added to this table. We want your child to have a long, healthy Life. Take a few moments, and Go have your test." And now they did... Their awareness raised, they are now changed people, including the teens.- How could they say no to a Mother who has lost a son, or to any parent whose child sits on this table... This was the 'no-brainer.' Up the stairs they went or told me quite genuinely, they would as soon as their child's meet was over.* The final figures showed they did take the trip up the stairs – parent(s) and athlete, and Dr. Abraham and Staff confirmed it.

One year, my good friend Stewart Krug joined me at the "Hopkins Heart Hype Screening" to help in our mutual cause. Stew lost his Son, Matthew, at age 16. Stew is a mild, gentle Father, and every time I see a picture of Matthew, I think of Stew and vice versa. They look so much alike. I think it meant a lot for people to know that it is equally painful for a Father to lose a child, and it means just as much to him to advocate for a cause that will prevent this from happening to any other child.

That year, I also spoke to a couple of our service people who were at the event in their uniforms. They said, "I think it's great what you're doing. We don't get these tests as routine in the Army." I was shocked that our Servicemen and Women don't get an EKG and Echocardiogram testing, and we send them into battle. ...Of course, my mind went to well how can we organize a screening for them and the Vets... But that's a whole new ballgame for another day. However, I was happy to screen one of our service persons on leave at one of the "Annual CHAD Volleyball Tourney & Heart Screening" events in Hermosa Beach, CA. (more on his results in Chapter 22, the Hermosa Beach screening.)

In the "Hopkins Heart Hype Program," out of 1,000 kids screened, 30% were found to have abnormalities that required follow-up. In one year's screening, two athletes were found to have had serious problems: one a heart valve condition, the other a possible heart transplant. In a recent study from Johns Hopkins, both the Echocardiogram and the Electrocardiogram are recommended. This dual heart screening gives the best chance to find both structural and electrical problems. Dr. Theodore Abraham says, "It has to be comprehensive. An EKG does show you a lot, but it doesn't tell you the whole story. The advantage of a comprehensive screening is that it is holistic, rather than being pinpoint."[2]

CHAD has used this dual-protocol based on the advisement of its Board of Advisory Members on both coasts: Dr. Theodore Abraham, Hopkins Heart Hype Director; and at Children's Hospital Los Angeles Heart Institute, Dr. Michael Silka, Tenured Professor of Pediatrics/ Cardiology; Dr. Pierre Wong, Director of Echocardiography; and, Dr. Alan Lewis, Professor of Pediatrics, U.S.C., whose focus is Cardiomyopathy and Myocarditis.

With these significant 'posts' anchoring our foundation, we forged ahead to the next city where hearts were calling.

CHAPTER 18

9-11 Hearts of the World Under-siege Screening New York's Finest - the NYPD

From anywhere in Manhattan, the perfection of blue sky hung like a painting, not to be outdone by the brilliance of the Sun that rose that September morn... – Images that are seared into our minds as every other crystal-cut memory that occurred that day: minute-to-minute, day-by-day, and for months and years to come. I recently met a woman who still recalls how she was riding on the elevated train that crosses the Manhattan Bridge on her way to work in the City. She saw the American Airlines 2nd plane, which she could identify by its logo—the thing she wondered was, why is this plane flying so low? It's almost on our level. She would not find out the reason until she reached the Manhattan side of the bridge. The rest of us, including much of the world, would see it in real-time through the global media of television and electronic devices–our *"Pearl Harbor of the 21st Century,"* as that American Airlines 2nd plane continued on its path and crashed through the 2nd World Trade Center Tower.

It is one of those once-in-a-lifetime occurrences, when every single New Yorker and much of the nation remember where they were, what they were doing, and perhaps what they were even wearing that exact moment. I was getting ready for an appointment with big round brushes in my hair when the phone rang. It was my son Collin calling from California. His voice was tentative, anxious; I didn't understand why, "Mom, is everything all right?" "Sure, Honey," I said, entirely oblivious. "I've been trying to get through…. Something's happened, a plane crashed into the World Trade Center…" and with more of a cautionary tone so as not to frighten me, he continued, "They said, it might be a terrorist attack…" Just then, what had been a morning show on the T.V., I think *The View,* changed instantly to live coverage of the *World Trade Center* showing the gaping hole in the shape of a plane on the side of Tower 1. "Oh my God, some idiot crashed his small plane into the side of it!" [That was my explanation… there was no worry of a terrorist attack in my voice.] But then the phone dropped or did I … much like that which happened when I received the indelible phone call which marked the 1st worst day of my Life. This time it was the surreal image of the American jetliner slicing through the wall of the sister tower marking the 2nd worst day … perhaps, for All of Us as Human Beings.

I remember yelling out, "The Firemen!!" It was my son's voice on some part of the phone, telling me, "Mom, be careful, your heart!" There was nothing wrong with my heart– that had been determined, no blockages, no anomalies, but I had learned [post-Chad] the heart can be hurt by other things, like overstress or emotional hurts. It was a muscle and, in my case, it tightened up when I got upset which would cause the blood not to flow as it should, and I would end up in intensive care for a week, so his caution was not unwarranted.-

I remember during one of these episodes looking up at the emergency room lights and saying to myself—as the gravity of the situation finally hit me– you have to learn how to deal with your emotions… or you won't be here anymore, and if you leave the Earth too early, your son, Chad, will say to you, "Mom, what are you doing here? I gave you the foundation…" –And, the other son on the other end of the phone and his brother won't be pleased either, so buck up sister and get your act together. Thousands of Families will lose thousands of Loved Ones today. They will need the love, prayers, and support from every person in this City and country to get through this. –And, of course, I thought immediately of CHAD, we must be able to help somehow. The Firemen or 'Firefighters,' as my friend who is one, refers to his profession came to mind– I would go to them immediately and see how we could help.

But first I had to call Carl and Sharen. Their loft was in Tribeca, only blocks away from the World Trade Center. Just their answering machine was on. I left several messages, each growing more frantic, – "Please, please come uptown to stay at my apartment [in midtown]." "Please call me to let me know you're all right." It would be hours before I heard from them, but when I finally did, Carl thanked me but said they would be staying at a hotel near their property so they could keep an eye on it.... in case of looters... Oh my God, as if there isn't enough to worry about, but thank the Lord that was something that never happened. I think even the criminal-minded folks had their humanity touched that day.

I next called Dr. "Archie" Roberts, my partner in the 1st Massachusetts high school heart screening. Just a few months prior, in May, we had done a shoot and an interview at the Marriott gym about "The CHAD Foundation" and his organization "The Living Heart" for *USA Today*, depicting one of the athletes having a screening there. The Marriot Hotel, where the gym was located, was attached to the W.T.C. (World Trade Center) complex; I had to make sure Archie wasn't there. When I reached him, he told me he was fine and hadn't been at the Marriott gym that day, but he said his daughter, who worked in the towers, had gotten out safely. She had thankfully exited the building. Praise the Lord! We then spoke about what we could do, and we would both be in touch soon. My son Curt finally reached me, and knowing all was well with the Family, I could now venture out to see the Firefighters. The nearest firehouse was just a few blocks away in midtown on E. 51st St. or so.

What every New Yorker also remembers is the moment when you first walk out the door. – This foreign smell hits you in the face straight on and does not abate– an odor that you have never encountered before and never want to encounter again. The burning smell of something you can't quite identify combined with the powerful overtones of acrid fuel would prevail the air for weeks. We were probably 70 blocks north of the Towers, but the malodorous offense permeated the entire length and width of our Island. I have a friend that lived in the far end of Brooklyn where not only the smell was apparent but also ashes blanketed the streets blown by the prevailing wind that day.

By the time I reached the firehouse, it was early evening, and I introduced myself and my son's foundation to the Firefighters on duty. ...Maybe, we could provide heart screenings to the Firefighters before or when they returned from what would be soon called *"Ground Zero."* They were polite, but I'm sure, on second thought, what I was offering as a helpful medical service to them might have seemed a bit irrelevant considering the emergent situation. I would later find that the brotherhood of Firefighters prided themselves in taking care of their own.

I also made a visit to the Police Station, which might have been on the same street. I think I met with a detective who took my card and said he would be in touch. He seemed genuinely interested, and that it was on behalf of my son. I know it touched him, especially considering the day...

After the screening which Dr. Archie and I would soon provide for the NYPD, the NYPD Benevolent Association made a donation to CHAD and gave us all a genuine NYPD cap that I will always treasure. I also have a commemorative NYFD hat from Ground Zero. I tried to meld the two, kinda like the double-billed Sherlock hat, but not a good look. Better to honour each by switching off because whose ever hat you had on during that exceptional time, you'd get a tip of the cap or a honk of the horn from your passing NYPD car or NYFD firetruck. Our Heroes appreciated the acknowledgment.

This was an overladen time for me, I was due to leave for Los Angeles in two weeks to host the *"10ᵗʰ CHAD Annual Volleyball Tourney and Heart Screening,"* to be held on 30ᵗʰ of September at Zuma Beach in Malibu- one of Chad's best-loved places. It would be like going back home. I had been working on this event for a year. We had the Mayor of Malibu planning on stopping by and two stellar co-hosts: Holly McPeak, 3-time U. S. Olympic Volleyball Medalist, and Gabrielle Reece, super-model and former professional volleyball player. I told Dr. Archie, I would join him as soon as I returned from the "CHAD Heart Screening."

While I was in Los Angeles, Dr. Roberts had begun the screening event down at one of the schools near Ground Zero, and, by the time I returned to N.Y. on the 3rd of October, the event had been moved to "The Police Academy" in midtown. I recall when I first walked into that building, it was like walking into a movie set with the massive wooden desk raised high above the ground, which caused you to look very high up to meet a very 'tall' robust Policeman who sat behind it to greet you...as well as make sure you belonged there.

During these 3 weeks, *The New York City Police Academy* became a veritable medical clinic with special screenings on several floors. What was once the Library might now hold medical personnel doing blood pressure testing and pulmonary function. A floor up, you might find several rooms now containing cots or tables where the Echocardiogram screenings were being held. On another level or down the hall might be the station for EKGs. The space where we registered the NYPD participants was a large room that contained a huge table that could seat 20 to 25. It is here we did the intake having the officers and, staff fill out forms which asked about their personal and family medical history, and included cardiovascular questions, as well as questions regarding lifestyle, physical activities or sports that they participated in. Dr. Robert's wife, myself, and two other family relations took over this section from 8 AM until 9 or 10 at night at times. Even my son, Curt, who was staying with me at the time, would come by and help out between his modeling go-sees.

As we began the process of registering almost 2,000 members of the NYPD for their cardiovascular screenings, never had I seen and heard so much wheezing and heavy breathing. These audible sounds were coming from the NYPD detectives and officers as they completed their screening forms. These were other heroes who were working in the Fish Kill landfill sites, hours on end, sifting through thousands of tons of debris to search for the remains of those killed on September 11th as well as any of their personal effects. All the while, they were breathing in noxious, perilous vapors their bodies had never been exposed to before, just like the first responders were experiencing at "Ground Zero."

Dr. Roberts worked tirelessly. One night, the always impeccably attired doctor, came out of his makeshift office with his stethoscope wrapped half-haphazardly around his neck, sticking halfway in and out of pockets. He never stopped, and he always had a smile on his face. I remember him sending a few patients straight to the hospital, whose testing showed dangerously high blood pressure rates or heart screening concerns. We provided near 2,000 heart screenings at this event to the Men and Women in Blue, civilians who worked there, and N.Y.C. Police Academy cadets and graduates. Every cardiologist in the City was volunteering their time and coming over after their hospital shifts ended to read the Echocardiograms and EKGS. This was an all-out fantastic show of community support on every level.

At one time, when it wasn't too busy, Dr. Robert's wife and I snuck away for a few minutes. We accompanied a van of Policewomen from the NYPD down to "Ground Zero." We were within feet of the greatest devastation and loss of American lives of our times. The site was utterly surreal, like walking into and viewing the Apocalypse. Everything was a smoulder, and there were great shards of graceful steel lattice that once belonged to the building façade reaching upwards, which made it seem like a church that had been torn asunder by some terrible force. The quiet, silent reverence was palpable throughout… It was prevalent in the utter devastation in which all the responders performed their determined mission without words, to find and raise Life again, and if they couldn't do that to find whatever they could for the Families' Loved Ones. …There was never a thought that they were putting their own Lives at risk searching for their fellow men and women. Hundreds would give up years of their lives performing this sacrifice for humanity.

As I looked to my right, I saw "the cross" - tall, iron grids in the shape of a cross. It stood at the edge of the rubble as if to say, "This signifies the perimeter of a Sacred Place, never forget that as you enter or look upon it." On the lateral side of the cross hung a

Firefighter's helmet. I turned to our Policewoman escort and said quietly, "Look what the Firemen did, they made a cross." Just as quietly, she answered me, "They didn't make it; it was found like that." It took my breath away. (Several years later, I would be in a cab driving near the new "Freedom Tower," and as we passed a building, I saw that same cross. Only this time, it hung proudly on the face of a building, draped in an American Flag that was fluttering. I think it may have had a tour across the country and then came Home.

If you are a New Yorker, you will have your own personal story of that day. Mine is always connected to my son, Chad: watching him that pre-Christmas day as he stood in Tower 2, looming over the historical plaque he read so seriously while looking down on the City he/we loved so much. On this our last Family outing together, he was seeing all that he was reading and memorizing the landscape to take with him forever.

On this never-to-be-forgotten day, the 11th of September 2001, I could see Chad and his young Friends welcoming into the Gates of Heaven thousands of Innocents who were just going to work living Life, and their Lives were sacrificed because they Live in a Land that was Free. Chad, too, had stood on that very same spot on Earth that was like no other. He would want to be there to welcome them to the next place.

Along with the Firefighters, there was another group of people I instantly thought of the moment the 2nd jet sliced through Tower 2. It was the staff of Fuji Bank, which was located on the 81st Floor of that Tower. Fuji Bank on Park Avenue had been my bank for years, ever since I moved to N.Y. and worked for Shiseido. It serviced both "The CHAD Foundation" and my personal account. But sometime after the 1st terrorist attack on the World Trade Center, Fuji closed their Park Avenue office, and all of the accounts were moved to Two World Trade Center. It was always a little difficult doing my banking there because I always thought of Chad and our last Family gathering at this place. Now, whenever I would go to Fuji Bank, I would have to use the same bank of elevators we used as a Family. After the 1st bombing, Security was tight. You had to show I.D., go through the metal detector, and get a special pass with a photo before you could even get in line for the elevators. Ironically, 6 weeks before 9-11, Fuji closed its doors to all personal accounts and small business accounts, which meant I had to move my accounts and would never have reason to go to the 81st floor of Tower 2 again.

However, I will always remember the Fuji Bank staff. They were was so gracious and friendly, and I remember one of them, S., told me he would be looking forward to seeing my off-Broadway play and CHAD production of *Welcome Home Kelly*, and he wanted a front-row seat. I kept my promise to him, and 8 months later, when *'Kelly'* opened, there was a front-row seat with his name on it. I tried looking for his name on the list of survivors but never saw it. I hope he and his colleagues made it out... A few years later, a friend was visiting someone in the hospital. He told me the person in the next bed had worked at Fuji Bank, and that man told him most of the employees made it out. I hope he was right.

Prior to 9-11, when you went to the bank, first, you had to take an elevator to the 79th floor. Then you take a short walk over to the other bank of elevators that would take you to Floor 81. For years, I would have this dream, that when the elevator reached the 79th Floor, I would go to step out, but there was nothing but sky and air.

We, the generations that followed World War II, never saw an event like Pearl Harbor happen in our lifetime. And though we looked with horror and sadness on this national tragedy which occurred in our own beautiful Harbour of Hawaii, we thought we would be safe from ever having to worry that this could happen in our Homeland. September 11th was the game-changer. But also on that infamous day, the adage, "The worst of times, brings out the best of us," became a shining reality. Unlike Pearl Harbour, this siege annihilated not military personnel, but everyday people who made up the entire world, who were just going to work that day, living and making Life in what is known as the Capital of the World.

But extraordinary heroes were born that day from everyday people. No one saw or cared what religion you belonged to, what your race was, or your nationality. You are my fellow Human Being, you need help, and I am here to help you. – 'I have gotten on a plane… from all across the country, and I have come to help you.' In our most tragic hour, the Heart of Humanity survived. I saw storekeepers giving away shoes to the survivors of the towers as they began their arduous trek home, maybe miles for some. Restauranteurs fed the volunteers and responders daily…for months. I saw actual footage of two men following the complete collapse of one of the Towers. One was helping another up from under an automobile. Both were covered in the cataclysmic gray soot that also enveloped the air like an apocalyptic movie. One happened to be a Hasidic Jew, the other of the Muslim faith. They walked away, hands around each other's shoulders; two Human Beings were helping each other stand up and survive.

CHAD and I were so grateful we could add our help in a small but meaningful way with Dr. Roberts and the "Living Heart." Hopefully, we identified the most severe and at-risk cases so they could follow-up and get the medical help they needed. I will never forget those brave Policemen and Policewomen we had the privilege of meeting and serving.

Following 9-11, I moved to Battery Park City in lower Manhattan, for I felt somehow I had been on the lucky side of the ship that day and was spared. This was my way of showing solidarity. For 7 months, I walked daily across the "Church St. Bridge" and watched with grave concerns as each beam rose from the barren Earth of "Ground Zero." I had to know we were going to be all right. – I had to know we were going to survive as a city, a country, a nation whatever happened. This poem came to me day-by-day, week-by-week, year-by-year, and was the answer to my query. It is dedicated to every Hero and Heroine that gave their Lives that day in September and all the 1st responders who tried to save as many as they could: NYPD, FDNY, Port Authority, E.M.S. and the many I have missed...

Home

It is the tip of the Island called, "Manhattan,"
Where I feel the most at Home.
It is here in the fetal position, I lay cradled
in the womb of the world.
Spawning new dreams of hope and splendour,
Amongst the dust where lies the battered
ruins of the new Rome.

Where brothers fought brothers spilling blood
that stained the terrain scarlet and future
generations consecrate sacred,
For it is to our Forebearers that we owe,
No knee will ever bend to Crown or the will
of one man or woman.

From the Gangs of New York to 9-11 to
Freedom Towers our challenges continue to
lay waste on barren ground waiting for the
Lifeblood of new explorers to rebreed
Hope amongst the ashes.

The mighty evolution continues spawning
everyday heroes, standing shoulder to
shoulder. And as the sun sets, the Phoenix
Will always rise, fueled by the fodder of
Dreams from every corner of the Earth.

Where Babel here defines a nation built on
the diversity of tongues from a thousand nations
Set sail for a mighty Rock called New York
Where they will chip away unceasingly to carve
a Life in this Land of Promise and pass their
own Life's blood to the next generation.

Step by step, the torch is passed from hand to hand,
lit eternally in the Harbour of Freedom,

Held forever high in a Lady's Hand.
The Price of Freedom is the heartbeat of
every man, woman, and child who plants
their Spirit in this Soil for the inalienable
Right to be Free.

- by Arista (N.Y. Artist/Writer)
Battery Park City/Ground Zero
11 September 2009
www.chadfoundation.org
copyright – Library of Congress, U.S.A.

CHAPTER 19

The Hearts of the Homeless
Graz, Austria &
Gothenburg, Sweden

In this journey of CHAD, it is wondrous where the *'Wizard of the Sky'* would take us next to find hearts that needed to be screened. But before I could take the 'next step,' the artist with now two post-ops of tibial-transpositioned knees must transition from being a makeup artist- standing too much, to doing something creative– whilst sitting more. Ah, let's see what's out there: selling elegant dinnerware to wealthy clientele whilst performing one's duties in a luxurious, upscale environment... or Director of Development at a bare-bones non-profit organization for the homeless, which entails raising monies, writing grants, creating events, press, and public relations. –Well, will you look at that? CHAD has prepared me for something else... What I have been doing and learning in his foundation for the past 8 years has provided another skillset. Besides, I truly wanted to know more about our people who are without a home– how and why this happens and what I could do to help. And so I chose the 2nd position.

One of the first charges I was given was to help raise monies to send our Team of New York homeless men to participate in the *"1st Homeless Streetsoccer World Cup,"* to be held in Graz, Austria with 16 other participating countries. The what? For who? Where?? Yes, those were the same questions I got when I presented the idea to prospective funders. Why not buy them clothes or a computer? Send <u>me</u> to Austria on vacation! But they had to let me explain the 'why.' There is a worldwide organization of homeless newspapers, and two of its organizers were hoisting a pint in South Africa one night and thinking of ways to "Raise Awareness of Homelessness." Eureka! "Football"! [which in Europe and the rest of the world means "Soccer"] "Let's host a Homeless Streetsoccer World Cup," and thus was born an inspiring, consequential event which is still going on until this day. But we had to get them there first.

The power of the press was the "launch-pad." One of our clients (as our homeless people were referred to) was selling our homeless street papers in the subway—something he wasn't supposed to do but guess who bought one? A New York Times reporter who called me immediately–could he do a story? Sure come to Baruch College on Sunday, only place in town who will give us a place to practice... He did come, and we were off to the races. The story broke on Saturday; HBO was calling me Monday morning for the exclusive story. I loved the Bryant Gumbel program, *Real Sports,* great human interest stories of the sports world. - They got their exclusive. Not only did they spend 2 months at our Drop-in Center following the players' journey, but they also came to Austria with us. Mary Carillo, sports correspondent, and former tennis pro would fly over and cover the homeless soccer event after covering Wimbledon. Wow.

We chose the talented, creative filmmaker, James Marsh, who would document the journey of our Team in N.Y. and Austria. Who would know that a decade later, he would receive an Oscar for his documentary, *Man on Wire*? But for these moments, he was traveling with the dispossessed in the bowels of N.Y. Subways as I took our Team for physicals, thanks to Bellevue Hospital, and capturing the moment in the Doctor's office, which would determine *if* we had a goalie as R. had been bashed in the head 6 weeks before we were to leave. (don't ask how...the stories vary) The Doctor kept us in suspense before he finally gave his approval.- Finally, "Yes, he could play... but we had to get R. special protective glasses to protect his eyes." Ah! Those Angels again.

Amongst this breathtaking mayhem, our enterprising Executive Director, J.G., one of the most innovative minds you will ever meet, poses to me, "Arista, why doesn't your foundation provide heart screenings for all the teams of the 16 countries participating?" "Why that would be fantastic!" I respond, smiling widely... quickly displaced with anxiety within. "How do I do that? There's an ocean between us!" You want hearts to safeguard – cross the big pond!

So, my days were spent trying to get our Team there, dress them, and help get them trained. Do they know soccer? Uh, not too well, they're from America. We play football here. Well, our Executive Director is a black belt; he trained them in discipline and drills. And well, wouldn't you know it, the Everton Football Team happens to be in town from Liverpool. They are exchanging community service programs with our Midtown Court, surely they will help train our boys. And they did at Chelsea Piers, what kismet! Do they have shoes? Well, not soccer shoes. I know who to call, well I didn't call him, but I wrote to Mr. Knight, C.O.O. of Nike (at the time.) "Sir, our New York team of homeless men, is representing the U.S.A. in Austria and they have not the appropriate shoes... (remember the 'Ask?') ...and then the 'Receive.' "Thank you, Mr. Knight!!! Just look at how great your shoes look on our Team!" I did send visuals from Austria to him. [The next year, Nike sent shoes for all 26 participating teams in Sweden for the "2nd Homeless Cup." Who says corporations don't have 'heart'!]

—And at night...the middle of the night, when the time was appropriate, and Austria could be reached during *their* business hours, I contacted hospitals given to me by the organizers of the tournament. Despite the language barrier–though most Austrians do speak English fluently, and after many attempts, I was able to reach Dr. Josepha Binder from Abteilingfur Kardiologie in Graz, Austria. How wonderful... she would love to be of service, but if given the bare minimum of 10 players per team times 16 countries, that still was too much for one cardiologist to do.

So... I called my loyal doctors in California, "Now, I know this is a longshot, but do you know any cardiologists who might want to come to Graz, Austria, for the *"1ˢᵗ Homeless Streetsoccer World Cup?"* And help screen athletes from 16 countries?" (Silence, pause, really – what did you expect?) Then Dr. Silka answered, "Well, it just so happens Dr. Luna will be vacationing in Italy at this time – and he does love soccer, let me ask Dr. Wong to ask him." (Are you kidding?? Of course, I believe in miracles!) Dr. Luna would drive over with his Family after vacationing in Italy… (How long would that little jaunt take? I'm thinking Julie Andrews traversing the Swiss Alps in *Sound of Music*.) –Dr. Luna must really like soccer, plus being an Angel as well as his family… Where are we going, Dad? To do what?? And he would stay a few days to help us… Help us? If it were not for both Dr. Luna and Dr. Binder, we could not have provided this event for our homeless teams of the world.

And of course, the echocardiogram machines were no problem, thanks to our community supporter, Philips, who has helped CHAD screen thousands of people, young and old. "Oh, you need two machines to go to Austria to screen homeless teams of athletes from 16 countries? Great cause." It seemed if I was golden! —Well, until we got to Graz's tiny landing field in the middle of the night, then a bit of the patina began to fade. "What are these?" said the inspector, peering at the big boxes containing the machines. Everybody explains. "Where are the papers?" he asks, sticking his hand out, waiting. Everyone points to me. I give the man the only paper they gave to me at J.F.K. and the paper from Philips. After reading quite carefully in the darkened airfield, he shakes his head, "No, Miss, these are not the right papers." "These are the only papers I have," said I, answering very politely as I would to a police officer. "I need the papers that say you are not bringing in these machines to sell." Now the politeness is wearing thin—a long trans-Atlantic flight, with long stops in London and Switzerland. "Who am I going to sell them to???" I brought them for the "Homeless soccer event –to screen the hearts–of the *homeless* athletes." Sixteen countries of them! This man seemed void of one at that moment. More speaking in Austrian with our young Austrian guide and as I watch, the stern man turns abruptly and takes my machines away. They would spend the night in a cold, concrete building- okay, I'm told it was a locked office… and it was July.

My face does not hide my disquiet, which the astute student guide quickly addresses, "The machines have to stay in the locked office tonight, but someone will speak to the Mayor tomorrow, and we will get it all taken care of in the morning." I was reluctant to leave the airfield without my machines. All I could see were athletes from all over the world playing their hearts out, without first getting their hearts screened!

Finally, my young diplomatic guide took my elbow, leading me to the van. I was a stranger in a strange land … but with a nice stranger leading me to my home for the next two weeks. But first, we had to stop at a beautiful Catholic boarding school with extensive tree-laden grounds. Here was where all 16 teams and their coaches would stay. (And for the N.Y. staff, a darling hamlet Inn dropped amidst a big green mountain. Austria was a polite, gentle, hospitable place… Did I mention charming? We all fell in love with it…and its people. (The woman desk manager even went into the kitchen which had been closed for hours to make us grilled cheese sandwiches once we arrived.)

Somebody did, in fact, know 'the Mayor' and my echocardiogram machines were released without further hindrance the following day, which allowed me to prep the rooms for the cardiologists who were to arrive on the first day of the tournament. We set up places in the boarding school so the location would be convenient for all the teams to get to, before or after practices. Outside we set up tables serviced by volunteers who would help teammates fill out their prescreening questionnaire forms when they were from countries who didn't read/ speak English well.

In Austria, they have a mandate after graduation from high school for compulsory military service, or an alternative option, community service. So most of our guides were fulfilling their obligations in social service but did so with such enthusiasm, friendliness, and genuine care. (I am glad that through the years, I have had our guide Gernot visit me twice in New York; he now has the title of Dr.!)

[...Who knew that as little Chad took my hand to bring me to see 'Arnold' at Muscle Beach in Venice, California, I would one day be visiting his hometown in Graz, Austria, screening hearts of the world. And we would be getting a letter of support from Governor Schwarzenegger for that little boy's foundation a year later. That *Destiny-Maker in the Sky* is so full of surprises...]

As for the actual games, people were tentative in attending the first few games, and athletes came in dribbles to the first day of the heart screening. It was suggested I go to the press room and send out press releases on the event and also attend the breakfast coach meetings for every country. I did both, and slowly the attendees began to increase, and whole teams would be lining up for their screenings! I think it was getting the word out more... but also a tragedy had occurred in June, just one month before the event, which emphasized quite soberly the importance of preventive heart screenings.

Marc-Vivien Foé, a Cameroonian soccer player, was playing in an international match in France in June, less than a month before our tourney. He collapsed midway through the game with no players near him and died shortly afterward. It was found on autopsy he had hypertrophic cardiomyopathy, the #1 silent killer of "Sudden Cardiac Deaths in Young Athletes." - This was the very heart anomaly we were screening for with this Echocardiogram test. Marc-Vivien Foé was 28 years old. He was playing in the *"FIFA Confederation Cup"* with professional soccer standouts from 7 continents. Our players were playing in the *"1ˢᵗ Homeless Streetsoccer World Cup"* hailing from 16 countries. They were being given the Echocardiogram test that just may have saved young Foé's Life.

The results for this segment of the population were fascinating. One might think because of the societal stigma, lack of adequate food, or housing, or healthcare, they might have more susceptibility to heart disease. But the stats stayed around the figure we have always gotten– 10 or so recommendations to follow-up for every 50 persons screened who are not homeless. We found the Europeans smaller in frame, shorter than our norm, and not overweight or obese. Is it the food they eat in their countries? Is it less fatty, lower in cholesterol? More natural? Less consumption of fast foods? Do they eat lesser quantities than the U.S.? And we are speaking about a homeless population. This would be a very informative investigation for future studies.

The screening was very comforting to many players and their coaches in the wake of the Foe Sudden Cardiac Death. One player told Dr. Luna about palpitations he had while running and climbing the mountains. After the exam, Dr. Luna told him his heart looked good. He left with a big smile and said, "Now I can run in the mountains all I want."

This was an extraordinary event on so many levels. Chad would have loved to be here seeing their love of their sport and playing their 'hearts' out but also having had the pre-testing *before* they took the field. With his love of people from every nation, he would have been the roving reporter. The opening ceremony was an event no one will ever forget, especially our players –it was truly like a mini-Olympics.

I was visiting with our staff in our players' modern-style room, furnished with blonde wood bed-frames, cupboards, and open-standing closets. Suddenly we heard the sound of instruments playing- perhaps ones we couldn't identify... then followed by robust and lyrical singing. We all ran out of the room. And on the steps, from the floors above, the parade of teams had begun. The sounds we heard first heralded the Swiss Team's entrance, announced with the beating of their unusual drum. They were singing happily and proudly their national anthem. Then came the Italian Team, dressed in their distinctive colours, singing beautifully in their native language. Then the South African Team followed. Dressed in bright, colorful headscarves, they were singing and dancing the most vibrant African songs which resonated throughout the hallways. The U.S.A. team would follow them.

As we reached the door of the boarding house on the main level, each Team was given their country's flag. Our Team had chosen their goalie, R. L., to carry it. As we ran down the streets of Graz to the mock stadium set up in the city square, it was a memorable, magical moment. Out of the corner of my eye I saw, the HBO producer T.W.

and his cameraperson, Al, running ahead of us so they could get the shot of the NY Team entering the stadium. For one sublime moment in time, 16 countries were just athletes representing their countries and so happy to make friends with all the neighboring nations of the world. They were not diminished by their homeless status. They were just human beings of many races, creeds, and nationalities saying hello through the game of sports, proudly, with dignity, and their self-esteem intact.

It was such an extraordinary experience I took a week of vacation when I returned to New York to write a screenplay about the event, titled *Ew-Ess-Ah*, the way the Austrians cheered the U.S.A. when they made their 1st goal.

They were the most hospitable people. Everyone cheered everyone. Someone with the initial, H., may be rolling over in his grave, as our American Black goalie shook hands with many Austrian children in the stands who wanted his autograph. R. was a "rockstar" that week with moves in the goalie net that would have the stands cheering. The event grew in popularity, and suddenly the organizers had to put large video screens outside the town square so all those who couldn't fit into the stands could watch the games. The Austrian Team was comprised of many Nigerian men who had taken refuge there…. and yes, they also knew how to play soccer, well, 1st place! The U.S. learned from and admired everyone else, although we did rank a respectable 8th out of 16 places. CHAD and I were privileged to be a part of this international sports event of goodwill and help their hearts feel healthy and whole again!

After the games, everyone gathered at the picturesque bars and restaurants, which were found by first walking through a narrow pathway between quaint 300-year-old buildings. Then it was like drawing that curtain again and entering straight into the painting, *Starry Night* by Van Gogh, which hung on my wall in my New York studio. Suddenly the poster came to Life, and another world appeared: Dimly lit outside cafes where people sat amidst cobblestone streets enjoying their repast. Conversations were happy but quiet and civil-rippled with occasional laughter but never unruly out of respect for the people who lived above the establishments. Their shutters were quite visible. Some were halfway open or some closed, indicating they had already gone to sleep.

It was here in this living tableau, alfresco, that the disenfranchised sportsmen got to know their neighbors of the world. I saw an English and an Irish player with their arms around each other's shoulders, each wearing their country's flag. I saw a Japanese player and an American player trading hats after the tournament. I had some South African players tell me they thought that the "Americans" would be arrogant, but after getting to know us, "You're not, you're some of the friendliest people here."

…And our American team also learned humility and compassion as they became aware of the 'levels' of homelessness on the day everyone was going home. The young Brazilian Team—many but teenagers, wandered into their room, and their eyes widened as they saw all the new traveling clothes our Team had, thanks to caring local merchants back home. All were freshly washed and dried by the Austrian volunteers. Our Big Boys seeing their reaction—to a person gathered up all their new socks and gave them to the boys who were thrilled. However, when one of the boys pointed to himself and then to our goalie 'Rockstar' asking, "Can you take me with you?" I know that broke R.'s heart when he responded, "I wish I could, Buddy, but I can't." I think it was a very good day for the planet.

Because of the grand success of the "1st Homeless Steetsoccer World Cup" in Austria, we were invited a year later to participate in the *"2nd Homeless Streetsoccer World Cup,"* to be held in Gothenburg, Sweden. Organizers were enlightened following the Austrian tourney as their analyses showed that a third of those athletes who had participated in the tourney found jobs, went back to school, and/or found permanent housing. The playing field had been leveled through the universal vehicle of sports. The dispossessed were able to find their humanity again and their confidence and desire to live again.

This time as twenty-six teams of the world came together, the terrain was entirely different, and went from the fairytale European village of Graz to the land of the Midnight Sun in Gothenburg where the Sun reigns until midnight during half the year. As the tourney was in mid-July, we were able to experience this phenomenon. Though perhaps for the Americans, we were too jet-lagged to notice and fell out at midnight even though there was still light in the sky. This time, newcomers were participating in the tourney like Namibia, Japan, Russia, and Slovenia. This upped the stakes and scope of the games, and there were almost half again as many hearts to screen. One of the organizers, H. Mied, C.E.O., felt the CHAD Heart screening was "a valuable initiative as it provided high-quality health care service of a preventive echocardiogram especially for disenfranchised people who have little access to this screening given their life circumstances."

This event was like our '2nd child.' Having made it through the first, we were better prepared, knowing what to expect and could organize and implement things easier. It was night time duty again to reach Sweden in search of cardiologists to help with our event. Organizers were kind enough to provide me with the names of hospitals in the area. Dr. Odd Bech Hanssen, Chief of Echocardiography - Lab, Sahlgrenska University Hospital, Gothenburg, Sweden, was the Doctor who took my call. He later told me when he had put the phone down following our conversation, that he looked at his staff and said, "I just spoke to this woman in America ….I'm not quite sure why we are doing this, but we are… providing Echocardiograms for homeless athletes from 26 countries ….They will be participating in the "Homeless Streetsoccer Cup.. - I know many of you are beginning the summer holiday, so we will do this in shifts." - These were Swedish Angels.

Gothenburg is an attractive port city with endless skies of blue and a profusion of fresh sea air that just makes you want to open your lungs as you would a jacket and greet the day. And Dr. Odd Bech would do just that before coming to the screening every day. He would kayak to his tiny private island. There he would breakfast on his brown bread and hot coffee while leisurely enjoying his morning paper; then, once on land, he would bike to the screening. ...We were certainly in a different kind of land, where everyone seemed more at ease, without stress, living and enjoying their Life and their world, which included the natural beauty of their country. – That gave me pause for thought... Everyone was so friendly and accommodating. The whole cardiology staff came and volunteered their time happily and professionally, even though they were beginning their summer holiday. Gothenburg, Sweden, is another world entirely.

At the heart screening, the entire Irish Team showed up led by their Coach. Besides being one of the most congenial, jovial teams, they also all wanted very much to take the screening test. As I have found in high schools and colleges in the U.S., if the Coach is behind the screenings, all the players will participate.

Another country that always fully participated was Italy. Their coach also signed up with his entire Team. They were one of the best soccer teams, but were they also more aware of their heart health as a country? The results of Dr. Gaetano Theine's Italian study, which took place during a 26 year period and screened 40,000 athletes, found the rate of Sudden Cardiac Death was reduced by 90% due to pre-participation screening. (We will discuss this study in the subsequent Chapter 27, "To Screen or Not to Screen.")

There was one country of athletes, as I remember–Namibia, who had a bit of resistance to taking the test. They asked me, point-blank: Why do they have to do this? Who is making them do this? I explained to them that no country or anyone was forcing them to take the test, not the US. The host country of Sweden had cardiologists and staff who were volunteering their time and help to administer these essential screening tests to all the athletes to prevent Sudden Cardiac Death. I further explained it was non-governmental, or not even sponsored by the tournament organizers. This was my son's charitable organization. – Think of it as a private citizen's gift for their hearts, my son's gift to them. I showed them Chad's poster and explained how he had collapsed on the field and reminded them of the Cameroonian soccer player who died similarly the year before. Finally, their suspicions seem to be allayed, and they agreed to take the tests. We all learned about each other by communicating with each other. Without newspapers or governments, we the people of many countries just met face-to-face as Human Beings and realized we are in many ways, just the same. We only live in different places. –And we all have hearts. And they all need to be taken care of.

The "Homeless Streetsoccer World Cup" in Sweden brought CHAD into contact with many more athletes of the world. There are so many diseases that can cause death and so many social dilemmas that can put extra stress and strain on the hearts of the homeless. If we could help alleviate their fears through a screening, and for many, there were no significant heart anomalies, they could turn their attention to other aspects of survival. That they could still participate in sports was a big concern because, for many, this is their only free source of enjoyment and physical exercise. For the 12% in which follow-up was recommended, they have a signed referral paper from a cardiologist that can start the ball rolling in their own country. And if that $3,000 echocardiogram screening is not available for them there, then aren't we glad we were able to provide this lifesaving test for them here –because their Lives to have meaning. Every Life is valuable.

CHAPTER 20

Western Massachusetts - A lot of 'Heart'

In this journey of CHAD, it seems the voyage has logged miles and miles, and years and years since its maiden voyage to North Hollywood High School in California...though it seems like only yesterday. And with every port visited there is found to be a different temperature to its inhabitants: flexibility or *not* to the way they think and accept new ideas, and a scale of priorities based on the culture of their community, which informs their own state of mind. Western Massachusetts was a most pleasant surprise. People are wholly ingrained in their communities there. Maybe it goes back to their colonial existence when everyone helped everyone... depended upon each other... cared about anyone who was a part of those early settlers that laid the foundation for our country.

People in this neck of the woods seemed to really care about their children's hearts. There was no hard-sell necessary. We had successful turnouts for all of our screening events. When parents found out there was a heart screening at the local high school, be it, Holyoke, Northampton, or Westfield, they came out, nor did their young athletes seem reluctant to have the test. No one was on the fence; parents/guardians/relatives, neighbors made the appointment to be there with their student-athlete(s) in tow. And they'd bring neighbors' kids if parents were working. This was indeed a family/community affair.

I found the townsfolk of western Mass think much like their 'far' country neighbors in Cali 3,000 miles away. Maybe, too, like Cali, it's just so darn beautiful naturally with plenty of space to run around that their offspring are more athletic… encouraged to be. It's generational, western Mass people are rooted in their land; they don't veer from home. So if they are a model community in many ways, they also became a 'model' for the necessity of preventive screenings in younger people, especially athletes. This fine, upstanding region lost three of their favourite Sons…to SCD, Sudden Cardiac Death.

It was a gorgeous Fall day when CHAD traveled by train to Holyoke, Massachusetts, for their 2nd heart screening there, which would take place the following day, October 29, 2011 at Holyoke High School. The brilliant autumnal colour, which is New England's signature painted our windows all the way to Springfield. There, Melanie Martin, the Head Athletic Trainer, picked up my volunteer, Peter and me—*and* our cholesterol and glucose machines—*and* our "Story Posters" *and* our many supplies as if she didn't have enough to do. She was an exceptional trainer. You could see how every student-athlete responded to her and how she really cared about each one of them in return. Her school was also one of the first to integrate concussion screening into their athletic program. She was one of the main reasons our screenings were always successfully attended. If their friend and trainer thought this was important, then her kids did it… and those athletes that had some problems in not being able to attend, she found solutions. (It was no wonder she would become the Athletic Director a year or so later.)

Despite the threat of an imminent blizzard the day of the event —the show, which was 9 months in the planning, had to go on. Staunch supporters of this community were donating their time and service to screen their hometown athletes. Cardiologists and cardiac sonographer technicians came from Holyoke Medical Center.

Nurses and PA's (physician assistants) from Pioneer Valley showed up to do support services, like administering the cholesterol and diabetes testing, blood pressure, and EKG. Philips supplied the ever-important Echocardiogram and EKG equipment. And Dr. Michael Willers, who could be counted on to attend every screening, always appeared towing his portable echo machine behind him. This incredibly efficient and professional team administered and read 100 Echocardiograms and EKGS for local Holyoke students and athletes. Local communities were also invited to participate. Ten anomalies were found that required further evaluation.

However, as the storm began picking up speed and headed for the entire northeast corridor, we made the call to shut down early that day at 2:30 PM, but not before we got a call from a Family who was driving from a neighboring city to bring their child to the screening. We made sure that one echocardiogram machine was still up and running so that the athlete could be screened. His Family made an effort to be there; we would not let them down. A few months later, as circumstances would emerge, we found that ALL of us wished we would have had the opportunity to screen just one more athlete that day who needed to be tested.

As Melanie raced us to the station, snowflakes as big as golf balls blinded the way, fueled by a furious wind. – Little did we know that our train would be the last to leave that station for many days hence. It was ominous from the start of the train ride, and I was wondering why I kept hearing thuds that sounded like blocks of wood being knocked about under the train carriage. It was Mother Nature's Way of showing what happens when you have a dead of winter storm before the leaves have naturally fallen; the limbs are over-burdened with their weight, now perilously wet with snow.

And as if to punctuate her fury of the unseasonal blizzard, an hour out of Hartford our train struck a fallen tree pitching us all forward.- Luckily no one was hurt, especially the engineer. It took hours for them to bring another train to pull our train to continue on its journey. Finally, in the howling darkness, the other train arrived, but they found so many broken trees in the path between both trains that they then had to call the tree-sawers. Good luck with that, it's 8:30 PM on a Saturday night in the eye of a full-blown Nor'easter. – 'Twas a challenging night indeed and a treacherous time for thousands of people for many weeks following, but more so, it seemed almost like a premonition of the sad tidings we would receive about that one athlete we wished we could have screened…

The one athlete who did not make the CHAD screening on October 29 was Jonathan Gray, known to friends and Family as "Jonno." Jonno had graduated from Holyoke High School in June, just a few months before our screening, and had just begun his studies at the University of Massachusetts where he planned to get an undergraduate degree and then attend the Firefighter Academy when he graduated. According to his brother, Mackenzie (Mac), Jonathan was tremendously hard-working in his athletic pursuits; he broke the school record in shot put. He loved the team aspect of the sport. With his help, the "Holyoke High School Track Team" went undefeated during the winter 2010-'11 and spring 2011 track seasons. The team won the "Western MA Track and Field Championships" at the end of the season in a tie with Northampton High School.

It's no wonder then when Jonno came home for Christmas break, one of the first things he did was head over to his alma mater, Holyoke High School, and help Head Athletic Trainer, Melanie, with some of the younger athletes. When he returned home that day, January 5, 2012, Mackenzie recounts, 'in an effort to stay true to his commitment to the team, Jonathan was completing an hour-long rowing workout on an ergometer he brought home from school when he experienced a severe and deadly arrhythmia. Attempts by his brother, Mom, and EMTs failed to revive him. Doctors and pathologists surmise that he died of a probable arrhythmia from an unknown cause.' –We could have detected these problems with an Echocardiogram and EKG preventive screening had our screening been a few months earlier or a few months later.

Can the light shine through such sadness? Jonno's 22-year-old brother, Mackenzie, says, yes. Because of the unknown cause of his brother's arrhythmia and the potential for genetic conditions,

Mackenzie was screened with an EKG, which detected an anomaly. An Echocardiogram determined an enlarged and mildly dilated right ventricle. Doctors initially believed that Mac suffered from a condition called ARVD, which can cause deadly arrhythmias with vigorous exercise- certainly a threat for a serious runner. A second Echocardiogram revealed an Atrial Septal Defect, which was responsible for the enlargement. As a 7-time marathoner and generally active person, Mac was stunned to learn that he had a nickel-sized hole in his heart without any symptoms. Mac credits his brother Jonathan with saving his Life. Mackenzie underwent open-heart surgery on April 19 2013, and was able to return to running without the fear of a stroke, right ventricular failure, or death caused by the defect. He is a survivor because of cardiac screening.

CHAD came back in 2012 to do a heart screening at Holyoke High School in especial tribute of Jonno Gray. Jonno's parents hold an annual sporting benefit every year, and "The CHAD Foundation" has been a chosen beneficiary. It is people like the Gray Family from Western Mass, who truly represent the 'heart' of our country. In remembrance of their son Jonno's heart, they do everything they can to help safeguard other young athletes' hearts. Thank you.

The "2011 Halloween Nor'easter" as it is now called may have been howling, but Mack Hale, a Junior from Northampton High School, who also attended the October 29 2011 "Chad Heart Screening" at Holyoke High, is a survivor because of it. Mack's parents braved that unseasonable blizzard to make sure their son attended that screening. And they are so glad they did because cardiologists found a potentially dangerous problem in Mack's heart, a dilated left ventricle, which warranted further evaluation. He was one of the ten anomalies found that day. Mack has been under cardiologist's follow-up care ever since and has learned to take his own pulse and monitor his pulse rate before, during, and after exercising. The excellent news is Mack has played a full season of sports during the 2012-1013 season.

As a senior at Northampton High School, Mack wanted to make sure his teammates had the benefit of the same screening tests he had, an Echocardiogram and EKG, which detected his heart anomaly 17 months earlier. So serious was he about making these preventive screenings possible for his teammates that he organized a "Homerun Derby Fundraiser" in October 2012 so that he could help bring the "Chad Foundation's Heart Screening Program" to Northampton High School. On Saturday, March 30, 2013, his wish came true at Northampton High School, and his teammates on the "Northampton Baseball and Basketball Teams" were offered free Echocardiogram and EKG screenings.

The great news is Mack Hale started college in the Fall, where he began his studies to become a doctor. "I wish there were more opportunities like the one that I had a couple years ago. I thought it would be great if I could offer a heart screening, no matter how large, to my community. I'm so glad to see it happen, and hope for good news for all that attend."

And while we were paying tribute to the 1st favourite son, Jonno Gray, with his own special heart screening at Holyoke High School, we sadly became aware of Western Mass's 2nd favourite son. His name was Kevin Major. Following Jonno's screening, I got in touch with Susan, Kevin's Mom, to see if CHAD could organize a screening in her son's tribute, and we did so at St. Mary High School in Westfield, MA on Saturday, September 8, 2012. Another young man would become part of our Family and travel wherever CHAD went to provide a heart screening and stand proudly at our Stories Table. – This was "CHAD'S Young Athletes Hall of Fame" – the 'honour guard of the young athletes and artists' who were just on the brink of beginning the quest for their hopes and dreams and had their lives cut short from Sudden Cardiac Death.

This is Kevin Major's story, which his Mom gave me for Kevin's poster: "He was born on April 8, 1992. His big brown eyes and infectious grin would become his trademark. Kevin started playing hockey at the age of three and played competitively up until his time of passing. Hockey was only one of Kevin's love for sports. He also participated in baseball, lacrosse, golf, and was a member of the Springfield & Massachusetts All-star Rugby team. Off the Ice or Pitch, Kevin would live by another Motto, "Live Every Day, Laugh Every Moment, Love Beyond Words." Everyone who knew or had an opportunity to meet Kevin knew he lived his Life and played with a "Big Heart." Unfortunately, on July 11, 2011, this physical "big heart" took our Son, Brother, Grandson, and Friend from this Earth. What we were to find out was Kevin actually had a condition that is called Hypertrophic cardiomyopathy (HCM). Kevin J. Major died of undiagnosed HCM while swimming on July 11, 2011. He was only 19 years of age. Kevin was a consummate athlete. As many of Kevin's teammates would say, his motto was "No Excuses, Play Like A Champion."[3]

A few months after "CHAD'S Screening for Kevin Major" in September, I got another call from Jonno Gray's Mom, Cindy, in January. Yes, another heart-dropping moment. Western Mass had just lost its 3rd favourite son, Patrick Ulias. As I called to speak to Patrick's mother, the pains to the heart return. They will never go away as long as young people are dropping on the fields and never getting up, or never waking from their sleep. CHAD wanted to pay tribute to Patrick, but his Family chose to help continue CHAD'S work of preventing Sudden Cardiac Death through preventive screenings and made "The CHAD Foundation for Athletes and Artists" the beneficiary in Patrick's name at his service. CHAD was very appreciative of Patrick's gifts. Here, too, is young Patrick Ulias's story which accompanies us everywhere CHAD goes:

Patrick A. Ulias of Holyoke, MA, was born on January 25, 1985, and died suddenly on Saturday, December 15, 2012, at age 27. As a young boy, Patrick Ulias learned the meaning of his name, Patrick Adam, "Noble man of the earth." He embodied it perfectly, and it was surely the young man he became. Active in a variety of sports, Pat was foremost an avid runner and hiker, encouraging others to discover the beauty and peace of the trails. Patrick had a way of bringing a smile to everyone he met. He was known for being a genuinely kind soul who made everyone he met feel special. He had a hilarious sense of humor, perfectly timed to have everyone rolling with laughter. A gifted artist and musician, Pat was generous with his talents; he played with a passion that could be felt by those around him. To quote a friend, "Pat's love of life through nature, art, and music was always inspiring." Patrick suffered a fatal arrhythmia just shy of his 28th birthday. He leaves behind his parents, two brothers, two sisters, and countless friends. In lieu of flowers, memorial contributions may be made in Patrick's name to The Chad Foundation for Athletes and Artists.

Bode well "3 Favourite Sons of Western Mass – Jonathan "Jonno" Gray, Kevin Major and Patrick Ulias." We wish you well on your next journey. You will be missed on Earth every minute, and we cheer on the Survivors – Mackenzie Gray (Jonno's brother) and Mack Hale screened at the CHAD Nor'easter screening. You are all why many of us parents have dedicated our lives to this work – to make sure we can identify problems early so that you all can live long, healthy lives.

CHAD learned about a significant component from the pilot screening at Holyoke High School from Dr. Arthur "Archie" Roberts, whom we partnered with. It was the importance of expanding our screenings to include additional tests that would screen for early cardiovascular risk factors: such as hypertension, high cholesterol, diabetes, and obesity.

The results from this comprehensive pilot program, which included 260 student-athletes from 3 high schools in the Holyoke area, were astounding: One third had abnormal results in either Echocardiogram, EKG testing, hypertension, high cholesterol, diabetes or obesity. (14% of all students had cholesterol levels higher than average for their age group; 10% had high blood sugar levels;

one had a thickened heart muscle; 8 had mild mitral valve leakage; 10 students had a left ventricular size equal or greater than 53 mm.)

It was clear from the screening results that preventive screenings in high school age students/athletes were a good way of identifying early cardiovascular risk factors that could cause problems immediately or in the future, and perhaps the not so distant future. If problems are detected early, a course of action could be prescribed: change in lifestyle, exercise, diet, or meds if required. – Are we then able to prevent future heart attacks, by-passes, atherosclerosis through early intervention? Can preventive cardiovascular screenings in high school-age children save monies for insurance companies in the long run?

Nationwide statistics are bearing this out. According to the 2012 CDC Report, 208,000 people in the 20 years and younger age group have been diagnosed with diabetes (type 1 or type 2). From 2008 to 2009, an estimated 18,436 from these 20 years and under age group were newly diagnosed with type 1 diabetes, and 5,089 young people in the same age group were newly diagnosed with type 2 diabetes on an annual basis.[4] In 2014, according to the Centers for Disease Control and Prevention, more than *7 percent* of *U.S. children and teens* had *high* total *cholesterol.* Approximately 12.7 million, or 17 percent, of children and adolescents are obese.[5] It is said that obesity extracts a high price annually from its society, an estimated $100 billion. As CVD Cardiovascular Disease is the number 1 killer of adults, the CDC recommends screening children and adolescents for risk factors associated with CVD.

Due to these significant findings, along with the standard Echocardiogram and EKG screenings, CHAD has integrated testing for: blood pressure, obesity, cholesterol, and diabetes into their cardiovascular screening program. This will provide more comprehensive tools to identify not only structural and electrical anomalies of the heart but also premature cardiovascular risk factors. Our findings continue to be very similar to those of the pilot program.

Western Mass, the community with a 'lot of heart,' taught us a lot about children's hearts today, especially young athletes that we can learn from, explore and expand upon. It is new ground, but there are a lot of us out there now, led by leading cardiologists from the country. It is a Movement of the Heart which continues to grow and help save Lives. We threw the first pebble into the pond, and now the waves are unceasing...

CHAPTER 21

New York, New York
A Big Bite of the Apple

Everyone knows the adage that has become an anthem in the world at large: – "If you can make it in New York, you can make it anywhere." As a New Yorker for many years now, I strive daily for that golden apple... watching this magnificent, hulking City made up of the world pounding its pavement, and its heart beating a million miles a second. But, I will confess with *slightly* bowed head and two feet *deeply planted*—nope—, I haven't made it here 'completely,' some 'big bites' – but still a "work in progress." You massive Rock, you are my lifelong challenge, but I'll get to you. I'll find your heart, what makes you breathe, and want to Live – and I will continue to safeguard your engine that makes Life possible, and I will screen as many of our children as I can... with your help, please.

Not that we don't have supporters/been supported in our great City, we do and have. Medical staff from exceptional hospitals in New York have led our screenings, and numerous volunteers participated, returning again and again. Both Mayor Rudolph Giuliani and Mayor Michael Bloomberg sent Letters of Support for respectively, the Columbia University preventive screening and the Harlem YMCA cardiovascular event. I just know we can do better in the attendance department. After all, this is "Emerald City," and if a cause shines big in "The Apple," it can shine its light all over this humongous country.

We've had a robust start, 1st screening Columbia University athletes. Then joining Dr. Archie Roberts, we screened the NY Giants at their Fall training camp, and during our national tragedy of 9-11, we tested almost 2,000 NYPD officers post-9-11. CHAD had near 100% participation at the "Rice High School" event in Harlem. Known for its famed basketball program, the school was run by Christian Brothers, who taught the young men self-discipline, respect, and the goal of a college education. The success of our event was attributable to one of these very Brothers, who was the basketball coach. Brother S. took our heart screening project under his wing, much like the Head Trainer at Holyoke High did. Watch how the kids respond to their coach and vice versa, and you will know how well-attended your event will be. There is genuine care and trust apparent, and what athlete is going to say no to his coach, especially this Brother, who was like a father-surrogate to many.

Another important factor I have found that garners successful participation is having the opportunity to speak to parents, teachers, coaches, and students before the actual screening. In Holyoke, MA, Dr. Archie and I addressed all three high schools, days before the screenings. In Baltimore, MD, the cardiologists from Johns Hopkins, and I talked to the student body in the gym where their favoured son, Reggie Lewis, had run the boards. Here, in New York City, Brother S. had invited me to speak to the parents at the Fall Orientation sessions for their boys. These personal talks proved vital in ensuring parents would bring their child to be screened because now they could be informed as to why preventive screenings are necessary. They would come to know that the HCM gene is present in 1 in 500 births, and young black men are more predisposed to this silent disease than whites, 44% to 26%. Parents and student-athletes' fears could be addressed or allayed. Here they could ask questions and receive answers from someone who had sustained the loss. All the while, they could see pictures and stories of young athletes facing them- as I bring as many of our Story Posters as possible to these talks. These youths looked very much like their very own children- vital, healthy with the promise of a great future ahead of them. The only difference is these children in the pictures did not have the benefit of the Echocardiogram/EKG tests that we were offering to their children.

We never charged for these screenings, which would have typically cost $2,500 to $3,000 each. However, in Western MA, with the support of the school and the community, we decided to ask for a 'suggested donation of $35 per child.' This would help bring the screening program forward to the next school, but more importantly, this became a way for parents to make a commitment to their child's health and Life. Was their child's health and Life worth $35? I would tell parents just don't go to the fast-food restaurant this week. Forgo that movie or a new item of clothing this month, and without exception, every parent made that commitment. Many expressed this was a small price to pay for the safeguarding of their child's heart and perhaps their very Life. And this was a middle-to-lower-strata community.

In Harlem, I was a little reluctant to suggest the same, but it was Brother S. who told me, no, I think you should. I have seen parents pay $200 for a pair of sneakers; this $35 shows they are making their child's health a priority, and they did! It was so beautiful to see, and for the few children for whom this was truly a hardship, Brother S. was like Mother Teresa, he found a way to make it happen.

At the Rice High School event, we had major support from the *"Mount Sinai Hospital Cardiology Division"* under the lead of Dr. M. G., who had worked with our screening program in Hermosa Beach, California. Dr. S. Priori, the then Director of the "Cardio Genetics Lab at NYU School of Medicine," lent her nursing staff for the cholesterol and diabetes testing at our screenings. We found five results at Rice High School that required further evaluation; one student had to wear a Holter monitor for several days as Mt. Sinai doctors followed his progress. He was thoroughly relieved when the doctors gave him the green light to return to sports. I was able to speak to Brother S. a year later, and he told me that the young man still talks about the experience and is so grateful he had the screening. He is looking forward to going to college in the Fall and knows he will be all right when he's playing basketball. These were all NY Winners. ABC Channel 7 came out and did a story on the "CHAD/Living Heart Screening for the Columbia University Football Team." I remember one of the players saying on camera that he thought 'Everyone should have some kind of pre-testing, it definitely helps. …Seeing Korey Stringer go down, that could be me.'

I thought I was being pulled along on a T-bar up the highest slope in our country. Why this isn't so hard, everyone is open to screening young people! But put on your headgear, Girlie, you're about to enter the big leagues of Science and Medicine. At one point, I had the excellent opportunity to have a meeting with the administrator of the organization that managed a large consortium of hospitals in New York, which has since changed ownership. The administrator saw actual footage of our screenings, which included TV stories from Los Angeles, Baltimore, and Western Mass. He was so enthusiastic about what we were doing, and he thought it was such a worthy community service to provide for the children of New York.

He introduced me to the cardiology staff at one of his hospitals, who also became very keen about participating in the upcoming CHAD screening. The administrator told me they had 7 hospitals throughout the boroughs, and he would like to get them all involved. Each hospital could staff our screenings for the high schools in their local communities and help to implement these preventive screenings. I thought this was extraordinary, the best I could hope for, and was very excited to begin. Oh my gosh, look at all the children we can screen!!!

– However, there was one official at the hospital, whom I had actually had a personal meeting with, well-versed in HCM (Hypertrophic Cardiomyopathy.) And when he found out we were really going through with our first screening in NY, he did not share the same enthusiasm about us using their hospital staff. Why? Two words–"low yield." For the neophytes like myself, I learned that means you're not going to find enough, in this case, HCM results, to warrant using their hospital staff… In order for their staff to participate, there was a special meeting scheduled with some significant heads of the hospital present. We had a steadfast ally in the administrator who fought for CHAD, *but* we didn't win that day. We lost 7 hospitals (and all the attendant schools they could have screened).

It was a valuable lesson for me to learn as I was venturing within the venerable halls of Science and Medicine, where everything happens slowly; all must be evidence-based and go through many layers and filters of testing and analysis. Pioneering new ways of thinking, treatments, protocols will take a passionate, rational belief that what you're doing is essential in safeguarding lives, and evidence to base it on. Finding like-minded partners distinguished in their field who support your mission through action is of utmost importance. And as the layperson advocate, having an unwavering constitution, perseverance, courage, and openness that lasts a lifetime carries equal weight as it is you who is leading the charge. I am brought to remember pioneers like Semmelweis, the Austrian obstetrician who first published evidence stating when doctors washed their hands before treating their patients, the mortality rate decreased for women in the birthing ward. A simple thing that was not readily accepted and has become a bedrock of its profession. So don your helmet and just keep chipping away at The Rock...

That's the mode I was in– rather a heavy drilling than just chipping– when I encountered the 'Father' at another of our screenings who wouldn't wake up his teen sons to come and have a screening. This screening took place at a major youth organization in Harlem. He happened to be walking past our screening event and popped in. It's a pretty impressive sight: starting with a "Sign-In" station where student-athletes fill out their pre-screening questionnaires– complete with Cardiovascular questions, the student's and family's health history, and also, permission and waiver forms. The second stop is a post where the height, weight, and B.M.I./obesity readings take place. Then comes blood pressure testing, followed by cholesterol and diabetes testing—all screening for early cardiovascular risk factors. Next, is the EKG to test for electrical problems, and lastly, the motherlode, the $2500- $3500 Echocardiogram. This is the gold standard for detecting HCM- hypertrophic cardiomyopathy, the number one silent killer of 'Sudden Cardiac Death in Young Athletes,' as well as a plethora of other structural anomalies that are found.

"What's all this?" said he, his eyes growing larger as he scanned the pretty elaborate clinic. "We're doing heart screenings for young athletes… you have any teenage kids?" said I, hopeful– we needed candidates! "I have two teenage boys." This time my eyes grew large too, "Ah, participants!" and my voice raised to an octave a decibel higher, "Well, where are they?!" He turned, not entirely understanding the exclamation point in my voice. "They're home sleeping." "Well, go wake them up and tell them to come here!!" Adamancy. "I can't," says he, "They'll get mad at me." - Time for battle gear. "Sir, come with me please, it will just take a moment." I lead him to my stable of soldiers that come with me to every screening – smiling, healthy, athletes reaching out to him from the poster easels they sit upon… Chad included. **They** never had the benefit of these heart screenings. He began reading some of their stories. He couldn't believe it. They were healthy, with no symptoms. He began to read more.

His face changed. Mine didn't, "Now, will you go wake them up? It's free, it's safeguarding their hearts, maybe even saving their lives." More hemming and hawing, they'll get mad at me. Drill hard, sister!! "Sir, this is important! Not to be rude, but who's the parent here??" "Maybe another time." "No, there is no other time. This is the time, 9 months in the making; everyone is here today for *your children.*" I even told him about our lead cardiologist, Dr. Robert Brown, from Lincoln Hospital, who was reading the Echocardiograms at this event. Just a few days before, he had been called on an emergency as a young football player had collapsed. He was able to save him; the young man lived for a few days, but then expired. It was found in the autopsy, he had HCM, the very thing we are screening for today. The man apologized, thanked me, and left. However, he did come back a half-hour later… sans his teenagers but asked if he could take some literature for their Doctor to have a look at. – It's a step.

It takes a lot of steps to make a screening, that's why you always want to see them filled to the maximum. Once the venue is secured and that's no easy task, first, you have to find one, and then a date that is convenient for all—the school/organization, athletic events, then finding out scheduling availability for cardiac ultrasound technicians, nurses, and volunteers. Then of utmost significance: what excellent cardiologists are available in the area and not on call that particular day which the school/organization has given us for the screening. (And they are exceptional, for they work tirelessly as cardiologists all week long. Who wants to give up 5 hours on a Saturday to provide screenings for young athletes? Well, look under Acknowledgments at the end of the book, and you will find the loyal, dedicated team of doctors, staff, and volunteers who give their gift of time and service just for that reason –to save a Life.) It's just this screening was particularly hard. There was a hospital at the end of the block; it was for their community. But no, they weren't able to help… and we had gone right to the top. How about cardiac sonographers? I called every local hospital and finally found a very accommodating one that was supportive of our mission.

And you must have backups. What about nurses to do the finger-sticks for cholesterol and glucose testing and blood pressure testing? Do we have enough funding for the glucose and cholesterol slides per student? They have to be pre-ordered ahead of time, and they are costly. What if the students don't show up? The slides can't be saved for another screening. What about the Echocardiogram/EKG machines? Would the manufacturer be able to contract with us for that date? Volunteers, for height and weight, and BMI? We lucked out with Citibank volunteers, thanks to my friend, R. Perez, and some of his fraternity brothers. And all these excellent medical staff and volunteers have to be fed! Step up, "Café Bonjour." And screening questionnaires, release forms/waivers, permission slips have to be disseminated and signed ahead of time, thanks to the Director of Development there, Charles Taylor. He did his best but also found an uphill challenge. Media and Press must be contacted…several times. And let's not forget the most important person, the student-athlete - and the all-important "Raffle Incentive." Lest we not forget the young athlete in Baltimore, who made sure he was the first to be screened and stayed all day just so he could see if his ticket won the Muggsy Bogues sneakers! (which thank goodness, he won.)

For our Harlem Raffle, a very kind volunteer's daughter was able to donate a selection of cool CDs the kids might like from "Universal Records." She was also able to acquire tickets to see *"Wynton Marsalis at Lincoln Center"* and a backstage pass to meet the Cast. (The young man didn't know a lot about Wynton Marsalis, but he wore a suit and afterward went backstage to meet the musicians; it was a night to remember!) I also received from an actor friend a signed poster from the Cast of *Xanadu* on Broadway. Lastly, a local designer, Khalil Jenkins, created a unique Custom Denim Bag for the event.

It was perhaps the lightest show of students we ever had. However, out of 28 persons screened, Dr. M. from North General Hospital had 4 recommendations for follow-ups; one finding was a thickening of the heart muscle. There were also high cholesterol and high glucose findings and 4 high blood pressure results. The young lady who won the Custom-designed Denim Bag was thrilled to win it but also expressed her thankfulness at getting screened because now she at least knew she had a problem and could do something about it by following up. The nurse counseled those that had findings of premature cardio risk factors such as hypertension, high cholesterol or diabetes/borderline diabetes, and or obesity and gave them recommendations for their diet and exercise. CHAD also donated the life-saving AED (Automatic External Defibrillator) to the organization's swimming department. Thanks to Cardiac Science, the AED was much appreciated because, in a big organization, there are so many departments that could use this device that saves lives.

When I looked out in the hall, I saw young people, and I was about to sally forth and retrieve them… but they were not attached to parents who needed to sign their paperwork if they were under 18, which they were. They got the notices, letters to the parents, the flyers, the pre-screening questionnaires weeks before. I was also told there was a practice of another sport in progress right across the street. Why are they not here? I even had a volunteer venture across the street with flyers to see if any of the players practicing there were over 18. He came back; no one followed.

Weeks before, I had even made an appointment to see a deputy at *"Congressman Charles Rangel's Office."* He thought what we were doing was very laudable, but after speaking for a while and sharing with him my inability to 'move the troops,' he looked me in the eye and told me straight up "The first one may not be successful... but every one you have after that will begin to become successful." This was his community; he had lived here a long time; he was wise and imparting that wisdom gained. That's all I needed to know... Yea., but I kept thinking of the ones we might miss. This was a community at risk for the HCM gene, the #1 killer of Sudden Cardiac Deaths in Young Athletes. That stat, which says young black men were more predisposed to it–44% to 25% white, kept hovering in the background. It is a hard fact to accept, but this is part of the landscape of screening. – In some parts of the land, you get 28 participating; in others, 100; in others 250; so you learn to make every single one matter. Because it does, every Life matters.

Sometime after that, through a good friend, I was introduced to a mid-town doctor, Dr. B. Paswell, who had just moved into an extensive suite of new offices in the mid-'50s. After we met, he showed me around his beautiful space, which had just gone through a total renovation, and then graciously offered it for our next heart screening. What a gift! I was ecstatic, why each patient could have their own examining room. There were rooms to do the Echocardiograms and EKGs separately and a big lobby for parents and students to wait. In addition, our volunteer staff could even use the vast wraparound desk for reception. They would have plenty of room for entrance and exit stations and all the paperwork necessary for both. NY1-TV was also coming to cover the screening as The CHAD Foundation, and I had been honourees a few months prior as "NY1's New Yorker of the Week." (CHAD was very proud to join the ranks of the chosen New-Yorker-of-the-Week.) So many volunteers are working relentlessly to make their communities better places on so many levels. The program had a substantial viewership in the millions, for it aired in all 5 boroughs. What was disheartening was not one person/school called asking for us to organize a heart screening in their school or community, and the great Host made a point of making sure viewers saw the contact information.)

But you keep plugging away. This community screening had a perfect mid-town location accessible by the subway. This had to be a successful screening. I targeted 50 highs schools from Washington Heights to Battery Park City that were known for their athletic programs. Dr. Brown would come from Westchester and Dr. Rotatori from Staten Island. The IAMP school of ultrasound technicians were coming from New Jersey. Dr. Bruce was lending his nurses to help with EKG administering. A kind Medical Rep was providing lunch for the Volunteers and Medical Staff. I even invited my union, "The Screen Actors Guild-AFTRA," after all we are "The CHAD Foundation for Athletes and Artists"... and there have been so many heart-related deaths of our actors. Several actors did take advantage of the opportunity.

I'm tenacious when it comes to calling, polite, but until I reach you personally, I will keep calling you – Athletic Directors, Coaches, Principals. Public schools or Private Schools. And I will also come to your school and stuff your mailboxes with flyers on the event with "Intro Letters to Parents and Coaches." I even posted to college boards on the internet... and got a college doctoral musician from Croatia who came for his screening...who ended up doing a benefit classic concert for CHAD (which we will hear more about in Chapter 29). Such extraordinary gifts we receive through Cyberspace and the people they bring to us!

But what about the student-athletes? Why did only 6 schools out of 50 send any of their student-athletes to be screened? I even contacted a school in Brooklyn who had recently lost a young athlete to Sudden Cardiac Death, polite interest, but no one took the subway to Manhattan.

It is a conundrum. I have asked people from all walks of Life why they thought this was. #1 answer – They don't want to know. It's Human Nature. Stick your head in the sand. What I don't know can't

hurt me... But we know it can, and can even kill you. #2 answer –
Denial. It didn't happen to my team, my school, my kid... happens
rarely. –No, the HCM gene is found in 1 in 500 births; the Centers
for Disease Control say 3,000 – 6,000 young people between the ages
of 15 and 34 years of age die annually from Sudden Cardiac Death.
Do the math; in 3 decades, that's a town.

And what about all the other anomalies we find in our screenings:
holes in the heart, Wolff-Parkinson-White syndrome, stenosis of the
carotid artery, valve problems, and on and on. It's the ultimate test to
identify the lethal HCM, and it's **FREE** (yes, donations are accepted
to pass the program forward but not mandatory). This test, by the
way, is one you can't go to your Doctor and request a preventive
Echocardiogram for your child. Typically, the $3,000 test will not
be paid for by your insurance company without a referral from a
cardiologist, which the CHAD Result Form provides.

But here today, for a subway ride and a few hours on a Saturday,
your child can receive a $3,000 test that is non-invasive, doesn't
hurt, and can identify deadly problems of the heart. And it also gives
parents and their children a tremendous sense of relief if the initial
screening is normal. And if further evaluation is recommended, the
parent will have the necessary referral form signed by a cardiologist.
We have so little we do have control over. At least with having this
preventive screening, one can have an excellent chance of knowing
your child will not collapse and die from Sudden Cardiac Death while
they're on the field, court or in the pool.

The # 3 answer I received was "Economics": I understand this
one. Take a drive through the ghettos of our society wherein some
areas, kids have to walk down the center of the street in groups to get
to school through the maze of rival gangs. You got one sure talent–
sports, and a ticket out - and, then, to have a test that shows you can't
play sports?? That's the worst-case scenario, and the best is with this
test, you have the best chance of not dropping from Sudden Cardiac
Death while you're playing the sports that you love.

But granted it takes a hero to hear this, and I saw such a hero
as I watched Isaiah Austin, make his speech of gratitude at being

honourarily drafted to the NBA in 2014. Isaiah was found to have a potentially lethal disease called Marfan's Syndrome, which is also one of the causes of Sudden Cardiac Death in Young Athletes. The NBA is the only professional athletic organization that mandates Echocardiogram testing for all its draftees. We are so proud to have on our back cover a quote from a letter Adam Silver, Commissioner of the NBA, wrote to CHAD stating why the NBA has chosen to screen their athletes.

In 20 years of screening, I have found an incredible thing - that young people want "To Live" today. Given either or— they choose "Life." To me, that is a very mature, heroic behaviour for a young person, for it is a massive blow if they cannot play sports professionally or even non-professionally. But the flip side of that coin is all the children across the country who come to our screenings have read articles about, saw TV broadcasts about- young athletes that look just like them collapsing and never getting up… These Kids want to get up, and they want to "Live." And when they meet me personally, or any of the other parents who are involved in preventive heart screenings who have also lost their Son or Daughter to Sudden Cardiac Death, they begin to see and understand what that means. –"If they were no longer here anymore, how would it affect not only them but their Family"? Everyone learns about Life participating in these heart screenings.

And just when I think my great state isn't listening, the phone rings. That phone again. It was a woman named Heather B., who heads a youth organization, *"H.E.A.L.T.H. for Youths, Inc."* She told me about another young warrior who had gone down at football practice, 16-year-old Miles Kirkland, who attended "Curtis High School" in Staten Island. Your heart sinks to the ground once more. You must understand that for those of us who do these screenings– we want this to be a closed club – no more members - no more children dying of Sudden Cardiac Death. My good friend Sharon Bates (who also lost her dear 19 yr. old son Anthony to undiagnosed HCM) told me the last time we had dinner in New York, "That is 'our ultimate goal': shut the doors down, *"Anthony Bates Foundation"*– out of business…

because we now have mandatory heart screenings for All of our Youth." – Maybe not in our lifetime, Sister Shar, but soon... With all the advancements our screening organizations and the scientific and sports community have made thus far, it is a vanguard of the heart that cannot be stopped.

When Staten Island called, I remember for my Manhattan screening, I had invited many of the high schools there, including one, where another athlete had collapsed and died. No one took the Ferry to Manhattan for our screening, but, well, I have no problem taking the Ferry to Staten Island ... I'll come to you. So CHAD organized a screening to bring tribute to young Miles. A volunteer, Peter J., and I took the Ferry and all our screening gear, cholesterol, and diabetes machines and supplies to provide preventive screenings for Miles' teammates for three years at "Curtis High School" in the borough of Staten Island. These young men had seen their beloved teammate go down; this would live with them for the rest of their lives. You bet we would beat a path to Staten Island, and screened as many athletes as we could, to make sure they would not have the same fate.

I came on ahead by Ferry to meet the Athletic Director, Eric Ritzer, and Head Football Coach Peter Gambardella, who pledged their 100% support. We had that and more with abundant participation. *"The Office of the Borough President, James Otto,"* got involved, along with Dr. Ginny Mantello, Director of Health and Wellness.

Dr. Mantello obtained great support for us– C.H.A.S.I. and staff to perform the cholesterol and diabetes testing and an enthusiastic team of student nurses from the *School of Nursing of Wagner College* who volunteered for 3 CHAD screenings. Several Staten Island cardiologists donated their time: Dr. S. Duvvuri, Dr. S. Swamy, Dr. F. Rotatori, Dr. Ayman Farid, N.Y.U. Langone, Dr. B. Co from New Jersey, along with his staff as well as Dr. Jared Lacorte, pediatric cardiologist, who has supported 5 of our high school screenings in S.I. Philips, SonoSite, and Terason provided the Echocardiogram and EKG equipment. H.E.A.L.T.H. for Youths, Trader Joes, A & C

Superette and Salumeria, and Fort Place Deli made sure the medical staff and volunteers were well-nourished.

One of the cardiologists on board told me he screened his own children, and while lending his support to the event, he had gotten a text message from his daughter. She had won an athletic competition, and he was so thrilled. He is one of the pro-sayers that feel children should be screened and was equally excited at the scope of the event, which included screenings for other premature cardiovascular risk factors. He told me if the major organizations won't help, there's enough of us [cardiologists], we'll do the screenings ourselves. Thank you, Doctor, we are only able to provide these screenings because of All of You.

And, boy, are we glad we took the Ferry ride. In the 1st screening at Curtis High School in 2015, we found out of 100 screened, there were 28 anomalies recommended for follow-up. Interestingly, the stats almost mirrored those of the pilot study we did in Holyoke, which showed nearly a third tested had findings of one or more cardiovascular risk factors.

I think young Miles was very pleased that day that his teammates had the benefit of the test he had never been given, a test that could have saved his Life. It was later found he had undiagnosed HCM. You find out a lot about your children from other children… I was happy to get to know who Miles was – a living, dynamic 16-year-old who touched many people in his short Life with his 'quiet' goodness. In speaking to his Mom, Tanza, she shared with me the stellar qualities of Miles for his Story Poster- which now comes with us to all our screenings. She revealed to me that it wasn't until his sudden passing that she began to see the full impact the gentle giant (as he was known) had on so many friends and the community. Councilwoman Deb Rose nicknamed Miles "The Shovel" for his work ethic in re-beautifying the plant beds near the precinct with such passion and care for the "H.E.A.L.T.H. for Youths" gardening project. Many teenage friends spoke to his Mom about the support and encouragement Miles had shown each of them. "Miles didn't brag about what he was doing; he just did it!" cites a young lady who Miles worked with, and who was struggling in nursing. Miles told her she could do it, and he would help, and they would do it together. There was a young man on the Curtis JV who told Tanza that even though others were discouraging and telling him he couldn't play, Miles took him under his wing and taught him what to do in the weight room. Another shared her story, saying how she and Miles had a special relationship because Miles didn't believe they could be friends because he was black and she was white. She let him know what a wonderful friend he was.

That's was this book is about the "Celebration of Life" – however many days or years it was. It meant something. Every day they lived counted. These young people were making differences at an early age. Can you just imagine how many more lives they would have touched, what ways they would have contributed to society, how they would have fulfilled their selves, and given their individual talents to the world... but for a screening test that would have detected the lethal culprit. Tanza sent me a heartfelt "Appreciation Award" shaped in a heart that I treasure: two mothers have lost their Sons and are just trying to prevent the same from happening to other Sons and Daughters. New York is my heart, and so many here have opened their hearts to me and our common cause. I will continue to chip away at the 'main' Island... This here is a city of walking, and I will keep taking the steps that lead to your hearts... if it takes a Lifetime.

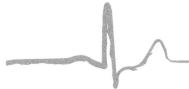

CHAPTER 22

–Coming Home to Malibu and The Annual CHAD Volleyball Heart Screening Benefit Hermosa Beach, CA

Three thousand miles away, a gala event was in the making! – Chad Butrum was coming Home to his beloved Malibu and his choice beach, Zuma… if in a very different way. This time CHAD was coming home to screen teammates from his other alma mater, *Malibu Park Junior High*- now transformed into *Malibu Park High School*. Coach Rich Lawson was instrumental in making this event a very successful one. He said his team was there not only to be screened but to help, and boy did they- from setting up early morning to making sure the event space was spic and span in the late afternoon when the event ended. Even if it was decorating the poles that held The Chad Foundation sign, the players did so with a smile on their face, enthusiastically looking for their next task.

Michael, our co-chair, set up us his white tents on the parking area adjacent to the beach so that our dedicated doctors from *Children's Hospital Los Angeles Heart Institute* could perform the Echocardiogram screenings. Even the Mayor of Malibu issued a special "Proclamation for the Chad Foundation Heart Screening Event." Local boutiques from Malibu donated terrific prizes for our "Opportunity Drawing," and Cali's famous *In-N-Out Burger* also provided many gift certificates. We even had celebrities: – Laura

Suico, Miss California, and two extraordinary women co-hosted the event - Holly McPeak, 3-time US Olympic Volleyball Champion, and superstar model and athlete, Gabrielle Reece. (Chad, I know you were watching from your unique vantage point and were very happy!) I also made sure we had something else at this event that had never been at another screening – our grand ole American Flag.

For you see, this event was on 30 September 2001, and we all know what shook our country to its foundation 19 days earlier, our generation's Pearl Harbor – 9-11. I had people from Cali calling me every day, first to find out how we all were doing, and then to find out if the CHAD Zuma event was still going on. Of course, it was going on! We were not fine on the East Coast...and wouldn't be for a long time coming but they were all good on the West Coast, thank the Lord, so all we needed to do was to get there on a plane.

-Well, that was a little hard. I think everyone was a bit skittish about boarding anything airborne at this time. But, hey, we're Americans, fear is not a part of our vernacular, so just get on with it. Though I admit, it was a little off-putting when we reached the gate. Smiling faces greeted our zombie-smiling faces... because I think my Friend, Noreen and I had worked 14 days straight at our makeup jobs so we could have 4 consecutive days off for this trip. (There is something to be said for sleep deprivation. She locked the keys in the rent-a-car, and when we finally straightened out that fiasco, we left half of the drinks for the event in the parking lot. –Yo! New Yorkers...) Nor was a wonderful friend who was flying to L.A. with me to help me with the multitude of tasks at hand. We did notice everyone was exceptionally friendly and welcoming at the gate, but where were all the other people? Maybe they were friendly because it looked like we were the only ones flying that day...gulp.

I wonder if Michael knew the night our feet hit the steps the same moment at *Yamashiro's* restaurant, how many steps we would be taking for his friend, Chad's foundation. I thought it sounded a little ambitious to say maybe we've been half-way around the globe, then I did the math: 26 r/t to LA, 6 to MA, 6 to MD, 1 to D.C., 1 to Austria, and 1 to Sweden – that's almost 6 times around the globe. What??...

and no end in sight... But today's event was an exceptional one. We had made it through our Day of Infamy and were paying tribute to each of Our Fallen by continuing to live our respective lives and save lives, here in this happy place- Malibu. My son had lived and laughed and played many sports here. And today, we were screening young athletes from his former school to safeguard their hearts so that they could live long, healthy lives and make their dreams come true. The American Flag flew high and proud that day.

A 3-time U.S. Olympian joined our Volleyball ranks that day, an extraordinary physical specimen. Holly McPeak showed us what a true champion was as she took to the sand and played with our teams. When asked why she would come out to an event like this (and it's hours travel time trying to get there on the Pacific Coast Highway especially on an *unusually* warm, sunny day in Autumn), she replied,

> "It seems like every week, I'm reading about a young athlete falling down on the field and never coming to. I think it's really important that we have these types of exams- Echocardiogram is very important, and if more young athletes have access to that, maybe we could prevent some of these deaths at such an early age. After the Echocardiogram and taking care of your heart, training hard, and following your dreams...and don't let anyone tell you, you can't do what you want to do."

(Chad would really like Holly...)

I am always amazed at how young athletes respond to their coaches and they to them. It's often like they are a second parent – the kids have such faith in them. Coach Lawson was one of those model coaches. I remember talking to many coaches, especially in the East. Some never really took advantage of our program; it was not a priority, but Coach Lawson went out of his way to help make this event successful. When he found out we needed certain height examining tables for the screenings, he contacted local spas until he found one that would lend us some. And the day of the event, he brought them early in his truck with many of his players in the truck bed ready to help. I think what he had to say regarding Echocardiograms says a lot about how coaches feel about their players and this preventive heart screening and why they wanted it for their team:

> "We had a number of young men lose their lives. They were all healthy, supposedly, and all had physicals, and everything was going all well for them, and something didn't work right. Unfortunately, a lot of those things have been traced back to the heart. – ... I'm responsible for the kids that push themselves physically and mentally, but the physical push they do, we want to make sure they're in top healthy shape. The heart is so obviously the most important part that needs to be functioning... many times gets overlooked. They do a blood pressure test, and that's about it.
>
> We overlook the fact that there's a need for an Echocardiogram that's done on the kids, and if it's a dollar figure, I think that's wrong, and I think we need to get people to step up...like the doctors here today. They donated their time, that's fantastic. If a kid came up with a red flag, perhaps couldn't participate because of that, there are other ways we'd bring him into the football family. We all want to do the best we can for our kids, no doubt about it, and this is just one more way of finding out if the kids are healthy and they can perform at their best level. So I'm going to continue with this crusade and get the other coaches involved, it's our fundamental responsibility."

Dr. Masato (Mike) Takahashi has supported so many of our events (until he retired a few years ago from *Children's Hospital Los Angeles Heart Institute*). He weighed in on what we were doing here today and why he, too, feels it's essential to be part of these screenings:

> "We're screening for structural abnormalities of the heart; specifically the condition called cardiomyopathy. It's a heart muscle abnormality. Most importantly, in the presence of a cardiomyopathy, the heart rhythm becomes irregular unexpectedly during a sporting event. So it's very important to make a diagnosis before the patient shows any symptoms because the first symptom may be a Sudden Death. –[We

participate because] we feel it's our social responsibility to reach out to as many young people as possible."

We also had a guest come all the way from Arizona. Sharon Bates, a dear Mother, and good Friend lost her 19-year-old son, Anthony Bates, to undiagnosed HCM (hypertrophic cardiomyopathy). Anthony was on his way to the University of Arizona, where he was to play football when his favourite red truck he was driving crashed into a barrier. Later findings would identify the lethal disease, hypertrophic cardiomyopathy. It was a privilege to be Sharon's 1st mentor, for she came to learn how to do heart screenings, and she only needed one look at it. Talk about someone running with the ball, she's never stopped running! Anthony is very proud of his Mom. You'll never get that ball away from her; she has a lifelong mission:

> "... I think if people would recognize this disease as something of a large magnitude. There is 1 in 500 people that are affected with this disease and don't even know it. That's a huge statistic, and we're not reaching those people yet, and we just need to do more, and we will. My glory and joy will come when we reach that goal and have Echocardiograms – proper health screenings for all athletes."

And why do celebrities get involved in such a cause? CHAD has no major presence, there are no paparazzi here. The beautiful and *tall* Gabrielle Reece (Gabby) … (my 3" wedges made no difference… I still looked like a hobbit as I proceeded to interview her), but the down-to-earth supermodel/athlete spoke from experience:

> "Your heart is incredibly important. They kind of talk about it as an analogy of all sports—'that team won because they had more heart.' - You can be strong, athletic, and powerful, you just want to make sure your 'engine' is healthy and taken care of."

And while the external event was in full swing, amidst the white sands and Malibu surf, the Doctors and Cardiac Sonographers were diligently providing screenings. Often the hospital sonographers are working with the cardiologists daily. They get to know their shorthand, and with their own experience at screening, they can detect signs which will call the doctor immediately. It is here that we found our first case of Wolff-Parkinson-White syndrome. Troy W. was a former USC Volleyball player. He had played at many of our Volleyball Benefits before we added the screening component. He would write to me a month later to thank The CHAD Foundation for this screening. He had further evaluation, as the doctor recommended. The diagnosis of WPW was confirmed, and he had scheduled surgery within a month of The CHAD Tourney. A year later, he would tell me he is playing sports better than he ever did.

(Troy's story can be found in Chapter 29, under Testimonials)

At the Zuma Beach event, there was another friend of our chair, Michael Tidik, who came and played and was very impressed with the event and the quality of the playing. I call him a 'scout location Angel' for he went back and told his good friend, Dave Najarian, about the tourney. Dave loves to play volleyball and has friends that love to play volleyball right in front of his house where the nets are, on the beach facing the Pacific Ocean.

In this journey of the heart, I have found from the very 1st step, Angels Abound, and some of them even play volleyball...quite well. (Chad's smile is quite broad now; it is one of his top 3 sports to play!) But do tell, what kind of folks just open the doors of their beach home for 17 years in a row and host the *"Annual CHAD Volleyball Benefit Tourney & Heart Screening"*? An incredibly generous family who let us turn their living room into a heart screening room for Echocardiograms and their sons even relinquished their bunk beds for our EKG examining room. The Family provided the most ideal setting and the most delicious food, year after year after year. Kristie's Dad was head chef at the barbecue for many years, and Ernesto, one of Dave's real Chefs, followed suit, and her Family brought and made the most delicious desserts and side dishes. Dave ordered a special secret chicken for the barbecue, 200 lbs. of it, which the doctors, always looked forward to. Safeguarding hearts and having a fun tournament that raised proceeds for "CHAD'S Gift of Heart & Art" and CHAD'S Annual Gift to the Children's Hospital Los Angeles Heart Institute" became a summer event of the year that everyone looked forward to. Our Doctors and Staff, Volunteers, Philips, and Mortara, who provided state-of-the-art equipment and, of course, all of the Players and Spectators had a superb day in the sun, while getting everyone in their family to have their hearts screened!

I have to believe that *Destiny Star Wizard* I mentioned in the chapter beginning Part II, was also looking down and said instructing his wand, "There. There in Hermosa Beach– that specific spot is where you will find many people who need your heart screenings." Huh? Fit, active athletes of every age… some even semi-professional. How could this be? But he/she/it, whatever the Keeper of the Wand was, the Keeper was right. Even though this is a smaller screening than most, under 100 participants, the results have always been between 13 and 20% findings for anomalies, from the age of 6 months to 60. In this screening, if you are playing in the tournament, or bring your children of any age, are a spectator, or attend a local high school, you can be screened.

We are so fortunate to have the screenings at this CHAD event administered by cardiologists from the *"Children's Hospital Los Angeles Heart Institute" and their Staff.* They have been supporting the organization's efforts to safeguard athletes' hearts for the last 20 years, screening near 1,000 hearts of every size, age, and shape. Here's a case in point: A father playing volleyball in one of the CHAD Tourneys had his 6-month old baby with him and took advantage of the opportunity to have him screened. The doctors spoke to the Father about the abnormal findings and recommended a follow-up. When he did indeed follow up, the baby was found to have a hole in his heart. The pediatric cardiologist waited a few months for the baby's heart to grow a little more, then performed the surgery. When the father returned to the CHAD tourney a few years later, he expressed his thanks because he told me he thought the baby just had a cold and didn't feel well. Today that baby is now a very active 7-year-old with an enormous smile, and he and his siblings and his father's friends and their children and siblings come to the CHAD Tourney to have their hearts screened. It's a beautiful thing to see! ...And a huge sigh of relief that they've taken the opportunity.

The "2010 CHAD Tourney and Heart Screening" was a banner year. Out of only 50 screenings on athletes, there were 18 anomalies. That's a whopping 36%!

> **Highlights: - 2 teens with both abnormal ECGs and ECHOS, 4 Abnormal ECHO Results, 3 Abnormal ECG Results, 3 Borderline ECG Results. One individual was found with significant aortic insufficiency and a dilated aortic root.– This person was advised to obtain formal cardiac follow-up; another individual was found to have Wolff-Parkinson-White syndrome – with potential risk for sudden death due to an arrhythmia. The second patient was scheduled for a catheter ablation, which Dr. Silka said should completely eliminate any cardiac risk and allow the patient to return to full athletic activities in a short period of time.**

In the "2010 Chad Screening," Lindsay S. was 12 when CHLA doctors found stenosis of the aortic artery. The doctors spoke at length to Lindsay's Mom. (That is why CHAD requires a parent to accompany every child under 18 to a screening.) The doctors recommended follow-up, and Lindsay's Mom Raecene wasted no time in making that appointment. A pediatric cardiologist confirmed Dr. L.'s findings determined at the CHAD Screening.

> "My daughter has Aortic Regurgitation with Stenosis. The doctor explained that my daughter will have to be very aware of her condition for the rest of her Life. The good news is that she doesn't have to give up Water Polo. He said that the chances of this ever being caught by a general practitioner or pediatrician was probably zero. In the words of our pediatrician, I do consider us the luckiest people for meeting you and being part of The Chad Foundation. Thank you."

Raecene, Lindsay's Mom, recently shared with me that Lindsay & her Water Polo Team won the entire Conference, and she just completed her 1st year at Whittier College. She is doing very well and will be released to an adult cardiologist for ongoing care and observation. Lindsay, herself, is also a young Angel, just like Mack Hale was in M.A. after his findings. The first-year, Lindsay saved all her babysitting money to make a donation to The CHAD Foundation, and last year she presented us with almost $2,000 in donations that she collected during the year amidst her busy 1st year in college and summer job. Lindsay sponsored her own *"CHAD Expanded Cardiovascular Heart Screening," with an Echocardiogram, EKG, Blood Pressure, Cholesterol, and Diabetes testing at Port Richmond High School in Staten Island, NY* on 2 December 2017. We thank you, Lindsay, for safeguarding young athletes from your own heart! You are why we do what we do. (Update: Thanks to Lindsay's 2018 gift, she also sponsored the *"CHAD Expanded Cardiovascular Heart Screening at Curtis High School in Staten Island, New York on 9 June 2019."* This event is in tribute to Miles Kirkland, 16-year-old fallen warrior athlete who died while practicing football drills at Curtis High School. Miles died of undiagnosed HCM, Hypertrophic Cardiomyopathy, the number one silent killer of young athletes.

Through preventive screenings, this event's purpose is to safeguard hearts, detect abnormalities that can lead to Sudden Cardiac Death, and identify premature cardiovascular risk factors that can prevent early heart disease. However, there is a third significant component to this equation – follow through with the "follow-up directive." At another CHAD Tourney Screening, the CHLA doctors found some anomalies in a friend of the CHAD movement. He was spoken to and told the doctors he would follow up as soon as he got back from the family vacation, which began the next day. When he did return, it was a holiday, and he was playing a sport, and he collapsed. And it was over. Our friend had the physique of a young Schwarzenegger and a smile you would never forget… It's as if he led us to the promised land of Hermosa Beach and then got called back somewhere else… just like Chad. Well, now K. you're that Coach up there on High for all the younger ones that also made that journey too soon. Hats off to you, dear friend, and athlete, we'll miss you terribly but will never forget you or how much happiness you brought while you were here. We are all heartbroken, especially your dear Family and close friends, but we promise to be better, to do a better job ... raise even more awareness and save more hearts because of you.

I wish we could get to see so many, many more, but every time we do have a screening, I ask God, please send me the ones we need to see. In this beautiful little enclave on Earth, the Maker has sent us a lot of them. Thank you for as we know more, and more and more, every single Life matters. M. K. you led us here. Please lead us to the next piece of Earth that has hearts calling for us to screen. God Bless until we meet again!

CHAPTER 23

"Mothers/Fathers"

In the early years following Chad's passing, it was like being frontiersmen and women on barren, Martian turf– no one to talk to, no one to ask for advice, not much information available. However, we did have another new, unfamiliar information vehicle that helped us all find each other – cyberspace, and we had a website, www.chadfoundation.org. Here, parents found me and Chad's story. Here, at least they could find someone who knew what they were going through—the worst thing they could ever go through. Every email I opened, it broke your heart- another dagger, another young Life lost, as priceless as your own child's. We all knew one thing – we were in extraordinary pain. Still, we somehow had to make it through this, and, simultaneously, we had to find how to prevent this from ever happening again to another child, another family.

It is a given in our society that the loss of a child is the most significant loss a Mother will ever know, and in this journey, I have felt and seen this anguish first-hand. I have seen the extraordinary strength in these women who balance marriage, their other children, single-parenthood, full-time, and/or multiple jobs to form foundations in honour of their children and dually – to save other children's lives… as many as possible.

For me, what was an eye-opener was witnessing the earth-shattering grief a Father experiences at losing a child, not something he or society as a whole is prepared to witness or deal with, especially emotionally. After all, they and society see themselves as the strong ones, the caretakers, the fixers. I spoke to one Father about a month after Chad passed rambling on at a break-neck speed about Chad's Foundation. He listened very quietly and finally said, "...and when did this happen?" I answered, "One month ago." He then was more animated, and his voice grew warmer in tone, "Oh, my Dear, you are still in shock. –It didn't really hit me for 5 years. I was driving on the freeway, and suddenly I had to pull over. It wasn't any particular remembrance or song, but I wept for hours..." I've never forgotten what that Father said to me, and have shared it with many other parents who have lost children...especially those whose loss has been recent.

I called this Father's office a year later, as his invitation to *the "1ˢᵗ Chad Foundation Volleyball Benefit for Children's Hospital Los Angeles Heart Institute"* had been returned. I was saddened but not surprised by the answer the receptionist gave me. "I'm sorry you didn't know? Dr. S. passed away 3 months ago." I knew then what 'dying of a broken heart' meant. I had heard it in his voice with my own ears. A few years after that, my Sons and I were walking toward Chad's gravesite, and I was relating this very story to them when my foot suddenly stopped at a new grave-marker. Unbelievably, it was the Doctor's final resting place, now located somewhat catty-corner from Chad's site with his own dear Boy's site to the north. I guess they were all bonded forever now –in Heaven and Earth... a Father and two young Sons who died of Sudden Cardiac Death in Young Athletes. This, for some Fathers, may be the most catastrophic thing they will ever face and have the most agonizing time verbalizing and even taking to paper... The boy's Father, who this book is about, had tried many times; some things cannot be shared...and must stay within the heart. We understand and respect – a Son and Father's Love...

Parents try in many different ways to deal with their pain. K. and R. Vargas created 2 scholarships in their son, Byan's honour. His Mom shared that it was fun to watch the Awardees and see what they do in their sport- transcending their loss to benefit other kids. I am so very grateful for those Mothers and Fathers who could and wanted to share their Child's story with us in Chad's Book, for I know it is the most heart-rending story they will ever tell... and yet in many ways, the most significant.

JANNA APRIL BECKER

April 6, 1987 - December 31, 2002
by Rhonda Foster, Janna's Mother

I am Janna's Mom. Janna was my gift for everything I'd ever done right in my life. From the moment she was born, I knew she was special. I loved watching Janna grow. Even at her young age, she was intuitive and sensitive, determined and capable, responsible, and caring. She had a twinkle in her eye and a quiet inner strength. I loved her smile. I loved to just watch her and listen to her voice. I loved watching her little hands grow. I marveled at her thoughtful opinions; I always took them into great consideration. She loved to just laugh and be silly. She matured with confidence and the resolve to create her own path in life. And I felt certain that she would be able to fulfill whatever goals she set forth.

As for myself, I had grown up fairly quickly at a young age when my Mom was very ill. When problems arose, I learned to fix them. I grew up feeling that I could fix just about anything if I put my mind to it. I became a Registered Nurse; nurses take care of everyone and everything. I was what most people call an "over-protective" mom, always believing that "an ounce of prevention was worth a pound of cure." But the one thing I couldn't prevent, couldn't fix, would never get a second chance at, and never even saw it coming, was a parent's worst nightmare...

On December 31, 2002, I got the phone call that drained the life from me. Janna was found unconscious in her bed. The ambulance came. I was told later in the emergency room that, "They were never able to get a heartbeat." *That was it??? Here one moment... gone the next?* In an instant my world, the entire world, changed. How on earth could life go on without her? How do you live the rest of your life with one foot on earth and one foot in heaven? I couldn't imagine... and I had NO idea what happened! No one did.

But now I know... Soon after Janna passed, I found out that what she had was an electrical problem with her heart, called Long QT Syndrome. It could have been detected with a simple, inexpensive electrocardiogram (ECG) read by a cardiologist. Devastated by this knowledge, I immediately founded "Take It To Heart"™ (www. TakeItToHeart.org), a program to help prevent sudden cardiac death in young people; I had learned too much not to educate others. How can a heart problem be treated when no one even knows it exists? For what other segment of the population do we completely ignore such life-threatening, yet detectable and treatable medical issues? I felt compelled to do everything I could to prevent my family's nightmare from becoming another family's nightmare. Take It To Heart™ is an educational program for those working with youth, and provides heart screenings focused on youth that includes an ECG read by a cardiologist.

Along this journey, I have met so many special and inspirational people... moms and dads tirelessly working to help others while building meaningful legacies for their own children who have passed. Janna is an integral part of who I am and everything I do; her essence is with me always. She gives me courage, strength, and patience. When one door closes, I know that another one will open. I realize that I cannot fix the past, but I can do my best to ensure that Janna's having lived on this earth will help light the way for others.

I love you with all my heart, Janna. Until we meet again…

In one of the stars
I shall be living
In one of them
I shall be laughing
And so it will be
As if all the stars
Were laughing
When you look
At the sky at night
~ The Little Prince
Antoine de Saint-Exupery

Rhonda L. Foster
Janna's Mom
October 7, 2007

LOUIS T. SAVINO, III

- October 12, 2000

The Silent Killer
by Toni Pellegrini, Mother, 2007

That night on Oct. 12, 2000, when the doctor came over to me and said: "I am sorry, Louis didn't make it"…I felt the life pour right out of me. I kept thinking it was a terrible nightmare…it was a terrible nightmare, a nightmare that was reality. Louis collapsed on the field while practicing soccer. His friends came running over to my car to tell me, and I quickly dashed to the site. I found the coach performing CPR and teammate on his cell, calling 911. In what seemed like an eternity, the ambulance finally arrived – but it was too late. This was all due to Louis being misdiagnosed with having physical induced asthma, I would later learn from the coroner that the autopsy report evidenced Louis had a heart defect known as HCM (hypertrophic cardiomyopathy). Within weeks, I soon realized my son's case was not isolated, and within two months, we had formed the Louis T. Savino, III Foundation.

Seven years ago, I would have never dreamed that my son was living with a silent killer. He was the picture of good health. He was careful with his diet and had a good exercise routine—he was practicing good health habits. He valued his life and well-being. We teach our children to take precautions in order to stay healthy. This is evidenced by the foods we eat, the medications we purchase, the doctors we visit…this becomes second nature to us. And yet, despite all of these precautions, I joined hundreds of parents throughout our country whose teenager succumbed to sudden cardiac death. Where did I go wrong?

As parents, coaches, & teachers, we place our children on the sports fields (some of us beg our children to play several sports—we push them to do better). We are also responsible for their safety. Unfortunately, it took a practice soccer session to turn tragedy for me to learn three important lessons. 1. What AEDs are and why they are needed and, 2. Why it is important to pursue heart testing as a result of certain symptoms, and 3. Why family history is so important to a child's physician.

Since 1982 thousands of high school and college athletes have died suddenly in the U.S., and most were victims of heart failure. We know that sudden cardiac arrest can happen at any place, at any time, to a person of any age. Our foundation runs daily Internet searches, and we continually find new cases. Sadly, that list of parents who face profound loss gets even longer. So what are we doing to get these numbers down? Yes, we need to be prepared with a strong chain of survival with AEDs and CPR, BUT we must work together in the prevention of sudden cardiac death in young athletes. We routinely screen for breast and colon cancer – neither of which kills instantly… why aren't we screening our kid's hearts? Prevention is paramount.

I am tired and disgusted with the headlines….High School Football player who collapsed at practice dies… Student collapsed and died while jogging…Basketball Practice Turns to Tragedy for a local teen…and the stories go on and on. My heart sinks every time I read such a headline. As a bereaved parent, you lose part of your future when your child dies.

My life every day is quite different now compared to seven years ago. I look to my dreams to share time with my son. My time here is spent on a crusade to spread awareness in the prevention of sudden cardiac death in memory of Louis and to spare parents from having to experience the same ultimate tragedy of losing a child to Sudden Cardiac Death. Part of our mission is educating young athletes, parents, coaches, and teachers regarding the extent of sudden cardiac death (SCD); providing funding to purchase AEDs to schools and sport's facilities; working for heart screening of high school athletes prior to sports participation; and working with the Commonwealth of P.A. for the revision of the school physicals. The Louis T. Savino, III Foundation is an affiliate of Parent Heart Watch…PHW is a national voice for SCD in children with a membership of over 150 advocates in 43 states. I am sure you hear the news and read the newspapers regarding placements of Automated External Defibrillators...there has been some movement regarding better physicals through a more comprehensive physical form….this is not enough…we need to arrive at the 21st century and start screening these young athletes prior to sports activity….that is prevention.

TAYLOR ALLAN

May 08 1991- April 26th, 2008
by Ken Allan, Father

Kingston Ontario, Canada

I am Taylor's dad. All of my adult life, I wanted a baby girl to hold and to nurture and to love. She arrived on the 08th of May 1991. I could tell that she was destined to be someone or do something to make a difference in the world.

Taylor walked and talked at an early age. Even when little, her sense of love and life was something that was evident. She loved life, family, friends, and the underdog. She excelled at everything she did. She was a star basketball player at all the schools she attended. Basketball was her sport. From the time she could bounce a ball, she never put it down. She was always practicing her shots, lay-ups, and plays she learned over the few years we had her. I was fortunate enough to be her coach for 4 years in public school and 3 years in a local biddy league.

Her health seemed impeccable. One day in 2007, she fainted at her high school and was taken by emergency to the local hospital. When I got there, she looked normal and just wanted to go home. The attending Doctor told me that fainting was a normal part of a young girl's life and not to worry. I wish I never had have listened.

At 11:15 pm on the 26th of April 2008, I was awakened by the parents of her girlfriend, where the teens were having a party. They told me that Taylor was on her way to the hospital because she had collapsed and was unresponsive. I grabbed my clothes and got to the road just as the ambulance was taking her to the hospital. I tried to follow, but with speeds reaching up to 150 km per hour, I opted to drive slower and safer.

When I got to the hospital, I was met by a Doctor who told me that Taylor was unresponsive and only had a "flutter" of a heartbeat. They asked me to come in the room and talk to her to see if that would bring her back. I knew then that she wasn't coming back. After working on her for almost an hour, the attending Physician came in and told me she had passed. He could not give me a cause of death.

At first, her passing was being determined as "natural causes." The Coroner in charge could not accept that diagnosis, and she was sent for further tests. After testing was complete at the Sick Children's Hospital in Toronto, it was determined that she had died from ARVC (Arrhythmogenic Right Ventricular Cardiomyopathy).

Thanks to all of the people I have met as a result of her passing, some good things have come out of it. I went on a media blitz and had many articles published, one in MacLean's magazine in the July 2008 issue. I have had numerous radio and television interviews. Taylor passing meant that public awareness about the "Silent Killer" that takes our children is no longer hidden. Doctors were not even aware of heart Arrthymias. They are now at least in Ontario. Through the SAD.CA foundation in Canada, we have managed to get 11 AED's installed in our local high schools. Kingston has declared the week of June-8-12th SADS week in Kingston.

Taylor, there is not a day that I don't think about you and who/ what you could and should have aspired to. My Angel, my baby, I miss you so much. We will meet again.

Love Dad

MATTHEW CHARLES KRUG

July 4, 1985 – July 18, 2001
by Stewart Krug, Father

My son, Matthew, was born on July 4, 1985, by way of a scheduled Caesarian section. As he grew up, we learned that he was truly a loveable firecracker. He was always a very happy and extremely active little boy. Kristen was the big sister, about 19 months older. She and her friend, Katie, could always convince Matthew to play dress up with them. He enjoyed attention, especially from his sister, Kristen.

As parents, we did not notice any issues in Matthew. However, in pre-school, we were first alerted that Matthew might have learning disabilities. The disabilities were further recognized in kindergarten. At open house, his teacher, an older lady who had taught for many years, told us that she had never had a student like Matthew before. We found that hard to believe, but she was very nice. [She sent us a very nice note after Matthew passed away. So, he definitely made an impression on her.] Matthew was formally evaluated by the school's REACH team and diagnosed with Attention Deficit

Disorder (ADHD). So began many years of academic struggles. But during this whole time, Matthew remained a very happy little boy. [In later years, after Matt's passing, I learned that it is not unusual for people with heart issues to have comorbidities - the presence of one or more additional disorders (or diseases) co-occurring with a primary disease or disorder].

In an attempt to help Matthew control his apparent attention problem, we eventually began using a drug called Ritalin®, [Ritalin® (methylphenidate) is a central nervous system stimulant. It affects chemicals in the brain and nerves that contribute to hyperactivity and impulse control.] The treatment seemed to help some. In later years, I learned that there were questions regarding the effect of Ritalin on young people's hearts. Whether this was a cause of Matthew's heart problems, we will never know.

Matthew loved sports. His favorite sports were football and hockey. His favorite athletes were Jerry Rice, wide receiver for the San Francisco 49ers, and Eric Lindros of his beloved Philadelphia Flyers. We never had a chance to attend a 49ers game, but I was happy that we did get to attend a Flyers game. Matt was so excited.

Matthew liked to play sports. He tried the typical sports that are available to boys; soccer, baseball, and swimming. Matt was not very good at soccer or baseball. He did enjoy his swimming. It was amusing that initially, he hated to get his face wet. However, thanks to good old peer pressure, eventually, he did get his face wet and, from then on, loved to swim underwater. He eventually was part of our community swim club's swimming team. He loved to swim the breaststroke and became rather good at it. At that time, little did we know that this same swim club would play a devastating role in Matt's life.

Matt was also an avid roller hockey player. He would play for hours with his friends or in a pickup game at the local recreation area. Eventually, he played in the YMCA's roller hockey league.

Although we were aware of Matthew's learning disabilities, we had no idea that he had a heart problem. In early 2001, I first observed what turned out to be a symptom of Matt's heart problem. Matt would frequently (at least it seemed to me) press on his chest (breast bone). When I asked Matt about this, he could not describe how often it occurred or how it felt. Unfortunately, he did not recognize this as an issue he should tell us about. [As I now speak to parents and youth about sudden cardiac arrest, I try to impress upon the young people to pay attention to their bodies. Do they hear the message?] In hindsight, he was most likely having an arrhythmia or palpation. I had an upcoming appointment with our family doctor, so I brought Matt along. We had a good relationship with the doctor. He was always helpful and friendly. The doctor checked Matt with a stethoscope only. The doctor heard a slight heart murmur. The doctor explained that a slight heart murmur was not unusual. He said that many people have slight murmurs that are not life-threatening. This is when without the knowledge I have now, I made a fatal mistake. I did not ask for any additional evaluation. I don't remember the doctor's advice, but he did not recommend an EKG or other tests. About three months later, Matt suffered his sudden cardiac arrest.

In his freshman year, Matt was part of the McKean High School chorus. At the end of the school year (June 2001), Matt and the chorus went to Disney World to perform in Epcot. He was so excited. I was glad and proud that Matt had the opportunity to enjoy this experience with his friends and school mates. I think back about that trip, what if Matt had suffered a sudden cardiac arrest at Disney World? [Disney is known for its exceptional emergency response system.] Maybe they would have saved him, maybe not. It would have been so far away [we live in Delaware].

On Friday, July 6, 2001, at about 2 pm, while very informally shooting hoops (basketball) with one of the lifeguards at our community swim club, Matt suffered a sudden cardiac arrest. The ball had rolled away from the boys, and Matt went to retrieve it. He collapsed on the grass. The swim club did not have an automated external defibrillator (AED). However, there were 3 sixteen-year-old lifeguards. They began CPR immediately. They phoned EMS. However, they lost time, some time due to miss dials in the heat of the moment. EMS arrived in several minutes (not sure the exact amount of time, but not more than 8-10 minutes). They shocked Matt three times and were able to restart his heart. He was then transported to Christiana Care, the local major hospital.

I remember arriving home at a little after 2 pm. I received a phone call from one of the family saying that something had happened to Matt at the pool. I don't remember if they mentioned that it might be life-threatening or not. I rushed to the hospital, not knowing what to expect, but very frightened.

When our family met with the emergency room staff, they asked us, "do you know why Matt went into cardiac arrest?" Of course, we had no clue to the problem. After initial evaluation in the Christiana Care emergency room, an echocardiogram was done on Matt. By this test, Matt was diagnosed with hypertrophic cardiomyopathy, a structural heart disease where the walls of the heart are abnormally thick. Matt remained in a coma but otherwise was stable. He was then transported to the State's only pediatric hospital, A.I. DuPont Hospital for Children. Matt was admitted into the ICU. He remained there for 3 days, still in a coma. Since his heart was functioning on its own, he was moved to the step-down area on the following Monday.

On day four, I broke down. Between the stress of the situation and being tired, I just lost it! Why did this happen? Why did it happen to such a nice, caring young man when there are so many evil people living? Of course, no one could answer the questions.

I remember during the days in the step-down area of the cardiac wing, we saw pictures of survivors on the walls of the hospital. Initially, that gave us hope. But, nurses and neurologists were quick to warn us that those cases were not the norm. The fact that with each passing day, Matt was in a coma was not a good sign. I remember asking if there were any special treatments that might help. I remembered that Tyrell Owens, the football player, had a hyperbaric chamber that supposedly infused oxygen to help him recover from injuries. I asked if that treatment would help. I was told no. In recent years, mild hypothermia treatment has become a standard treatment for sudden cardiac arrest victims. It has helped save many victims and limited loss of brain function of others. Would this have helped Matthew? Again, we will never know.

After about 8-10 days, Matt's body lost temperature control. His temperature spiked high. They applied cooling pads to Matt's body. Soon after this happened, testing was done, which showed Matt had no major brain activity. This was devastating news. His mother and I were asked by hospital staff to decide if Matt began to fail, did we want life support treatment. It was a hard decision, but each of us finally agreed that Matt would not want to live as a vegetable. In trying to maintain hope, we prayed that we would not have to enact that decision.

On July 18, 2014, twelve days after his SCA, Matt's body showed signs of shutting down. We had learned that the body can function for a few days with minimal brain function, but will eventually shut down. That evening Matthew passed away. The hardest thing that **I will ever have to do** was watch Matt take his final breaths. I will always have that painful image etched in my brain. As technology has advanced, and I hear stories of miraculous survival stories, I often wonder if we did the right thing by not keeping him on life support.

During the days in the hospital, I went online to learn as much as possible about this terrible event and the cause, hypertrophic cardiomyopathy. At that time, I found Lisa Salburg and the Hypertrophic Cardiomyopathy Association. Lisa was informative and supportive. I decided in the hospital that I needed to be an advocate to help prevent this horror from happening to other families. To this end, a couple of years after Matt passed away, we created the Matthew Krug Foundation. The mission of the Matthew Krug Foundation is to Protect Children and Youth from Sudden Cardiac Arrest.

Over the next several years, I have met many families, including the families who have contributed their stories to the book. I am amazed at the caring and love that these folks show not only for their lost child but for the children of other families who they meet along our journey. Arista and Sharon Bates were two of the first new friends I made. I consider them my mentors. At the time of this story, I have made many friends, too many friends. Many of these families have joined together to form Parent Heart Watch, our national voice. Through Parent Heart Watch and our individual efforts to educate the public about sudden cardiac arrest in youth, place AEDs, train people in CPR and use of an AED, passing legislation and providing heart screenings, I believe we have made a difference in saving lives. This we do in memory of our lost children.

In closing, I thank Arista for this opportunity to tell the readers a little about Matthew. Our dear Matthew, my little buddy, may you rest in peace. We miss you so much.

CHAPTER 24

"Brothers/Sisters"

R. ANDREW HELGESON

03 March 1987 - 25 May 2005
by Jennifer Helgeson

Sister to Andrew Helgeson

"Thank you for being such a wonderful sister to Andrew, even though he is not with us. It is something I admire and appreciate. I think very highly of you." That is one of the nicest things anyone has said to me in the last ten years. (It came to me in a Facebook message from one of my brother's friends a few years ago.) It is nice to get some recognition because it is not a simple situation and well, all I can do is try. It is a fine line to walk. When you first meet Americans, they love to ask you about family. I always honor my brother by mentioning that I had a brother who passed away. This is a challenge to people out of the blue, and I have to prepare for comments, such as "welcome to the only child club" from near-strangers.

May 25, 2015, marks the tenth anniversary of me walking into my brother's room to wake him and instead finding him kneeled down next to his bed, dead. I will go to great lengths to repress the memories of the EMTs stopping at the wrong house, forgetting to bring in their AED, and ultimately invading our home and barring my mother and me from the room for hours. I would give anything to have never seen my father's face, stricken as he rushed in the house after driving home from work frantically. He lost what was most valuable to him in the blink of the eye; that is the only time I have seen my stoic father shed tears.

This all happened just two days after my early graduation from University and one of the happiest moments in our family's history. Andrew had a scholarship to his choice college and would get to continue playing lacrosse. And then Sudden Cardiac Arrest came in the night, claimed him and the first and last sign was death. Andrew was the picture of health and the pride of our family; and he was my best friend. He was my side-kick for 18 years; we did it all together from running around the house as the Teenage Mutant Ninja Turtles to shopping for Mothers' Day. He was exactly three years and two days younger than me and 9.5 inches taller. He maximized on our Norwegian genetics with the look of a real Viking.

So, at the age of twenty-one, I learned the fragility of life in a somewhat brutal and graphic manner. And as modern medicine has not caught up to heart health, doctors wanted to take all kinds of preventive measures so I would not share Andrew's fate, though all indications are such that my heart mis-beats about as often as the average person on the street. Thus, one month later I found myself on the operating table getting an Implantable Cardio Defibrillator

(ICD) fitted in my chest. The ICD has never been called into action. There was that one time a few years ago that it went off falsely due to a manufacturing defect and I was shocked repeatedly on a London side-street...but that is another story...

That summer my parents visited Andrew at the cemetery every day, sometimes more than once. My father read him "The Hitchhiker's Guide to the Universe" as my mother, and I sat with him. The scariest thing was that I hadn't just lost my brother, but in many ways, I came to realize that I had lost the family I had always known. Every dynamic was destroyed by Andrew's absence and by the end of that first summer, I was deeply engulfed in what felt like freezing dark waters without a paddle and was in need of an escape plan. I had been awarded a Fulbright Grant to live and research in Norway starting in September, and against much of my protesting, my parents got their passports and took me to the small village of Aas, Norway, just outside of Oslo, where I would learn to swim against the frozen tides of my present circumstances.

I could write a novel about my adventures there, so just suffice to say here that from reindeers and hitch-hiking to wacky roommates, crazy bike-rides and fishing, I waded in the engulfing waters. My closer friends and housemates there knew what had happened just a few months before, but most did not. Sometimes I would take the train into Oslo alone early in the morning and walk around those streets; I would see Andrew all over – tall, blonde young men. The only trip he ever took abroad was to Norway with me and my father a few years previous. And in a country so far away, it was strangely comforting to walk places I had with him before.

In the end, when I look back over my journey thus far, the most important lesson has been to hold those who care about me close; to love and support them in return. As for the others who have nothing kind or supportive to add, even if they are blood relations, let them live their selfish lives, be careful not to wish them ill, but hope that they realize one day the power of compassion and become self-aware of their personal limitations. It is the intangible gifts that we are given in life that matter the most. I have been blessed with a great many true and sincere friendships. And without those angels on Earth, I may not have made it this far or at least not to feel happiness and hope again.

We all have problems on some level or other. Sadly, some close friends have now also lost parents and siblings, battled illness themselves since the time of Andrew's passing. And since my first Norway adventure year I have lived abroad in the U.K. and France; I have travelled all around Europe, as well as getting as far as Uganda, South Africa, and China for work assignments.

I like to think that I have really touched lives in a positive way in my field of work and that I attribute in part to wanting to live in my brother's image. I know that post vita most people's memories are idealized excessively by family and friends. But, the number of people who came forward as being touched for life by Andrew during his short 18 years in this world is proof that he was angelic in nature. The truth is he was much cooler than was I in high school (I wish that I had actually told him); that attribute combined with a big heart made him lovingly known as "Helge." And thankfully some of his friends are in touch with me today and tell me how much his memory still resonates with them. I like to think that in some way Andrew, who didn't live one full life, actually lives hundreds of lives…in a way, he is a teacher of autistic children, a public defender, a taxi driver, a search & rescue aviator...

I have missed a lot without my side-kick little brother, and deep down I know that there will be hard times ahead because of his absence. In a way, I lost my past, as there is no one to reminisce with over childhood memories, and I have lost elements of my future; all the happy occasions will always feel a bit bitter-sweet without him.

I am writing this during a visit back to my family home. Memories flood back and though I cannot say I am at peace with the fate dealt to my brother, I am at peace with how I can handle this challenge and the scar – both the internal and external (from the ICD operations) ones – that will always be with me.

I will always have a hole inside me, but over time it is not filled in completely, since there is no replacement [for] Andrew, but it does get patched over from love and trust of wonderful people. And well, I have found it to be true of many who suffer great loss, myself included: I have a lot of love and support to give to those who deserve and welcome it. I made it out of the deep, cold engulfing water in time; and I thank the Universe every day for those who have helped me along the way.

Richard Andrew Helgeson Memorial Foundation, a 501(c) (3) Public Charity, to raise awareness of Sudden Cardiac Arrest in children and young adults. P O Box 4024, Silver Spring, MD 20914. Contact: 301-236-0448; rahfoundation@comcast.net http://www.andrewhelgeson.org and http://silverchips.mbhs.edu/ story/5424.

> *I am a curious, cautious guy.*
> *I wonder what life will bring.*
> *I hear the sunrise.*
> *I see tomorrow's destiny.*
> *I am a curious, cautious guy.*
> *I pretend not to care.*
> *I feel fear about what is yet to come.*
> *I touch my crystal ball.*
> *I worry about what I may miss.*
> *I am a curious, cautious guy.*
> *I understand actions have consequences.*
> *I say I will make it fine later.*
> *I dream that I will be successful.*
> *I try to make the wrongs right.*
> *I hope I will end up content.*
> *I am a curious, cautious guy.*
> -R. Andrew Helgeson, Jan. 2004

EMILIE PURICELLI

Feb. 26, 1975 - Aug. 30, 1997
Anne Skebba, Sister to Emilie
(by Arista)

I am so appreciative to Anne Skebba for sharing her story with me about her sister Emilie. It was the summer after she had graduated high school, and her big sister, Emilie, then 22, had just returned home from living with her boyfriend. It was the 30th of August, and the two girls were looking forward to a sisterly trip to see their brother in college in Flagstaff. They were to leave that morning. Anne had already been out earlier and had just slipped into Emilie's bedroom to grab the phone and thought she was still sleeping. The alarm clock kept going off continually, which brought their Mom into the room to find out why. That is when Mom, Christine, discovered her daughter, Emilie, was not breathing. Anne remembers flying to the neighbor's house to call 9-11… why she went there and didn't call them from home, she doesn't remember.

It's hard to imagine being 18 years old, discovering your sister is not breathing, and how-where-what to do next, and you and your

Mom are the only ones in the house. The police and paramedics came and would not let them into the room. Anne doesn't remember much after that… She was lying on the couch in a state of shock. There were 4 years between she and Emilie, so growing up, that's a big difference, and as Emilie had just moved back home that summer, Anne was so looking forward to forging a relationship with her sister.

Following the trauma of losing her sister and before she knew it, Anne found herself away at college, and there she recounts is where the loneliness set in – far from family and not readily able to talk to anyone, especially 19-year-olds about this tremendous loss. She even stayed and went straight through to summer school. But without a support system there, she began to imbibe in alcohol more than she should as a way to cope.

One of the reasons I decided to write this book is because early on in my journey, I received emails from mothers over the years who would tell me they've lost their best friend, their neighbors or their relatives. They just didn't want to hear about the loss anymore – time to move on, time for closure. Anne, at 19, experienced the same thing; she lost her best friend for two years. They have since reconnected, but then it was hard to connect to anyone. For Anne, they don't know what to say, so why even discuss it. When I asked her what would you like to hear people say, she answered, "Just a normal conversation, not sad, not focusing on when and why it happened. Ask about the person and their relationship together. Keep it positive and not focusing on 'the day.' After a pause, she told me, "If I mention my sister passed away, that means I really trust you." When she married her husband, she was able to reconnect again…

For siblings, there is an added layer of protection they must face as parents are doing everything possible to make sure this doesn't happen to their other children. Anne remembers after her sister's passing, there were genetic testing and the wearing of a Holter monitor to monitor the heart rhythm, but as a young adult, all she could think of is 'I'm gonna drop dead of LQT syndrome.'

However, as time passed, she learned meds change, and bodies change. As an adult, Anne had been taking beta-blockers for 18 years, and then she met a physician who told her the beta-blockers, along with the anti-depressants, were a *bad combination*. So in March of 2016, Anne made the decision to remove herself from both of these medications, and for her, it was like also removing the daily reminder of fear since Emilie's passing.

I found Anne's career choice after college very interesting- as I had met a sibling once who had lost his 13-year-old brother from Sudden Cardiac Arrest in the school pool while he was playing water-polo. This older sibling became an EMS worker because of what happened to his 13-year-old brother.

Anne became a probation and parole officer for 10 years, an occupation she told me could be very dangerous – you might have an attempted murderer parolee in your car. And when I asked her why she chose that profession, she said she loved criminal justice. It was just trying to help people, understand what they are going through, talk to them, and teach them. She even said she loved that population. I'm sure this is just who Anne is, but I can't help but wonder if it gives some sense to her life. She lost her sister at a young age from heart disease: she can't talk to her sister about it, she couldn't help her, and she found that people couldn't really understand what she was going through... In working face-to-face in this population, maybe she can be that person for them.

When I asked her to tell me about Emilie, she responded, "She was 6'2 ½", very pretty, with long, brunette hair. She was shy, awkward with boys, played basketball, always athletic, and always wanted a boyfriend. She wanted to be accepted/fit in; never said anything mean about anyone; didn't have problems, and never argued with parents or friends. She was a NICE person, everyone liked her. When she was in 6th grade, because of the age difference, she remembers she'd say like any big sister, "Get out of my room! Or gross!" But when Emilie moved back in, and she was going over to her boyfriend's house, she started to see her as an adult sister. "We were just beginning to be friends. She snuck a dog into my parent's home, and it was a 'secret,' and we were bonding."

Anne told me her sister's last gift to her was a pair of shorts. Emilie was always telling her, "Wear shorts! You have good legs"! Anne also has Emilie's gold necklace that her sister wore every day. When I asked her what she misses most about Emilie, Anne responded, so honestly, it hurt, "I'm envious of anyone who has a sister, and I get angry when I see people angry at their sisters and yelling at each other. To have a sister around would be such a neat relationship. I think to myself, what would Life be like if I had a Sister..."

CHAD ALAN BUTRUM

April 23, 1994
by Curt Butrum, brother

Curt's Story on his Brother, CHAD

My Big Brother Chad. That's what he was to me. I followed in his footsteps. Where was he going? What fun was he having with his older friends? When you're young, you just HAVE to be wherever your older brother is. Chad was like my commanding officer in the military. I did whatever he told me to do. "Hey, Curt! Jump off the roof of the garage into an empty plastic swimming pool." Did that, without hesitation, and almost broke my ankle. Try explaining that to your parents without incriminating your brother. "Why would I do something so idiotic?" my Dad asked. Not wanting to jeopardize my loyalty to him, I said nothing to my Father and Mother as to why I did what I did. Or the time he convinced me to eat fifteen little flowers to be in his "Club." Did that got violently ill. As I wretched in the backyard, all I could think of was, "Man! I'm in his super-secret fraternity!" What kids will do just to get their older brother's respect and be with his "In" crowd. Or the time he told the next-door neighbor's kid to refer to him as "God" when in his presence. Good Lord, he had a willful personality! Of course, he never had malicious intent with regard to others. I just think he wanted to exercise his persuasive charm. See if people would follow him. And we all did. Now all kids can be precocious when they're young. Hell, Chad and I almost burned down an entire condominium (by accident, of course!) when we lit a little fire on the floor of the garage, to see, well, what the heck fire was all about. We were dumb preadolescent teenagers getting into mischief (Sorry Mom!). I was always following his lead to prove I was worthy of his trust. You know so he would bring me on all his adventures. Damn, I miss him.

Chad had a very prominent birthmark on his face. One that kids (they can be so cruel) love to make fun of. This alone could make any child grow to become a hateful, bitter person. But Chad directed all that venomous teasing right back to those kids. His good looks, winning smile and charisma, even at that young age, made the blemish disappear. You see, he turned it around. His birthmark made him unique. He stood out in the crowd. Because of *who* he was. Kids were like, "that has to be a lucky mark. I want one!" This "Lucky" streak grew as he did. Every school we went to, Chad, was the most popular one in it. The power of truly believing in oneself, as he did, is well, amazing.

Chad always had *others'* best interests in mind. Always treated those around him with respect. And *always* made you feel better about yourself. He gave of himself like I never did, and to this day, I wish I had been more like he was. His "Cult of Personality" was infectious. But hey, not everyone can be like Chad. One in a Billion.

Now back to the popularity thing. Chad had near one thousand people at his funeral. And he was only twenty-six years old. Being a charmer super looks AND being good at sports? All you have to do is look at someone like Tom Brady, to say, "Wow. That guy's got it all." And he did. Starting Quarterback on the Football Team. Voted best looking his Senior Year. I tell you, *I* was jealous. "Why can't you be more like Chad?" I was asked, as I got into more and more trouble during my early high school years. Shoot! Chad didn't even drink when everyone else did. And smoke? He'd rather die. He never followed the crowd. It didn't ostracize him. It set him apart and made his "Myth" grow even more. Yah, that's right, myth. He was like the Sphinx. Nobody could figure out his secret to his celebrity. Envious ones would say, "How can this guy get all the hot girls in school with that damn mark on his face?" The adoration of his legions would confound these naysayers. Simply astounding, he was. That was My Big Brother Chad.

CHAD ALAN BUTRUM

April 23, 1994
by Collin Butrum, brother

Collin's Story on his Brother CHAD

So I want to talk about what my brother Chad meant to me and my family in the 26 years he had on this planet. From the time we were young, he was always what you would think an older brother would be. He was strong, dominating, caring, and always wanting to bring out the best in you even if it meant hurting your feelings from time to time. He would say, "Well, why don't you try doing this instead of that, and you might find a better result." It would have an effect on me as a person because he was all about being healthy. Chad was really into smoothie drinks after exercising, and he would take a half an hour to enjoy the drink, I mean every sip he would take his time and enjoy it. He would also do the same at every meal, always the last to leave the table. He really enjoyed his meals like it was the last supper, and don't get me started on his love for milk!! I feel like Chad had this ability to almost stop time and enjoy the moments in life. When you were done with the meal and ready to move on, he would still be half-way through the meal enjoying every bite.

He had this great attribute of taking the time to let you talk about yourself, and ask people all kinds of questions about themselves and their interests, and would never talk about himself. He wanted to know all about you.

Then there was the "Sports Chad," nobody got ready for a game like Chad did! He loved baseball, volleyball, football, and, most of all, Wiffle ball. He would duck tape the bat so you could see the ball sail into the next yard. Even if you were too tired to keep playing after 2-3 hours, he would find in a nice way, or an insulting way to motivate you to keep playing the game. He would not take no for an answer when it came to getting a game together, you got your ass up and played. I always loved that about Chad, he just wanted to have fun playing sports, going to a dinner, or a dance club. Another great attribute was when you would go to any event, if it was not what you expected, he would say, "We are here, let's make the best of it!"

One of a kind, my dear brother Chad! Love you and miss you, Collin.🎾😊🏈🏀

CHAPTER 25

"Relatives/Friends"

LOUIS T. SAVINO, III

- October 12, 2000

Our Call to Action
by Lorraine Sikora

Aunt to Louis Savino

Soon after the shocking death of my 15-year old nephew Louis Savino, it was inconceivable for me to think that a young life could end so abruptly. I had seen him only days before. I remember it like it was yesterday. We chatted about his sophomore year, which he had only started one month prior. He was excited and looking forward to what was ahead. He even sat down at his piano and played several tunes for me, and I enjoyed every minute of it. I would never have believed what was to come just four days later.

On Thursday, October 12, 2000, I awoke to the news that the USS Cole had been hit by a suicide bomber. Seventeen young crewmembers had been killed, and many others injured. Their lives ended suddenly and abruptly, along with their plans and dreams. I can recall thinking of the pain those 17 families were feeling after hearing that horrible news. Who would have guessed that just twelve hours later, my family and I would learn just how painful that loss was? I got that horrible call from my sister-in-law, Toni, frantically telling me that Louis had collapsed, and he was critically ill in the hospital. That sinking, sick feeling one never forgets at the time of a tragedy will forever remain in my memory. By the time a kind neighbor drove me to the hospital, this young, vibrant, intelligent, compassionate, beautiful young person had gone away. He looked so peaceful, just like he was asleep. His life ended suddenly, along with his plans and dreams. And on that night, he joined those seventeen other young souls whose journey began just twelve hours before. I can only hope they were there to usher Louis into heaven.

How incredibly painful to realize I would never see my only nephew live his dreams. How was I to explain to my son Christopher, then six, that his best friend had left our world? How do you break the news to his four grandparents that they out-lived their grandchild? How do you tell his classmates that their fellow student won't be coming through the doors of the school the following day? How could this be? Kids just don't die suddenly – there's nothing "natural" about it. This was too unsettling and disturbing to ignore. Within days of the tragedy, I began conducting Internet research to determine the frequency and cause of sudden cardiac death in young people.

I found that it is difficult to obtain statistics regarding the frequency of these deaths other than the fact that it occurs in "1 of 200,000 young people". I quickly realized these tragic deaths were more common than I ever thought possible. I've since learned that those cold and inhumane "statistics" cannot possibly capture the pain and overwhelming grief of losing a vibrant, young person. I was no longer searching for numbers; instead, I stumbled upon far too many news articles with the horrific title, **"Student-athlete collapses and dies."**

Relying on those articles, I began building my own registry of cases–reading painful stories of parents, students, teachers, and coaches who witnessed the sudden death of a young person whose heart ailments had gone undetected. I would meet Toni for breakfast in the mornings and show her what I had found the night before. A common thread in nearly all of the sudden death cases that I located was a type of heart condition. I also located many articles that addressed the importance of thorough physical examinations, family medical history, and the history of sudden cardiac death in a family member under the age of 30. Sadly, seven years later, the file filled with media stories is larger than two telephone books – each representing the life of a young person lost to sudden cardiac death.

Ironically the very first time I searched the Internet, I located the story of young Chad Butrum and his mother Arista's quest for awareness and detection of the horrible silent killer that robbed her son's promising young life. She was, perhaps, the pioneer who paved the way for all of us who have now come together as members of the national sudden cardiac death advocacy group, Parent Heart Watch.

Our call to action became apparent within two months of that horrible day. Toni and I were inspired by Louis' spirit of community service to move forward with our crusade. In December 2000, we formed the Louis T. Savino, III Foundation.

The Foundation raises funds for lifesaving devices known as Automated External Defibrillators (AEDs). In keeping with our fundraising mission, our focus is on yet another type of AED: Awareness, Education and Detection

Awareness: providing information about the warning signs of sudden cardiac death;

Education: sponsoring CPR and AED training programs for teachers, coaches, and students to provide essential lifesaving training.

Detection: crusading for comprehensive school physical examinations and to fund heart screenings that would detect previously unknown heart symptoms in the student population

On October 19, 2000, I delivered the eulogy for the young man who was the light of our family. He was the boy who brought tremendous joy and pride to each of us. While writing the eulogy, I prayed for inspiration and out flowed the following words about the many gifts this wonderful young man had to offer.

Louis gave us many gifts.

He gave us the gift of unending humor; he not only laughed a lot, but his witty sense of humor was infectious.

He gave us the gift of service. He volunteered many hours of his time as he tutored children, read to the elderly, served as the Penn Charter Choir Librarian, tutored his fellow students in Latin, and offered help to his family.

He gave us the gift of intelligence, and he shared that intelligence with everyone in his path in a very modest way. His remarkable memory enabled him to recall countless sports statistics, sports team trivia, historic events in our world, and specific details about every American president.

He gave us the gift of music. He played the piano eloquently since the age of 4, and he hoped to someday to form a band with two of his best friends. He loved all types of music, especially the music of the group No Doubt.

He gave us the gift of the spoken and written word. He had the wondrous ability to speak to people at any age about almost any topic – a sign of true maturity. His ability to express himself in writing was truly exceptional. His ultimate "dream" was to become a Sportscaster for a major television network.

Louis gave us the gift of unselfish love and patience – the precious gifts of our world. He was an exemplary son, grandson, nephew, cousin, and friend.

God could have easily called Louis into his kingdom when he was first born as a "preemie" weighing only 4 pounds. Instead, he gave Louis a golden opportunity to build his legacy in just a short period of time. What he **could have done** and what **he chose to do** in his 15 years is what made him such a wonderful example for each of us. We are hopeful that the Louis T. Savino, III Foundation will not only keep Louis' spirit and legacy alive but also hopefully save precious, young lives.

"Chad's Friends"

I never realized the impact of losing a young Friend and the effect it could have on people for the rest of their lives. These many years later, I still see and feel how Chad's Friends are still in miss of him. They have taught me how a Friend, whatever age can impact your Life for the rest of your Life."

"Chad was such a special person to me. He actually lived with my sister, Stephanie, in the Agoura/Oak Park area for a while. She went out with Kevin Simmons too. Even though I didn't get to spend as much time as my sister did with Chad, the times I did spend were great. He would always make me smile and laugh, and his positive energy was contagious. My sister was lucky enough to spend the last night of his life with him. That night he had my sister come over an hour early to show her the suit he was going to be wearing for his upcoming birthday and gave her a picture of himself. He said he "just wanted her to have it." Steph thought it was a little strange that he had her come over early and gave her the picture, but for some reason, Chad felt he needed to do that, and I guess there was good reason, looking back on it.

A group of them all went out that night, dancing, of course, and at the end of the night, he said, "I had so much fun tonight that if I never went out again this year, it would be okay." Chad wanted me to go with them that night, but I didn't, and I still regret it. His passing had such an impact on me. Anytime I hear a bagpipe, I completely breakdown in tears because it takes me back to his funeral. My sister and I always talk about Chad, wishing he was here and think about him when we're someplace we know he would love. Fortunately, I did get to see him in a dream a few years ago, looking just the way I remember him!

I hope you are doing well. It's so great to see all that you have done in his honor.

Sincerely,
Stacy M."

Sean, Chad, Louis – Graduation Day

North Hollywood High School, North Hollywood, CA

"I will forever cherish the fond memories and wonderful times
I shared with Chad. I was truly lucky to be a part of his Life! I

will remember him as he was, A Gentleman, Scholar, Athlete, and above all else the Most Special Friend I've ever had."

All My Love,
Sean [Smith]

"Chad was for Jr. High School and all of High School…and parts of college, the closest friend I ever had. He was like a brother to me. Even though he had 3 brothers of his own, I never had one, so I sort of adopted him as my brother. Whenever Arista sends me the information on what the foundation is doing, I pin it to my bulletin board so people come up and ask, Oh, what's that picture of a heart doing? Who's that guy, and it always comes out. I've actually mentioned it to the writers of the show as it might be an interesting topic for an episode since our show's about forensics and death and solving crimes. [Lou was a former producer for CSI.] It's such a mysterious way to die - never drank, never smoked, no body fat – the epitome of health to actually drop dead for nothing. – I think my wife Veronica and I actually started to have a family earlier than we planned after Chad's death… Veronica also lost her brother shortly after Chad – it would be a way to replenish the holes they left. …The only thing Chad ever asked of you was your *time*."

-Louis Milito

Hello,

I just came across this site while looking up an old friend on Facebook. I played football with Chad at North Hollywood High school. I had no idea what happened, I am stunned, to say the least, and I am so very sorry. I remember Chad as an absolute standout, he had class from a bygone era, even though it might not have been "cool" at the time. We would tease him about going home to wash his uniform when we had split practices during "hell" week because he was so meticulous about his appearance, sometimes calling him "Mr. Clean." I was working out really hard back then, and I remember Chad nick-naming me "body," and that's what he'd say whenever I saw him, as in "what's up body." He was obviously such a handsome guy that I would usually say something like "nothing much face." Thanks for taking the time to read this, it made me feel a little better writing my thoughts down and hopefully sharing a few very positive memories about your son who we all looked up to.

Sincerely,
Michael G."

"Chad and I actually met through a mutual friend, Sean Smith, through Lakeside Golf Club. Then Chad and I really hit it off and played quite a bit of volleyball together –played some beach and grass tournaments. That's how we became close friends. Chad just had a passion for everything in Life, whether it was volleyball or any other type of sports.

This is the Annual Volleyball Tournament Benefit we started in Chad's memory. He was a very good player- a very skilled player, so we put together a group of guys [and girls] who really like to come out in his memory and play volleyball. Chad would have been a kid in a candy store on a day like this, right down his alley. And we keep doing it every year in his memory, and it keeps growing. We started the tournament initially at Lakeside, then Zuma, now Hermosa Beach for many years now. It continues to grow, and we have wonderful people that come out every year to help with it.

Chad was the guy who wanted to start the game first in the morning and wanted to play till dark and so I just really have fond memories of the time we spent together playing in the tournaments. We'd play from morning till night. It was just fantastic. He had a great spirit and passion for life."

Michael Tidik
[Chair (25 yrs.) – *"CHAD Annual Volleyball Tournament Benefit"* – Hermosa Beach, CA]

"When I'm with the brothers, Curt and Collin, I say, "Hey, what do you think Chad would have done in this situation and that situation, so … he's here [at the CHAD Tourney] you just can't see him. For people who don't know him, he's just one of those type people who you automatically feel you've known him for years. He was very unbiased, you know you could be black, white, yellow, green.

He'd make the best of every situation, talk to everybody, and just wanted to know what you were about – very seldom spoke about himself. He always wanted to know what was going on in your head. What do you think, Jay? What do you think about this, think about that? What would you do? Just endless curiosity and endless knowledge of history – world wars… all the way back to the beginning of time. He knew it all."

Keven Simmons
(a great best friend who was playing football with Chad his last game on Earth)

…And in Chad's yearbook, I found the words of two friends~

Dear Chad,

…I just want to let you know that you've been my Hero for the past three years. I can't understand why you even talked to me, I was a freak. You helped me get self-confidence and overcome my super-shyness…

And thank you for your ragging powers. I never knew how to handle myself when it comes to a fight with words, now I can hang with the best of them.

Mister D.

Dearest Chad,

You're definitely one of a kind and your definitely not like the other guys in this society. I think people don't know the meaning of friends until they have you…

Miss S.

CHAPTER 26

"The Gift of Art" and "The Chad Safe Driving Campaign"

When people are curious and ask me why we chose the combination of "Athletes and Artists" for our foundation's focus, I revert to our initial mission statement. "…To inspire youth to live as Chad did - vibrantly and with a generosity of spirit, without substance abuse - "Healthy Body/Mind/Spirit." We did not begin as a screening organization but evolved into that entity. Remember, when our organization began, there were no preventive screenings in high schools. It would take a few years for the concept to take root. It was then we organized the *"1ˢᵗ Preventive Echocardiogram Screening for High School Athletes"* in the country in July 2000 at North Hollywood High School, North Hollywood, California. So though Chad clearly loved athletics and a 'healthy body,' he also loved the mind and spirit of all people from every descent, religion, orientation, and age. He truly cared about their hopes and aspirations, their potential in Life, and thus the holistic "Healthy Body/Mind/Spirit" became the core values of his foundation. He wanted to know *your story:* – where you came from, what you're all about, where you've been, what you wanted to do with your Life, and what challenges you were facing that clouded the track. What better way to explore and continue what was important to him than through the ubiquitous language of Art. If then the *"Gift of Heart"* safeguards the physical heart, the *"Gift of Art"* cares for and nourishes the mind and spirit getting to the 'heart' of the matter.

I think you will see Chad's spirit of Love and Life, and People reside within all the chosen projects and productions of the foundation. Our mission as artists is to create/produce/sponsor Art: - film, theatre, and books that celebrate American and global stories of all ancestries, which mirror Life in all its angst and glory and provide inspiring insight and role models. CHAD is dedicated to showing the inherent diversity of our country - the struggles, joys, and dreams of all Americans and providing a format for artists of all ethnicities to showcase their talents. Through our CHAD productions, several hundred artists have found a platform onstage and off to give their beautiful gifts of talent to New York and New Jersey, and someday we hope to the entire country. Actors, Directors, Stage Managers, Costume, Set, Lighting and Music Designers, PR and Graphic Designers have all donated their talents, wisdom, and professionalism to *"Chad's Gift of Art."* CHAD is forever grateful to The Chad Players and the Artisans of New York City for making our productions possible to entertain, inform and inspire.

The original play *...ALL ABOUT SNEAKERS* was our first theatrical project. An old-fashioned story of Love, it follows a couple's journey to re-find the long-lost steps of Love and the discovery that loving oneself first precedes loving another. It is a truth that comes slowly and not painlessly to surface when two earthy denizens and two rather unlikely candidates for higher growth evolution - an N.Y. cocktail waitress and a gravedigger come together. They find they no longer want the shams, cover-ups, game-playing, and undealt with pain and bitterness that have become the fabric of their respective lives.

Although it mirrors to a high degree the world they live in, they are ready to take the next step beyond that existence, which they find leads to the door within. *'SNEAKERS'* premiered off-Broadway at "The Shooting Gallery" Theatre in N.Y.C., and was reprised at the "Wings Theatre" in the West Village and "Theatre 603." It has also been performed for 300 homeless men and women at "Grand Central Neighborhood Social Services" and the "St. Martin de Porres Women's Residence" in Brooklyn. A homeless woman resident came up to me after one performance and said, "Now I know what I need to do about my relationship… but first I have to take care of me." D. Friedman, director at "Castillo Theatre," said of the play, "A beautiful love story with many deep levels," and S. Udolf, [then] Director of Social Services, felt, "Taking laughter on one's journey is a great lesson of the play."

Another original play performed by The Chad Players was *WELCOME HOME KELLY!* - a story about an Asian American daughter's quest for Father, Family, and the American dream. The story deals with attorney, Kelly Liu's return home to New York City's Chinatown after a 20-year absence, and the challenges of re-finding father, family in a home which now seems foreign to her. It is a timely play that reminds us all why we are here…because of the aspirations and courage of our ancestors. We are the beneficiaries of their long voyage…toward freedom. '*KELLY!*' won 1st place in the "Women's Empowerment Writing Awards," and "Columbia Pictures Minority Writing Competition." It is based on the original screenplay by the same name. In 2003, Arista was invited to Harvard to be a panelist in their annual "APALSA Law Conference," and was also asked to perform a reading of '*KELLY!*' at the opening reception. Its inaugural off-Broadway performance was at the "Sande Shurin Theatre" and was received enthusiastically. One lady recognizing the author at another event, commented, "You wrote the coming home Kelly play, and acted in it; it was excellent! We need more plays, which tell you, "You must leave home and explore." She was a retired schoolteacher. An Italian woman, who was a nurse, was crying after the play because it reminded her of her own father, who had said, "You've broken my heart, marrying a non-Italian." An African-American woman said, "Wow, even Asians have fathers that can give guilt trips…," and our African-American Stage Manager thought it was very educating as he never knew that Asian gang members didn't speak with thick accents, but were wild and spoke with the same vernacular as "the brothers." *WELCOME HOME KELLY!* transcended ethnic roots and touched universal values that people of all ancestries could relate to and in many different ways than anticipated.

And once we did integrate *"The Gift of Heart and Art."* The nurses from "Capuano Home Care" who had worked so diligently at the CHAD Heart Screenings in Holyoke, MA, organized a bus trip from MA to NYC to attend a Saturday night performance of *WELCOME HOME KELLY!* First, they had a wonderful pre-theatre dinner at *"Ruby Foos,"* a famed Times Square restaurant (where Chad's Father and I also had dined on our first trip to NYC.) Then had bought a significant part of the house that night with their generosity of tickets, and after our theatrical performance came backstage to meet the Cast and get autographs. HA! That was fun for the Cast too!

~ ~ ~

The two dozen 'Roses' Chad presented to me at my first play in Los Angeles are etched into my memory forever, and would eventually lead to another play where roses were a central theme. I remember the first scene-work of *Days of Wine and Roses*, which I performed with a young actor named Nick in Wally Strauss's Thursday night acting class in NYC. During the scene, my shoes kept slipping off my heels when I walked. Nick told me afterward, "Even your shoes seemed sad…" Actually, they were too big… much like the role which would take me 15 years to really grow into and perform in New York and Atlantic City.

In JP Miller's award-winning play *Days of Wine and Roses*, the lead characters, Joe and Kirsten Clay, are faced with the challenges of the real world today. - They find denial, alcoholism, and the journey to find one's way through this maelstrom of powerful addictive forces can raze one's Love to its core. However, as the author himself writes, it is not a story of drunkenness but 'a story of Love... don't forget the Roses,' and we never did. That is what informed our performances. *Days of Wine and Roses* has had 3 Off-Off-Broadway productions performed by the multi-cultural Cast, The Chad Players, in New York City: at "Chasama Performance," "The Sanford Meisner Theatre," and the "Lion Theatre" on Theatre Row, and in Atlantic City, New Jersey at "Dante Hall." At a Meisner Theatre performance, there happened to be in the audience a Board member of the *"Atlantic Commission on Missing and Abused Children/Dept. of Family and Youth Services,"* thanks to our cast member, J. Furey and his good friend B. Sherman. So moved by the performance was the Board Member that she brought The Chad Players' production of *Days of Wine and Roses* to Atlantic City's beautiful "Dante Hall." It was the community event of the year to show families the deleterious effects substance abuse can have on all the family members.

The community at large was invited. At one of the performances, we heard the teens fidgeting before the curtain went up, "Come on let's start the show…this is boring.-" But once the play began, they were gripped by every moment. And when the pivotal motel scene came where the lead character, Joe, is tempted by his wife, Kirsten, to take a drink after being sober for 3 months, the teens could not help themselves and utter out loudly. "No, man, don't take that drink… - Don't do it!" When Joe finally succumbs and takes the drink, the teens were devastated and spoke out-loud again – "Oh, why did he take that drink?? Why did he do that!" Afterward, the young people told the hostess that this was the best play they had ever seen; they loved it.

It was wonderfully received. Commented, J. Hall, producer, "Honest and sensitive portrayals, not a dry eye in the house, a well-deserved standing ovation," and Maggie Stone, TV Correspondent, Sinovision said, "I loved the performance …powerful stuff." Another patron, C. Lenz, from Drexel Hill, PA, wrote, "The chemistry between Joe & Kirsten was amazing, great ensemble cast. I came back a second night."

The reaction to our performances from adults and, especially, the teens and pre-teens taught me how much Art can genuinely impact people of all ages, perhaps even having more prolonged effects than a 30-second T.V. commercial airing to dissuade drinking. For we saw firsthand when young people *see* live theatre, they identify and relate to the characters – a real Family in Love, a Child they both Love, and the journey of alcohol testing Love to its core. It will resonate with them for a long time. In another performance of '*Roses*' at the "Lion Theatre" on Theatre Row, we had a "Talk Back with the Actors" following a matinee. A New Jersey High School student was in the audience. She said her school was about to start random drug testing, but she thought to see this performance would be a far better deterrent. My good friend Stew Krug brought his daughter all the way from Delaware to see '*Roses.*' Stewart wrote me a letter and said his daughter told him of a student from the University of Delaware where she also went [at the time] who died on the railroad tracks a short distance from her dorm. The student had been too inebriated to move from the oncoming train. His daughter, who attended the matinee, said sadly, "I wish more students could have seen this play."

Seeing the teens' intense reactions to our play and seeing the continuing rise of alcoholism and substance abuse in this age group and college students, it has been a goal now to do such a Community Benefit performance of our production of '*Roses*' in N.Y.C. At a venue like "The Apollo" [Theatre in Harlem], we could invite numbers of high school and college students, and even some of our Veterans. In my years working with the homeless, I met many Vets who had often fallen prey to drugs and alcohol upon their return to society. There was an inability to reintegrate into their community for many reasons, including PTSD, and they found very few who could truly comprehend what they had been through.

Also, with Chad's last writings and respect for the Native Americans and the fact that the very last film we saw together was *Geronimo*, we know his spirit resides within one of the foundation's film projects *EARTHEN*.

The indie screenplay, *EARTHEN*, is a romantic dramedy and a contemporary love story. It revolves around a down-to-earth cowboy who brings a New York cocktail waitress away from the glitz, materialism, and promiscuity of their society and back to the Earth and their real selves through the discovery of the meaning of their partial Cherokee heritage. The particular beauty of this Indian story is it portrays the Native Americans today, not in the 18th century. It obliterates the "all-noble... arms-raised-to-the-sky mentor" with a modern-day mentor, who's hip, witty, and loves Marvin Gaye interspersing sagely wisdom with his Motown lyrics. It is a quest made by a Mother whose loss of a child she cannot face grieving for. However, it is the Cherokee traditions and final purification ceremony in the river which help to show her, allow her to accept the full circle of Life: birth, death...rebirth. She can finally put her child to rest and accept the Love of man. In a traditional Cherokee wedding ceremony, their Love, too, comes full-circle. *EARTHEN* also has the official blessing of the Eastern Band of the Cherokee Nation. Our Chief Consultant on the script whom we worked with on the reservation in Cherokee, North Carolina, is Myrtle Johnson, producer/actress, and the author's spiritual Cherokee Mother.

"U.S.A. (EW-ESS-AH) A Year with The Homeless" – is a screenplay based on the real-life event the "1st Homeless Streetsoccer World Cup," and a New York artist, jobless after 9-11, who finds a fundraising job at a Homeless Drop-in Center. It becomes an unforgettable adventure as she helps to raise monies to take a team of N.Y. men to participate in the "1st Homeless Street Soccer World Cup" in Graz, Austria, with 16 other participating countries of homeless athletes. In real life, we were accompanied by HBO, who aired a segment about it on the stellar Bryant Gumbel *Real Sports.* It was a life-changing experience for all who participated. It illustrated how the vehicle of sports can be a universal leveler and bring back the self-esteem and confidence of the dispossessed...to *want* to get back into Life again. It was remarkable to learn homelessness existed in every country. It was even more remarkable to see that stigma disappear, as athletes ran down the streets of Austria wearing their colours, bearing their country's flags like Olympians. Observing the English team with their arms around their Irish comrades, and all coming to learn the American team was not a bully or felt superior as we found many countries had expected us to be- was a lesson for us all. Some of us even had to learn there was a country named Namibia!

On the last day of the event, the American team learned a great lesson on compassion when the young Brazilian boys came into their room to say goodbye. Our team watched the boys' faces as they looked with awe upon all their new traveling clothes, and clean underwear, and socks. Then without words, the New York team—to a person gathered many of their new clothing up and gave them to the boys. One boy looked up and said, "You take me with you?" And one of the players responded, "Buddy, I wish I could." He was the New York Black goalie who had become a "rock star" that week, cheered on by young, blond Austrian boys in the stands asking for his autograph. Hitler would have rolled over in his grave witnessing this, and that the 1st place team of Austrians was comprised almost totally of refugees from Nigeria. For a moment, it brought the whole world together. People shared humanity, not homelessness or hopelessness, and the new generations of Austrians cheered all the teams, and when they cheered for America, they cheered, *"Ew, Ess, Ah."*

I never got to share my stories with Chad about my days spent working with and for the homeless citizens of New York. But he would be proud to know his foundation provided heart screenings for 16 countries of athletes participating in the *"1st Homeless Streetsoccer World Cup" in Graz, Austria;* and, the following year, for 26 countries of athletes participating in the *"2nd Homeless Streetsoccer World Cup" in Gothenburg, Sweden.* If Chad had been with me, he still might be there… There were just *soo* many stories of athletes around the world … and he would have wanted to hear each one of them.

And how do we get from a screenplay on homeless Streetsoccer in Europe to *"From the Heart ~ A Night of Opera & Classical Music Benefit"*? Why from a Chad Heart Screening, of course. Enter a handsome young man named Javor Bracic, who saw our notice, *"Chad Free Heart Screenings for Athletes and Artists"* posted on the CUNY (City of the University of New York) website. "Thank you for coming, are you studying to be a Doctor, or in the medical field?" I queried when I saw him. "No," says he, "I am a concert pianist from Croatia studying for my doctorate in Musical Arts." "Oh!" exulted I, clearly surprised and thrilled an 'artist' would take the time to have his heart checked… But, simultaneously, a light bulb was going off. And I continue not 3 seconds later, "We are the Gift of Heart and *"Art."* – Would you ever consider doing a classical benefit concert for Chad?" He, with perhaps a 2-second pause, responded, "I would be glad to do a benefit concert for your organization… You're doing something wonderful, giving free heart-screenings." "Really??" (we only met two seconds ago…) I am profusely appreciative and rush to the large reception desk where sit all the Volunteers doing sign-in and exit paperwork. (By the way, this vast, wrap-around desk and spacious office with actual patient rooms were donated by Dr. Bruce Paswell.) And I excitedly tell everyone about what this generous artist is doing! Suddenly, one of the volunteers pops up and volunteers her boyfriend- again, within 2 seconds.—"Eric is a harpist for the U.S. Airforce. – He'll do it." "Really?" She confirms, going back to her task at hand. Well, what can I do?? Oh, I do have a friend that's an opera singer… maybe– And that is how *"A CHAD Night of Opera and Classical Music"* came together in 10 minutes, 15 minutes tops with extraordinary "Artist Angels" 'volunteering,' no less at a Chad Heart Screening. Take a look at the talented gifts they would give:

Croatian pianist Javor Bracic is the first prize winner of international piano competitions in Italy, Croatia and Belgium. Most recently, he gave a critically acclaimed solo recital at Weill Hall, presented by New York Concert Artists. His first CD album Performance was broadcast on WQXR. He was invited to give recitals and perform at festivals and conferences throughout the U.S.A., Europe, China, and South Africa. Javor has given a series of concerts for the humanitarian organization, "Yehudi Menuhin's Live Music Now," which brings music to nursing homes and hospitals. He has also given a series of lecture-recitals under the title the "Art of Listening" aimed at promoting the interest and understanding of classical music. Javor has a Bachelor's and Master's degree from the University of Mozarteum in Salzburg.

Mezzo-soprano Caterina Secchi feels equally at home in Europe and in the United States, where she was born. She began her vocal studies with the late Elio Gennari, a pupil of Arturo Melocchi, at the

"Rossini Conservatory" of Pesaro, Italy. Caterina made her debut as a very young singer at the "Teatro Regio" of Parma and progressed to sing with the major opera houses of Europe. She specialized in dramatic mezzo-soprano roles of the Italian and French repertoire, such as Azucena in *Il Trovatore*, Amneris in *Aida*, Ulrica in *Un Ballo in Maschera*, Santuzza in *Cavalleria Rusticana* and Dalila in *Samson et Dalila*. Tara Werner of the *New Zealand Herald* wrote: "..Secchi is a dramatic mezzo-soprano with a rich sound which could fill any venue."

Eric A. Sabatino was the harp soloist for the "United States Air Force Band" in Washington, D.C. Originally from New York City, Eric Sabatino completed a Bachelor of Music degree from "The Manhattan School of Music" & a 2-year scholarship in orchestral performance. He was principal harpist with the orchestras of the Empire State Opera, Amato Opera Company, and the Island Lyric Opera of New York City. His civilian accomplishments include performing as principal harpist with the Atlanta Symphony, Baltimore Opera, Kennedy Center Opera House Orchestra & Washington National Opera. He was featured soloist with the St. Petersburg Chamber Symphony, when he was invited to perform for the Diaghilev Festival in St. Petersburg, Russia, to include two solo recitals.

For this outstanding group of artists who were donating their tremendous Gifts, I had to find the most beautiful… 'affordable' venue for them, and the "Angels" were with me again. *"The National Opera Center"* in N.Y. had an intimate room under 100 seats with perfect acoustics. Backlit lighting on the side walls brought a softness to the contemporary style of the modern décor.

When I looked out into the audience to give my opening introductions, and saw the elegance of this room and felt the artists waiting expectantly in the wings, my voice shook for the first moments. I wanted so much for Chad to be here, to see what a beautiful new place we had arrived at in this– his journey that he left us to uncover and discover. … And I remembered what his good friend Keven had said on camera about Chad, "He's here – ya just can't see him," and he was.

One must learn to see things not visible with the eye, listen, and see things with your heart. Presence is an undefinable energy you can feel… He was seeing the faces of every member of his audience.– They were made up of all kinds of people of all ages. And, he was wondering about each of them, wanting to spend time with each. In this private, personal setting, I knew he saw what we saw, only with his inscrutable, detailed observations as was his mark. He saw Javor's fingers leaving the keys so elegantly as it brought the music with them. He heard Caterina's soul filling her voice, which started and ended not at her diaphragm but from the very soles of her feet, surging through her heart and lungs before it filled the room. And he felt invisibly the magical strings of the harp played again not just by Eric's fingers but the entire man; music so beautiful we had never heard or expected from this instrument. Many were seeing 'the harp' for the first time, up close – and would have a newfound delight and interest in it now.

At one time, I found myself at the back of the house. The music and sound did not diminish, not an iota, for the acoustics had been constructed as such. You could hear the music in any part of the house you stood in. What was amazing to me is the magical sound of silence that every actor can also feel and hopes to sense. –It is that singular moment where there is no physical sound or movement, no coughing or rustling because there is an invisible connection- the kinetic energy between artist and audience. That is what I saw. There were rockers and jazz aficionados in the audience who came not so much because of the music but to support, the college student, and the volunteer who had never heard this kind of classical music in an intimate setting. – Yet without exception, they were all utterly enthralled. And there was a special guest there, too, a "2nd generation guest." Her father, Louis, always thought of Chad as the brother he never had. Chad had been Best Man at Louis and Veronica's wedding. I just happened to be in Los Angeles when Zianna, their 1st daughter was born, and Curt and I were visiting her at the hospital when she was only a few hours old. Tonight she was attending the *"1st Chad Classical Concert,"* a freshman at N.Y.U.

–I love that *Star Person* up there that aligns the stars precisely and makes irreplaceable moments that will never be replicated again. Your journey has been magical, Chad. We all learned, experienced, enjoyed so much that night. –I attended the unparalleled *"Alexander McQueen Exhibit"* at The Met, twice; an experience that is impossible to duplicate. And our little concert was in a similar space… if on a much smaller scale. It is another world you step up to and know you are transported if just for a moment in time to an astonishing level you've never been. Thank you, our three Angel Artists, for sharing your exceptional *"Gifts of Heart & Art."* They were a moment of sublime beauty that has enriched us and won't be forgotten.

"Life is a Gift - Chad Safe Driver Campaign"

Lastly, our newest project, *"Life is a Gift - Chad Safe Driver Campaign,"* was inspired by an unfortunate story I happened upon on one of the court television programs. It was about a very wealthy man who was inebriated and driving at night on a pitch-black road and plowed into another car. So drunk was he, he didn't realize he had hit the car and pushed it into a creek, so he left the scene. Later, it was found the driver of that car, subsequently drowned. He was just a young college boy, who had *not* been drinking, and was on his way home to celebrate his sister's birthday. As soon as I heard this tragic story, the walls started reverberating…and yes, I think the heavens opened. Here was Chad calling to me, "Mom, you got to help these young people (O.M.G., another project…) But he was right, if any story had Chad's name on it, it was this one…

As we all know by now, Chad, in his 26 years of Life, never drank an alcoholic beverage, smoked a cigarette, or did drugs. It was just his own personal code, which he forced on no one, and his Friends can attest to that. They also know Chad cared about their Lives and what they were going to do with them, so he always made himself "the designated driver" when he and his friends went out to the clubs dancing- something Chad loved to do almost as much as playing sports. And another thing, you always had to wear a seatbelt when you drove with Chad...or the car didn't start.

To inspire youth to live as Chad did, "...without substance abuse and with love for all people of all ages and nations –Healthy Body/ Mind/Spirit," we are happy to launch his newest project. *Life is A Gift - Chad Safe Driver Campaign"* is a program which asks people to safeguard their own Life, their child's Life, and the Lives of others by joining Chad's new program on his website, www.chadfoundation. org, and ordering the special *"Life is A Gift" Keychain Shield."* It is a great-looking, heavyweight, curved shield pendant with an antique, pewter-like finish which says on the front of the shield: *"Chad – Life is a Gift"* and on the back, *"Save Lives, don't text/drink & drive."* In joining the program, one takes the pledge of the same, I promise to: *"Save Lives, don't text/drink & drive."* We are happy to tell you we now have drivers in 12 states and 10 countries as far away as England, New Zealand, and Paraguay, who have taken the pledge. They are using the *"Chad – Life is a Gift"* shield not only as a keychain, but a medallion in the car, or creatively as some form of jewelry.

When we take a look at some of the sobering statistics that follow, it is a no-brainer that we must all get involved. We must all be the example; 5 seconds in texting while driving could and has ended Lives. - *"Life is A Gift."*

Texting, Drinking and Driving and Not Wearing Seatbelts

Texting

- 23% of all car accidents each year involve cell phone use –**that's 1.3 million crashes.**
- Drivers distracted by talking or texting on cell phones killed an estimated 16,000 people between the years of 2001 and 2007.[6]

- **Texting while driving kills 11 teens each day**, says The Insurance Institute for Highway Safety.
- 5 Seconds is the minimum time your eyes are taken away from the road while texting. At 55 mph, that's driving the length of a football field.
- Teen drivers aged 15-17 are eight times more likely to be in a fatal crash if they have two or more teen passengers (aged 13-17) in the car.

Drinking and Driving

- 30 people die every day from drunk driving, that's one death every 48 minutes.
- 82% of accident fatalities are caused by drunk drivers
- 34% of drunk fatalities are 21-24 yrs. old; 18% of drunk fatalities are 16-20 yrs. old
- 70 percent of all teenagers drink alcohol
- 60 percent of all teen deaths in car accidents are alcohol-related.
- 18 percent of alcohol fatalities include other drugs, e.g., cocaine, marijuana
- Perhaps, the most significant influence on teenagers and their drinking and driving habits is Peer Pressure.

Not Wearing Seatbelts

- In 2009 (56 percent) of teens and young adults ages 16 to 20 that died in crashes were not wearing their seat belt.
- A study in 2013, shows teens who view their parents as involved (set rules and wear seatbelts) are twice as likely to wear a seat belt as a driver or passenger as teens who say their parents are uninvolved.

- At least 98 of the 176, 16- to 19-year-olds, killed on state roads in 2004-6 were not wearing seatbelts.
- Oct. 7, 2013, the only teen not wearing a seatbelt died after a pick-up truck carrying 4 teens crashed in Butler County. The other 3 teens lived.

What We Can Do

- Value Life at any age, at any cost. There is nothing "Cooler than Courage." Be your own quiet Hero, and Live and safeguard others.
- Be a real Friend, take the keys, and either drive your Friend home or call a cab for them when they are in no condition to drive.
- Parent involvement stats show if we wear our seatbelts, so will our teen drivers, and they will require their friends to do so.
- As parents, we can set an example at our own parties, by making sure guests who can't drive have a safe way home or spend the night.
- Always have cab-fare and be able to call a friend or family member, and be there on the other side; take turns.
- Organize a *"Life is a Gift – Chad Safe Drivers"* campaign in your school or community. Give everyone you care about a *Chad Safe Driver's Shield.*
- Be informed, access sources like, <u>Welcome to SADD,</u> or <u>Century Council: Fighting Drunk Driving & Underage Drinking</u>
- Be aware: 44 states and D.C. have 'graduated driver licensing Laws,' which restrict the number of passengers that new teen drivers are allowed to have in the car.

CHAPTER 27

"To Screen or Not To Screen – That is the Question..."

The Question

As preventive Electrocardiogram and Echocardiogram screenings can detect unknown lethal heart anomalies and prevent Sudden Cardiac Death, should broad-scale screenings be administered to all student-athletes at high schools and colleges before sports participation?

The Answer

Though many of us would consider the question of screening young athletes a "no-brainer," and answer with a resounding "yes," the issue becomes more complex and controversial when it rises to the arena of science-based evidence. Dependent upon which organization or governmental agency is providing the incidence statistics, it is said that between 3,000 and 6,000 young people between the ages of 15 and 34 die annually from Sudden Cardiac Death. Hypertrophic cardiomyopathy is the most common cause of heart-related sudden death in people under 30 and the most common identifiable cause of sudden death in athletes. One in 500 births has the HCM (hypertrophic cardiomyopathy) gene, the abnormally enlarged heart muscle, which is the leading silent killer of Sudden Cardiac Death in Young

Athletes. Other causes of Sudden Cardiac Death in Youth (SCDY) are structural cardiac anomalies such as Arrhythmogenic Right Ventricular Cardiomyopathy, Congenital Coronary Artery, Mitral Valve Prolapse, Aortic Stenosis, Marfan Syndrome, and Dilated Cardiomyopathy. Some electrical abnormalities that can cause SCDY are Wolff-Parkinson-White syndrome and Long QT syndrome. Other causes like Commotio Cordis (lethal disruption of heart rhythm due to a sudden, non-penetrating blow to the chest, specifically in the precordium area above the heart) and Myocarditis can also cause Sudden Cardiac Death. (Many of these anomalies have been detected in Chad Heart Screenings, such as HCM, Aortic Stenosis, Mitral Valve Prolapse, and Wolff-Parkinson-White syndrome.) Logic would tell us that by employing advanced screening methods to detect fatal heart abnormalities, the occurrence of sudden cardiac deaths among the young would be reduced. Why then is the preventive screening measure such a matter of debate?

Firstly, one of the most significant barriers to determining the best approach to the prevention of SCDY (Sudden Cardiac Death in Young) lies in the inability to assess the number of incidences accurately.[7] Figures range from 1:200,000 to 1:2300 athletes per year, while some subpopulations of athletes report at even higher risk with a frequency of 1 in 3000. The Harmon, Drezner review says to fully understand the cardiovascular risks in athletes and prevent SCD through screening, incidence estimates should include sudden cardiac arrest (SCA) survivors. They should consist of other SCD cases that occur at any time (sleep, rest, exertion/exercise, walking) and not just those occurring during sports participation. Based on a comprehensive evaluation of Sudden Cardiac Death information, their incident rate in college athletes is 1:50 000 and 1:80 000 in high school athletes, and their review says this should be considered a minimum[7]. Some subpopulations such as males, African Americans, and basketball athletes appear to be at higher risk. They also conclude that accurate SCD incident figures are necessary for determining the most effective preventive strategies in screening programs.

As we delve more into the incidence rates of SDY (Sudden Death in Young), we begin to see the complexity of the issue. According to the NIH (National Institute Health) Epidemiology Study, Sudden Cardiac Death in the Young estimates from research studies vary widely, from 0.5-2.3 per 100,000, depending on the location, age range sampled, and definitions used. If survivors of sudden cardiac arrests as well as the deceased are added, figures can increase to as high as 8/100,000.[8] It was in 2013 that the first "Sudden Death in the Young Registry" was instituted by the cooperative effort of the National Institute of Health (NIH) and the Centers of Disease Control (CDC) to compile such incidence stats. The registry is a national repository for sudden unexpected deaths in young people up to 24 years of age due to conditions such as cardiac disease and epilepsy. Before that, in its real infancy days, SCDY stats were often obtained from newspaper clippings, obits, and media. Autopsies were rarely performed on young SCD victims. It would be interesting to know how many of the 50 states are currently participating and reporting their SCD stats to the national "Sudden Death in the Young Registry."

To further illustrate this variance in SCDY statistics, let's take a look at the results of a study that occurred over a 7-year-period in the state of Michigan. The Michigan Department of Community Health (MDCH) put out a report on young people under the age of 40 who have died of sudden cardiac death in Michigan. The report notes the state's "grave concern for this issue, not only is it a tremendous loss to families but also communities losing children in the prime of their lives." As a result of a new state surveillance project, trends in Michigan SCDY cases are being identified. Analysis of mortality data for the years 1999-2006 reveals as many as 326 out-of-hospital sudden deaths occurring each year to individuals under age 40. The statewide age-adjusted mortality rate was 5.5 per 100,000, [in comparison to the 2.3 per 100,000 stats in the NIH Epidemiology Study], and 13 counties in Michigan reported even rates higher than the 5.5 per 100,000 state average. Overall in this report, atherosclerotic cardiovascular disease was the most commonly reported underlying cause of death, followed by dilated cardiomyopathy.[9] (Chad died from undetected dilated cardiomyopathy). It is interesting to note that with atherosclerosis being the #1 cause of death in the under 40 age group here, it underscores the need for screenings for early cardiovascular risk factors such as high cholesterol, diabetes, obesity, and high blood pressure screenings. These are additional tests that CHAD includes in its preventative heart screening program whenever possible.

Secondarily, although the issue – "To Screen or Not To Screen"— has now developed its place in society as significant enough to warrant science-based studies, it has as many doctors who believe the evidence shows we *should* screen young athletes to as many doctors who believe studies *don't show* it's warranted. The latter feel the testing procedure is too costly on a broad scale and results in too many false positives. Let's take a look at what some of the studies have found on both sides of the aisle:

"To Screen…"

In the NCAA (National Collegiate Athletic Association) Electrocardiographic Screening Study, which took place from August 2012 to June 2014, athletes from 35 NCAA institutions participated. Their screening protocol included a standardized history, physical examination (PE) as recommended by the American Heart Association as well as a 12-lead Electrocardiogram (ECG) utilizing the Seattle criteria for interpretation. The study tested 5,258 athletes from 17 intercollegiate sports and concluded that the electrocardiographic screening of the National Collegiate Athletic Association athletes had a low false-positive rate and provided superior accuracy compared with just a standardized history and PE to detect athletes with potentially dangerous cardiovascular conditions.[10]

A prior survey done some years before by researchers from U.C.L.A. and the Minneapolis Heart Institute Foundation found that more than 800 National Collegiate Athletic Associations have campus screening programs for potential heart problems that are inadequate. The programs used doctors without cardiac training and failed to ask critical questions about family history, such as a history of fainting, dizziness, exclusion of sports, and history of premature cardiac death under 35 years of age. The Electrocardiographic Screening of the National Collegiate Athletic Association Athletes, which took place in 2012-2014, shows there is progress in the arena of screening athletes in just a few decades.

Italian Study

Perhaps the study that has gained the most global attention on the success of its pre-participation screening for athletes is the Italian Study, which took place over a 26-year-period from 1979 to 2004 in the Veneto region of Italy, screening over 40,000 athletes (12–35 years old) utilizing the 12 lead Electrocardiogram. In the study, Domenico Corrado et al. found that participation in competitive sports increased the young athletes' risk of sudden death two and a half times. As well, the study discovered it was not the rigorous activity of the sports itself that caused the sudden death, but the event could set off extreme ventricular arrhythmias in undiagnosed lethal cardiomyopathies, which after a few moments are no longer compatible with life.[11]

The long-term follow-up portion of the Italian study found that there were no additional deaths among those athletes who had been screened and found to have Hypertrophic Cardiomyopathy and thus eliminated from play. Therefore, the study concludes that early detection of HCM, the number one killer of Sudden Cardiac Death in Young Athletes, along with appropriate managed healthcare, can save lives. Dr. Gaetano Thiene of the Padua Center for Sports Medicine said, "In over 26 years of pre-participation screenings, Sudden Cardiac Death was reduced by 90%, which proves that pre-participation screening is a life-saving tool."[11]

It is also noteworthy that the country of Italy actually mandates by law that all its athletes must have pre-participation screening using the 12 lead ECG protocol. Italian physicians who conduct pre-participation screenings must attend four-year postgraduate residency training programmes in sports medicine and sports cardiology. As highly-trained specialists in this field, they work in the country's sports centres screening and evaluating athletes for at-risk silent cardiomyopathies.[15]

The European Protocol

The European Protocol was created when a consortium of experts issued a consensus document supporting the pre-participation screening of young athletes utilizing the 12-lead ECG in conjunction with a family history and physical examination to prevent sudden cardiac deaths. They were comprised of The Study Group of Sport Cardiology of the Working Group of Cardiac Rehabilitation and Exercise Physiology and the Working Group of Myocardial and Pericardial Diseases of the European Society of Cardiology.[12] The consortium further recommended the use of the 12-lead ECG as it enhances the screening protocol. It can identify HCM, the leading silent killer of SCD in young athletes, which shows up abnormal in 95% of those diagnosed with HCM. It can also recognize other at-risk cardiovascular abnormalities like ARVC/D, which is another cause of SCD and has also presented in abnormal ECGs.

It is said that the Italian Study did much to inform and confirm the efficacy of pre-participation screening and laid the foundation for forming the European protocol. Due to the longevity of the Italian study- 26 years and the fact that it was population-based, led the experts to agree with the success and efficacy of the results of using this screening methodology to identify athletes at risk for undiagnosed lethal heart anomalies and reduce sudden cardiac death.

A study in the European document cites 134 high school and collegiate athletes who died of SCD. They were screened with a standard history and physical exam only. In only 3% of those examined by this method were cardiovascular anomalies suspected resulting in an accurate diagnosis of less than 1%.[14] The proposal also stated that by just increasing the athletes' awareness of symptoms that may precede sudden cardiac arrest is not enough to prevent fatalities as Sudden Cardiac Death is most often the first outcome of these undetected lethal anomalies.[13]

What says, "The Public?"

In 2013, the public was given a forum in the New England Journal of Medicine to voice their opinion on the issue of pre-participation screenings. It took place by way of an online poll kicked off by the query of a high school athletic director who wanted to know if he should require pre-participation cardiac screenings for all of his athletes before their athletic season. Four medical physicians considered experts in this field participated in the debate. The same discussion with the same experts was presented at the annual American Heart Association meeting. The views of the four participating physicians were as follows: Dr. Sanjay Sharma of London stood on the side of pro-screening young athletes and felt preventive screenings would save lives; Dr. Mark Estes of Boston took the opposite view and argued it was not scientifically proven that screenings reduce Sudden Cardiac Death in Young Athletes. Dr. Victoria Vetter of Philadelphia presented the case for screening with a history and physical examination only, the same view recommended by AHA the American Heart Association; lastly, Dr. Domenico Corrado of Padua, Italy supported the stand that screening with the ECG protocol enhances the identification of unknown cardiac abnormalities.[17]

At the AHA annual session, those audience members attending voted 70% in favour of screening young athletes for cardiac problems, and 60% voted to include the ECG in the screening. In the NEJM online poll, there were a total of 1,266 votes from respondents in 86 different countries. The consensus overall was only 18% felt young athletes should not be screened before athletic participation, while 24% favoured the AHA screening recommendations, utilizing history and PE- physical examination. Lastly, 58% of the respondents had a preference for screening with all three: a history, physical examination, and ECG.[17]

Of interest was the online voters from the United States who voted less for young athletes to have the ECG screening than their counterparts from other countries who were pro-screening. 35% of U.S. voters chose the screening model using only a history and physical examination, while 45% of the respondents voted for screening with the ECG.

In comparing voters from Europe with the U.S., 66% of the European voters chose the ECG screening protocol while only 13% voted for screenings using just a history and physical examination. Given the 26-year Italian Study and the country that mandates pre-participatory screening by law, it isn't surprising that Italy comprised the most significant percentage of voters in the European respondents. Of the 95 respondents from Italy, 74% recommended screening with the ECG.[17]

Now that we have heard from those who are on the side of screening young athletes before participating in athletics, let's hear from the other side of the aisle.

….or Not to Screen

In a U.S. study in which 4,052,369 athletes participated, 182 sudden deaths occurred: 47 athlete deaths were attributable to cardiovascular causes, the most common being HCM hypertrophic cardiomyopathy, and a higher incidence in African-Americans; 52 deaths were due to suicide. Thus in 30 sports over a ten year period, mortality rates were: suicide and drugs combined, 1.3/100,000, and documented cardiovascular disease, 1.2/100,000 athlete participation which led to the conclusion that there is a low risk of sudden death due to cardiovascular disease with mortality rates similar to suicide and drug abuse.[18] "A substantial minority of confirmed cardiovascular deaths would not likely have been reliably detected by pre-participation screening with 12-lead electrocardiograms."[18]

Likewise, in an analysis of 1,866 Sudden Deaths in Young Athletes during a 27 year period (1980-2006), 56% of these deaths (1,049), were attributed to cardiovascular disease; HCM (hypertrophic cardiomyopathy) was the most prevalent cause (36%). This U.S. national registry-based study concludes that young athletes' sudden deaths due to cardiovascular disease was higher than prior estimates but still considered low, with 100 SCD per year. However, the analysis also concludes that a more standardized methodology is needed to collect SCD data and mandatory reporting should be required to the Sudden Death national registry.[19]

The NIH Epidemiology breakdown for similar causes of death in 15-24-year-olds was as follows: 1) Motor Vehicle Accident Deaths – 9 in 100,000, 2) Violent Deaths (Homicides/Suicides combined) - 10 per 100,000, and, 3) Sudden Cardiac Death in the Young: 0.6 – 2.3 per 100,000. Based on these numbers, the NIH deems Sudden Cardiac Death rare in comparison to Vehicle Accidents, or Violent Deaths/ Suicides combined.[20] In the CDC "2018 - 10 Leading Causes of Death by Age," the 1st, 2nd, and 3rd causes of death in a similar age group are unintentional injury, suicide, and homicide. The 4th and 5th causes of death are Cancer and Heart Disease.[21]

If you ask Dr. Barry Maron, a leading specialist in hypertrophic cardiomyopathy, his answer is, "Screening large populations is a complex public-health problem," says Maron.[22] "It's deceptively complicated." Two of those indicated drawbacks are that screenings are expensive, and they've shown to yield a high rate of false- positives.

Let's take a moment to address the three major issues that non-advocates of mass screenings often base their stance upon: 1) Too costly, 2) Too many false-positive results, and 3) Low Risk of Sudden Cardiac Death, similar mortality rate to Suicides/Drug Abuse. You will see some answers below that address more than one of these issues.

(1) *Too Costly - The Cost of Preventive*
Heart Screenings in the Young

The cost of mass screening has always been a prohibitive factor in the ongoing debate. According to the American Heart Association (AHA) estimates, the overall cost of screening roughly 10 million U.S. high school and college athletes could be at least $2 billion in the first year.[23] However, in the Italian pre-participation screening program, mass screening was found to be economically feasible due to the limited cost of the first-line cardiovascular evaluation.[26] As well, the percentage of high false-positive rates that were anticipated and would require further testing with an Echocardiogram was less than 9% with very little increase in the cost factor. The average cost per athlete was €79 which was broken down to €64 (80%) for first-line evaluations and an additional €15 (20%) for further investigations if required.[27]

Halkin et al. state that incorporating the ECG as a screening tool to screen 8.5 million U.S. athletes annually who are of high school and college-age would cost the US Healthcare system anywhere from $2.5 to 3.5 billion dollars annually.[24] Stretch this to two decades, and out of approximately 170 million athletes who received ECG screenings, 4,831 lives would be saved at the cost of 51–61 billion dollars for a 20 year period.[24] This amount of life-years saved is a positive factor in the cost-effectiveness of the screening process, with cost estimates per year of life saved consistently below $50,000. A program is considered cost-effective in the U.S. if the cost of saving a life is less than $50,000 to $75,000 per year.[29] A recent US analysis estimated that adding ECG to history and physical examination in the screening protocol of athletes aged 14–22 years saves 2.06 life-years per 1000 athletes, at the cost of $42,000 per life-year saved.[82] "ECGs can detect up to 94% of most significant heart conditions; it is non-invasive, and considered cost-effective when compared to other tests such as Pap smears, mammography, and Prostate- Specific Antigen."[26]

Halkin concluded that more research was needed regarding the false-positive aspects of athlete screenings before the cost-effectiveness of routine ECG screening could be determined. The study also found that without the addition of the ECG screening, the 14-element checklist created by the American Heart Association as a guideline for screening young athletes for unknown cardiac disease is not adequate enough, and has a low sensitivity factor.[82] However, when screenings were implemented, the use of the Seattle protocol was recommended.

In 2016, similar questions were asked in the United Kingdom, "What are the cost implications of Athlete ECG Screening Criteria?" Relative to our discussion, the UK Citation addresses both the No. 1 concern of screenings 'being too costly,' and the No. 2 concern of 'too many false positives.' In the three-year study (2011-2014), 4,925 athletes between 14-35 years of age received screenings with history, (PE) physical examination, and the ECG utilizing the 2010 ESC recommendations for interpretation. Those athletes with abnormal screening results received further evaluation and testing. Here are the findings: 1,072 (21.8%) athletes had an abnormal ECG based on 2010 ESC criteria.[28]

However, utilizing the Seattle and refined criteria reduced the number of positive ECGs from 21.8 to 6.0%. "The overall cost of de novo screening using 2010 ESC recommendations was $539,888 ($110 per athlete and $35,993 per serious diagnosis".) The Seattle and refined criteria reduced the cost to $92 and $87 per athlete screened and $30,251 and $28,510 per serious diagnosis, respectively.[24] The use of refined criteria for ECG interpretation that are more specific to the detection of cardiac disease in athletes helps lower the cost of additional testing. Of paramount importance is the use of established ECG criteria specific to athletes. These studies are showing how the medical community around the world is working to demonstrate scientifically that screenings for young athletes can be economically feasible when using refined criteria specifically relevant to athletes.

(2) Too Many False Positives

The rate of false-positives has been reported as high as 30% in 18 ECGs administered during a study conducted by the Western Society of Pediatric Cardiology.[33] Perhaps the high rate of false-positives can be attributed to a lack of standardized screening protocol. And, too, there is a need for more physicians with experience and training in sports medicine or sports cardiology who can read the ECGs and perform a more cardiovascular focused physical examination. Recent findings in the states that do offer pre-participation physical examinations estimate that 35% allow non-physician examiners with inadequate training in cardiovascular evaluation to perform these examinations.[30]

However, by utilizing the New 2010 electrocardiography criteria from the European Society of Cardiology (ESC), false-positive incidence rates in pre-participation screenings are being reduced. Corrado et al[31] used the new ESC criteria on 1,005 athletes, which increased the specificity rate of the ECG screenings by 70%. In another study, Weiner et al. utilized the new ESC criteria on athletic subjects previously screened by traditional methods. They found the false positive incident rate was reduced from 83 of 508 (16.3%) to 49 of 508 (9.6%) while still maintaining sensitivity level.[31] What is indeed heartening is that medical and scientific investigations are taking place worldwide to reduce false-positive results without loss of the sensitivity level.

And in the 4-year study that took place in the UK, led by Dr. Harshil Dhutia and Professor Sanjay Sharma, both cost and false positives were addressed in their screening research. Near 5,000 athletes were screened, using as their base the 1) The 2010 European Society of Cardiology (ESC), 2) the Seattle Criteria developed in 2012 to increase the specificity of prescreening athletes, and 3) the refined ECG CRY-teria. Results showed that false positives were reduced from 21.8% to 4.3%.[28]

Grassroots organizations are also working toward solutions to diminish the rate of false positives such as twenty-year veteran screening advocate, Sharon Bates, who founded the Anthony Bates Foundation (ABF) in honour of her Son, Anthony when he died of undiagnosed hypertrophic cardiomyopathy. Dr. Marti Coombs created an online course that all ABF volunteers are required to take when they work at ECG stations. Through the ABF ECG Certification Training Course, volunteers were able to improve their electrode placement and reduce the artifacts on ECG tracings by 25%.[32] Sharon said in a recent article that she authored and which appears in the Journal of American College of Cardiology. "We hope to remove the 'roadblock' in the medical community as it relates to "false positives" in screenings."[32]

Another more known screening that has come to light with a substantial increase in false-positive rates is mammography screenings and overdiagnosis of breast cancer. Utilizing data from US healthcare insurance companies, the estimated cost of overdiagnosis from false-positive mammograms was an annual cost to the country of 4 billion dollars.[34]

Here is a case in point, just like in SCDY, it is known that preventive screenings can detect potentially lethal disease and save lives. The issue becomes not to discontinue preventive screenings because there are 'too many false positives' but to refine and change the criteria to make it more cost-effective for mass populations while losing none of its sensitivity, just as they are doing for mammography screenings. That is precisely what the scientific communities are working on in SCDY.

3) Sudden Cardiac Death- similar mortality rate to Suicides/Drug Abuse

First off, it is such a disheartening fact that in our country, according to a 2013 study, the second leading cause of death in 15-24-year-olds is suicide (4,878). The number one leading cause of mortality in this age group is unintentional deaths (auto accidents-16,191). The number three cause is homicide (4,329.) It is only when it comes to the 4th and

5th causes of death in this age group, do we approach real disease-cancer and heart disease, respectively.

I had approached a physician recently to participate in one of our screenings, and he posed the same statistics to me – only as many teens die from Sudden Cardiac Death as suicides/ substance abuse. I think he might have added lightning, what do you tell these people? Why should your cause be funded over theirs? I remember merely answering; all these causes are important and deserve funding-because they are and do.

After I lost Chad to SCD, I understand more the meaning of the following wise adage and have expanded upon it, "If it takes a village to raise a child, it also takes a village to save a child." To the doctor's query, I think I also added: "But at least in SCD, we have a concrete preventive screening methodology– the Echocardiogram and ECG." Unfortunately, there is no simple invasive or noninvasive test we can apply to these non-disease causes that are equally deadly. However, at least we know for these causes there are hundreds of people in many different disciplines working on preventive and treatment solutions in both the governmental and private sectors, and funding is allotted for most of them.

In our small, grass-roots organization, substance-abuse and accidents due to alcohol consumption are important issues because they were important in Chad's Life, and he tried to impart the values of anti-substance abuse while he was here. Our programs, *"The Chad Safe-driving Campaign: Save Lives – Don't text/drink and Drive"* and *"The Gift of Art,"* show the damaging effects substance abuse can have on yourself and your family. Through the vehicle of live theatre, they carry on Chad's legacy of anti-substance abuse. Every single cause that endangers our children's lives needs to be addressed, including our own, "Sudden Cardiac Death in the Young."

And in that vein, let's take a look at the funding our country apportions annually to these priority causes of Substance Abuse and Suicide which have similar death rates to Sudden Cardiac Death:

Funding for Comparable Death Rates:
Anti-substance Abuse, Suicide

According to NIDA, the National Institute on Drug Abuse, the costs society must bear due to the multitude of effects from drug abuse regarding health, lost production, and crime fall-out can exceed 600 billion dollars annually.[35] For FY 2017, the President's Budget for NIDA is $1,050.550 million.[36] Figures released from the National Center for Health Statistics show a continued rise of teen deaths due to a drug overdose- 19% from 2014 to 2015, up from 3.1 deaths per 100,000 teens to 3.7 per 100,000. And what is our country spending annually on Substance Abuse programs? According to the 2017 NIH (National Institute of Health) categorical spending report, $1 billion, 304 million was budgeted for Substance Abuse. An additional $46 million was allotted for Substance Abuse Prevention and $28 million for Screening and Brief Intervention for Substance Abuse, for a total of $1 billion, 378 million dollars. In September 2019, President Trump announced 1.8 billion dollars to combat the opioid crisis. Here it seems we are making inroads in funding for this massive societal problem causing death in our children.

How about suicide in our teens, the second leading cause of death in our 15-24-year-olds? What type of funding is allotted for this devastating cause? In the category of suicide, it shows the 2017 NIH has apportioned 42 million dollars plus an additional $26 million for suicide prevention for a total of 72 million dollars annually. It's a start to such a far-reaching, complex problem that intersects with so many layers of society, and perhaps it's a different kind of a 'heart problem' we face as a society.

And what about the Sudden Cardiac Death in Youth category in the NIH funding table, what is its annual budget? Remember, SCDY is seen as a rare occurrence – compared with a similar amount of deaths that occur annually from suicide or substance abuse. There is no category listed in the NIH table for Sudden Cardiac Death in Youth or Young Athletes. Therefore there are 0 dollars allotted for this silent killer of 3,000 to 6,000 young people annually, aged 15-24 or more if you count those who died while not engaged in sports. Twelve-year-old Kyle Morell succumbed while he was walking home; his brother Mitchell died a short time later. Or what about those who died in their sleep like, Emilie Puricelli, 22-years-old, and Patrick Ulias, the 27-year-old musician/athlete from Western, MA, or 18-year-old Jonathan Gray while exercising at home on his rowing machine, or 14-year-old James Cenney who was running with his family. They all died from unknown heart anomalies they never knew they had but could have been detected with a preventive screening test.

For those 6,000 lives that could be saved annually through early detection, there needs to be, and I project will be a category in the NIH for Sudden Cardiac Death in Youth/Athletes in the near future. No doubt, it also took many years for the baby counterpart SIDS to fight its way to funding, and now SIDS (Sudden Infant Death Syndrome) receives 23 million dollars annually.[37] "In 2015, there were about 3,700 sudden unexpected infant deaths (SUID) in the United States. These deaths occur among infants less than 1-year-old and have no immediately obvious cause."

This is the same number of young people said to have died from Sudden Cardiac Death in the 15-34 yr. age group annually. Let's be clear that it doesn't mean we take SIDS funding and apply it to SCDY. But continued research is also needed to prevent further SCDs in the 15-34 year age range. Perhaps funding research could be allocated on how to refine and standardize the Incidence Reports of Sudden Cardiac Death in this age group, making it national and making it mandatory to report it to the national register. Also, funding a study which includes youth in this age-range, who were not only participating in sports when their SCD occurred, but were doing other things: sleeping, walking, exercising at home, out for a run, at a sleepover, or having a meal. (On the other hand, we are grateful to see $43 million in the NIH funding apportioned for another urgent issue that concerns us- the 21st-century dilemma of Underage Drinking – Prevention & Treatment (NIAAA Only).

Although Sudden Cardiac Death in the young, SCDY may not yet appear on the funding budget for the NIH, I am hopeful that it is only a matter of time. For in 2013, The National Institutes of Health and the Centers for Disease Control and Prevention and National Institute of Neurological Disorders and Stroke (NINDS) partnered to create the "Sudden Death in the Young Registry."[38] It has begun to research sudden deaths due to heart disease and epilepsy and thus set future priorities for future funding. "This registry will collect comprehensive, population-based information on sudden unexpected death in youths up to age 24 in the United States. It is a critical first step toward figuring out how to prevent these tragedies best," said Jonathan Kaltman, M.D., Chief of the Heart Development and Structural Diseases Branch within the Division of Cardiovascular Sciences at the NIH's National Heart, Lung, and Blood Institute (NHLBI). "The sudden death of a child is tragic, and the impact on families and society is incalculable."

I would also like to see a study done to see if there were any common denominators that SCD youths experienced shortly before their first and final onset. Did they have a cold or fever? Did they have asthma? (Chad had asthma as a child and teen and took Prednisone. We found a prescription of this in his desk. I had even called his childhood pediatrician to discuss.) Were they taking any over the counter meds, such as aspirin, pain relievers, cold or cough meds? Were there any performance-enhancing agents (like ephedra) or red bull or caffeine used? How about steroid use, or asthma meds, or inhalers? Was there any unusual fatigue, headaches, chest pain, fainting, or blackouts? Nightmares? Further research is the only key we have to help us unlock the silence of this deadly disease. Before we try to assemble all the pieces, let's take a look at one last screening tool that's also up for debate.

One more controversy: Echocardiograms (Echos)
vs. utilizing just ECGS

The Chad Foundation has utilized the Echocardiogram (Echo) methodology since day 1 of its 20-years of preventive heart screenings for youth. This heart test uses ultrasound waves to produce images in real-time –think of a Mom having an ultrasound showing her baby. It is considered the gold-standard of detecting structural abnormalities of the heart, such as HCM, hypertrophic cardiomyopathy, the number one killer of Sudden Cardiac Death in Young Athletes. (Note: For all of its screenings the past ten years, CHAD has also incorporated the Electrocardiogram (ECG) as well as the Echocardiogram (Echo). The ECG detects electrical abnormalities, such as Wolff-Parkinson-White syndrome and Long QT syndrome, other potentially deadly heart diseases that we have identified in our screenings.)

As we have heard much on both sides regarding the use of an EKG in pre-participatory sports screenings, let us see what studies have to say about the Echocardiogram. In a study published in 2013, a total of 2,688 professional athletes or those participating in competitive sports were screened using family and medical history, exercise testing, Electrocardiography, and Echocardiography. Although 92.5% of the echocardiographic screenings tested normal, there were 203 (7.5%) showing changes, the most frequent being left ventricular hypertrophy, which was seen in 50 athletes. There were two that had HCM hypertrophic cardiomyopathy; changes demonstrated by the ECG did not meet criteria. The study concluded that although a small percentage of some cardiac structural changes can miss detection by physical or ECG testing, the Echocardiogram screening, especially in the initial phase of pre-participatory sports screening, can enhance the screening process in helping to prevent Sudden Cardiac Death.[39]

Children's Hospital of Philadelphia did a study that showed that pre-participatory testing utilizing an ECG screening was three times more likely to find potential SCD abnormalities than using the PH-physical exam and history, with a reported specificity of 93% and a false-positive rate of 7.8.[40] Their study, which also included the Echocardiogram, found that testing methodology had a specificity of 100%.[40]

Researchers at Johns Hopkins Hospital performed a study that took place at Morgan State University in Maryland, which The Chad Foundation for Athletes and Artists was also there supporting. The

Hopkins research team performed screenings on 134-star athletes from Maryland high schools utilizing an ECG to detect electrical anomalies and the Echocardiogram to detect HCM and heart valve abnormalities. A blood pressure test was also administered. Results found irregularities in 36 out of the 134 high school athletes; high blood pressure and elevated blood pressure were found in 29 and 19, respectively, requiring follow-up. Two athletes were found with serious and asymptomatic problems – one may require a heart transplant from an unknown existing issue, and the other had undiagnosed heart valve disease. Dr. Theodore Abraham, Director of the Heart Hype program at Hopkins, said when screening young athletes for heart defects it, "has to be comprehensive. An EKG does show you a lot, but it doesn't tell you the whole story. The advantage of a comprehensive screening is that it is holistic, rather than being pinpoint."[41] Researchers of the Heart Hype program say an EKG testing alone may miss heart defects in young athletes. Screening should be combined with an Echocardiogram, and it also impressed the importance for athletes to report symptoms of fainting, shortness of breath, or chest pain with activity.

The last study we'll look at using the Echocardiogram is "The ESCAPE protocol -The Early Screening for Cardiac Abnormalities with Pre-participation Echocardiography." ESCAPE was developed by Northeastern University and uses a portable Echo for screening and a frontline physician/sports med physician (PEFP) to view specific structures of the heart and take particular measurements, rather than a cardiologist.[42] Their study showed that the ESCAPE protocol could be done in a shorter time-frame than by using the AHA List, PE, and ECG, and it also decreased the cardiology referrals by 33%.[30] This led some experts to see this model, using a trained primary physician and a portable echo, as a cost-effective solution to using a full Echocardiogram performed by a cardiologist. (Note: The Chad Foundation, with the recommendation of its Board of Advisors, has always chosen to have a cardiologist present to read the screenings in real-time: 1) The cardiologist can also detect other heart abnormalities, (as well as HCM) that may be of significance now or in the future. 2) If a potentially dangerous problem is found, the parent of the child can consult with the doctor in real-time, and 3) A board-certified cardiologist is there to sign the athlete's Result Form, documenting what is normal or abnormal, and can recommend additional testing based on their initial findings. The CHAD Result Form also acts as a physician referral if further evaluation is required.)

Secondary Reasons for Cardiovascular Screenings in the Young

The primary reason for screenings in the young is to prevent Sudden Cardiac Death by detecting lethal anomalies early. However, there is also a significant secondary reason and, that is the early detection of cardiovascular risk factors in young people such as obesity, high cholesterol, diabetes, and high blood pressure along with unknown heart anomalies. Early testing can prevent premature heart disease 10 or 15 years down the road. Early intervention can thus help stave off triple bypasses, heart attacks, and chronic debilitating conditions like hypertension, diabetes, and high cholesterol. Then managed care, such as dietary change, exercise, or medications, if prescribed, can prevent major cardiovascular episodes or disease in the future.

Today, one in three kids born in 2000 will develop diabetes; about 176,500 people under age 20 have diabetes. It is said the indirect costs from diabetes today, such as disability, loss of employment, even death is 69 billion dollars. A recent study of 249 teenagers found that 80 percent had an unhealthy buildup of cholesterol on artery walls, often attributed to eating high-fat foods. Current statistics show that 30% of kids in the United States are obese, foreshadowing increased heart attacks and diabetes as these children reach adulthood.

These alarming statistics are the impetus for expanding CHAD Screenings to include Diabetes and Cholesterol Screenings. Dr. Alan Lewis of Children's Hospital Los Angeles Heart Institute, who has performed echocardiographic screenings for Chad the past 20 years, concurs on the need for expanding screenings that also include

Electrocardiograms, BMI, and a lipid profile. He cites a report in JAMA that found 75% of hypertensive children were undiagnosed and estimated millions of children were at risk. He also notes that the inherited disease of familial hypercholesterolemia is 1:500 in the population and is a significant risk factor in premature coronary heart disease. Dr. Lewis said, "Expanded screenings as proposed by The Chad Foundation can have a significant impact on finding important cardiovascular risk factors that are currently under-detected in otherwise healthy children." Dr. Theodore Abraham of Hopkins' "Heart Hype" program said of his screening findings, "We've found maybe 30%, so several hundred kids who have conditions which needed attention, like obesity, high blood pressure which, if intervened upon at this early age could save them from heart disease and kidney disease."

Also, in earlier times, when a young person died suddenly, the cause was often attributed to having a heart attack. However, a study conducted by our U.S. military of deaths in recruits aged 18 to 35, shows 28% had coronary atherosclerosis, 33% had anomalies of the coronary artery which they were born with, 20% had inflammation of the heart muscle, and 13% had structural abnormalities of the heart muscle.[43] So in this younger, seemingly healthy population, lethal problems are lying in wait, in wait for preventive screenings that could detect them.

Dr. Francesco Fedele, a professor in the cardiovascular department at Sapienza University of Rome and president of the Italian Federation of Cardiology, states another reason for the importance of preventive heart screenings – that is, saving other family members' lives as well as the affected member. Dr. Fedele said during the American College of Cardiology Scientific Session, "The benefit of screening goes beyond the identification of the student's risk of [sudden cardiac death] because it often triggers the evaluation of first-degree relatives who may also be at risk from inherited cardiac diseases. Cardiac screening with ECG has the potential of saving additional lives."[44]

(The Morrell family has lost five members of their family to HCM, hypertrophic cardiomyopathy. Tyler and Holly Morrell have ICD's because of genetic testing, which may save their lives. Mackenzie Gray credits his brother, Jonathan, with saving his life. 'Jonno' was home from college, completing an hour-long rowing workout on an ergometer when he experienced severe and deadly arrhythmia. But because of Jonno's sudden death, his 22-year old brother Mackenzie was screened. A second Echocardiogram revealed an Atrial Septal Defect, responsible for the enlargement in his heart. As a 7-time marathoner, Mac was stunned to learn that he had a nickel-sized hole in his heart without any symptoms. He underwent open-heart surgery to close the hole and will be able to return to running without the fear of a stroke, right ventricular failure, or death caused by the defect. He is a survivor because of cardiac screening.)

Putting it all together…

Complex, indeed, but Sudden Cardiac Death in Young Athletes is not a new phenomenon. In the year 490 B.C., the famed Greek soldier/messenger, Pheidippides, less than 20 years old, is said to have run the "first" Olympic marathon. However, after reaching Athens and proclaiming his important news of the Greek victory over the Persians, he immediately collapsed and died. And there is A. E. Houseman's elegiac poem, *To an Athlete Dying Young*, written in 1896 about townsmen paying tribute to a young champion athlete whom they hoist high on his funeral day just as they did the day he won their town the race. It is the solution that is new –that being "Heart Screenings for the Young Athletes to prevent Sudden Cardiac Death." Too bad we couldn't have known what to do sooner. But that is Life: awareness/observation of a problem, technological advances in science/medicine, pioneers that forage new paths against the established criteria, trials, more trials, proof, and refinement. – It is a continuous process and journey, but we have finally thrown off the covers of darkness to a disease that has been silently killing our youth for centuries.

We have learned from the "To Screen" or "...Not to Screen" studies cited earlier that the pre-participatory issue of screening athletes is a controversial one. And it probably will be so for a long time to come - as more reviews come to light, the screening mechanism continues to be refined, more countries and athletic organizations enter the field, and the critical factor of incidence rates become systemized and mandated by states to help the ongoing research. And, also we search for universal questions that specifically relate to cardiovascular issues which can be incorporated into prescreening questionnaires for all school-aged children. The creation of a shared repository is also needed, where screening organizations using standardized protocols can deposit and document their results for scientific research.

We have found some studies that did not endorse prescreening; however, their research often showed more SCDY victims than anticipated. Some stated the need for a more standardized way of documenting incidences of Sudden Cardiac Death and mandating reporting in the U.S. Sudden Death in the Young Registry before they could make a more accurate evaluation. Some researchers felt SCDY athletes who succumbed while at rest, or exercising, or in their sleep should be documented as well; one study also suggested including Survivors of SCA (Sudden Cardiac Arrest) in the incidence reports.

We have seen that the studies that support pre-screenings, which show using the Electrocardiogram (ECG 12-lead) with PE (physical exam) and history have far better results than just using the PE and history as the American Heart Association recommends with their 14 element checklist. Many researchers feel that although the answers to the AHA questions may raise a red flag, it is not sufficient enough to prevent SCD as 80% of the cases of SCDY are asymptomatic, and Sudden Cardiac Death is the 1st and only sign. In the question of using advanced screenings, many physicians feel the inclusion of the Echocardiogram gives more comprehensive testing and has a high specificity level, especially in detecting HCM, hypertrophic cardiomyopathy, the number 1 silent killer of athletes.

We also learned that a high rate of false positives is one of the significant obstacles those on the "...Not to Screen" side of the aisle have voiced due to some of the research in the field. However, studies utilizing the new 2010 electrocardiography criteria from the European Society of Cardiology (ESC) show false positive incidence rates in pre-participation screenings are being reduced.[45,46] Corrado et al. used the new ESC criteria on 1,005 athletes, which increased the specificity rate of the ECG screenings by 70%. In another study, Weiner et al. utilized the new ESC criteria on athletic subjects previously screened by traditional methods and found the false positive incident rate was reduced from 83 of 508 (16.3%) to 49 of 508 (9.6%) while still maintaining sensitivity level.[31]

The second obstacle to mass screening for athletes was Cost. One study put the cost factor annually from $2.5 to 3.5 billion dollars; it would save 4,831 lives at the cost of $51–$69 billion for a 20 year period.[24] (Figures say the US spends 40 billion dollars annually for the prevention and treatment of drug problems.) At this calculation, screenings to prevent Sudden Cardiac Death seem to be a comparatively low-cost burden for the country.)

And with studies using the refined criteria rate applied to ECGS to lower the false-positive rates, the cost figure is only getting lower. Utilizing the Seattle and refined criteria reduced the number of positive ECGs from 21.8 to 6.0% and the cost from $92 and $87 per athlete screened. Another study said ECGs could detect up to 94% of most significant heart conditions, it is non-invasive and considered cost-effective when compared to other tests such as Pap smears, mammography, and Prostate-Specific Antigen (PSA).[28,30] We found as a comparative, the cost of overdiagnosis from false-positive mammograms was an annual cost to the country of 4 billion dollars.[34]

Lastly, we saw that "Sudden Cardiac Death in Young Athletes" is often depicted in some studies as a cause of death that has a low mortality rate in the 15-24 years old– a similar number of deaths as those who die from Suicide and Substance Abuse in the same age group.[19] However, when we look at the NIH table for the various diseases and health issues that the government funds annually, we find there are categories for Suicide and Substance Abuse funding as well as their prevention. But, there is no category for Sudden Cardiac

Death in Young Athletes. There is a category for SIDS Sudden Infant Death Syndrome. But what about the 3-6,000 young people that die annually from undetected Sudden Cardiac Death in the young and early adult years?

"To Screen or ...Not to Screen - that is the question." I always remember one of the most important things I learned at university, and that is something I was privileged to hear from Barry Commoner, considered by many to be the father of modern-day ecology. As he wrapped up one of his lectures, which I was wholeheartedly buying– not seeing any holes whatsoever, he said, "But don't take my word for it, go out and investigate for yourself. Find out everything you can about both sides; then you can make an informed decision."

Last looks...

Statistics, science-based evidence is essential in evaluating this decision. But when we wrap a body, a mind, and a soul around each one of those numbers, it becomes something entirely different. It becomes a Human Being... not a commodity, a house, a stock, a theory, a business transaction, a forecast, a profit margin – but a Life. And that begs the real question - What is the value of a Life? What will we do to keep it living? If you look at your children- at any age, for most parents, the answer is instantaneous, "Anything." Listen to the beat of your child's heart. –That's not sappy -that's real. It is the most significant, astounding sound there is. That heartbeat will inform how you will spend the next 25+ years of your life working for, investing in, even where you plant your house and your career.

When I look at the lifespan of my own small foundation, I am still in awe of why so many physicians, technicians, manufacturers, volunteers give a better part of their Saturday to work assiduously screening 50 to 200 kids when they work all week, often very long hours. But when a physician says to me, as many have, "If we save one Life, it's worth it all," he answers the question for all of us.

315

I remember watching one physician enter the gymnasium of one of our recent Staten Island screenings, and he was so amazed at all the stations—just like a real clinic, he said. Another doctor felt exhilarated as he had wanted to screen athletes for a long time. Later in the day, as this doctor left the Echocardiogram station having just read an athlete's Echo, he took out his phone, read the message, and pumped his hand in the air. His daughter had just won a sports competition. He told me proudly about it and, without missing a beat, said, "I screen all my children," and went back to his happy text. A heart doctor and Father who had a daughter who was an athlete, and you can be darn sure he cared about her heart and every athlete's heart, he was screening that day.

Life is instinctive. We hear stories about strangers saving stranger's lives every day. A child, a miner falls down a hole, the entire community gets involved. A multi-million dollar machine may be required from 2 states away to save those lives. It somehow appears and as quickly as possible. Someone falls into the water, another human being goes in after him, not thinking he is also a father, a husband, a son. It is instinctive, hard-wired in our DNA, not only to survive ourselves but …make sure another human being does the same. We, who do this work, are just doing what the Walsh's and Amber's Mother did before us: – This can/should never happen to another child, and we will take whatever steps to make sure it doesn't happen again. These children become all our children. Life must be protected, whatever the cost.

When we hear about the 8-year old that succumbed from undetected heart disease, our hearts drop to our feet – why couldn't have we gotten there to screen him? Yet it makes us work harder to raise that awareness, change laws, and find more funding. There are so many things we don't have control over. This is but a simple preventive, non-invasive test that would cost us $82, the cost of *half* a pair of athletic shoes, and could save your child's Life. And I wish you could see the number of relieved children, parents, coaches, and school staff I witness following these screenings. They now know at least they have taken a step to give their child the best chance at not becoming a tragic statistic of a child that falls on the ground and never gets up again.

The Cost of High School Sports Participation

It is important to underscore the beneficial effects of sports and exercise. Physical activity is an essential component in the prevention and treatment of chronic diseases such as diabetes, heart and pulmonary diseases, hypertension, obesity, and osteoporosis. So it is vital to promote a physically active lifestyle and not scare people away from becoming and staying physically active.

Sports have become a significant part of our lives all over the world. A family in the U.S. spends $400-671 a year on average for their child to participate in sports.[47] At an $82 cost for a heart screening, that's $6.83 that could go into the heart kitty every month to ensure their child not only has the best equipment but the best heart. We must keep in mind that that figure will only decrease with advances in technology. There are already portable hand-held EKGs, and with appropriate expertise could be quicker and more efficient.

Sports are a massive enterprise. "Data from 231 NCAA Division I universities show a whopping 9.15 billion dollars generated in 2015."[48] It is laudable that many of the studies on prescreening are using NCAA athletes and that their at-risk health concerns are being assessed.

The economic loss of 6,000 young lives from Sudden Cardiac Death

What is the annual economic loss of 6,000 young lives lost from Sudden Cardiac Death per year? Let's say 6,000 people worked 50 years each, 300,000 people-years, at $65,000 annual salary $19,500,000,000: total loss $19.5 billion dollars. *There might even be some Steve Jobs or future presidents amongst* them and their heirs, but regardless they would each be giving their unique contributions that enrich and perpetuate our country.

Statistics show that participating in sports can have a positive impact, which can manifest valuable contributions to our society. According to the Women's Sport's Foundation, girls participating in sports are 92% less likely to get involved with drugs, 80% less likely to get pregnant, and three times more likely to graduate than non-athletes.[49] 95% of Fortune 500 executives participated in high school athletics. 96% of dropouts in 14 school districts in seven regions of the nation were not participating in an athletic program.[50] Through sports, young athletes learn skills such as teamwork, cooperation, self-esteem, and team spirit, which can build guideposts for life.

Where do other Nations and Organizations stand on Mandatory Screening?

Some nations and major organizations are not waiting for more statistics…more deaths and have already made their stand on the issue of pre-participatory screening for athletes. The U.S. does not require compulsory heart screenings for its athletes. And the AHA (American Heart Association) and the AMA (American Medical Association) do not support mandatory heart screenings for all high-school and college-age athletes. In their guidelines, the Personal and Family History, PE (physical examination), and AHA 14 question guidelines are sufficient to prevent SCD. However, nations such as Italy, Israel, and Japan already have mandated heart screening programs in place.

Israel enacted the National Sport Law, which mandates Electrocardiographic screening and exercise stress testing of all athletes, and Japan has implemented a nation-wide school-based heart screening system, which includes ECG screening. In Japan, Sudden Cardiac Death under school supervision has decreased since the school-based heart screening began. Known abnormalities that may cause SCD, such as CHD, HCM, Kawasaki disease, WPW syndrome,

Long QT syndrome, and Brugada-like ECG patterns have been detected through their program. The school-based heart screening in Japan has demonstrated its usefulness for identifying high-risk subjects among both athletes and non-athletes. All 1st, 7th, and 10th graders undergo heart screenings. Japan's program started in 1994, and the program's cost-effectiveness is considered appropriate.[51]

The Japan mandatory school-based program includes populations from different age groups. Their program found, like many other countries' studies, that the sensitivity and specificity of the screening system need improvement. Like many organizations, including the American Red Cross and the American Heart Association, they believe that the Automated External Defibrillator (AED) can be a life-saving tool in Preventing Sudden Cardiac Death in children. Also, the creation of a nation-wide electronic ECG database to assess cardiac safety is in Japan's future for their school screening program.[51]

In the U.S., bills mandating ECG screenings are in the process of being passed in various states, including Illinois, South Carolina, Texas, and Washington. Students in Texas who are currently required to get a physical exam before participating in the University Interscholastic League (UIL) will find the electrocardiogram ECG mandated as well in their freshman and junior years if the legislation passes. Wayne Smith, R-Baytown, brought the bill to the floor, which also made provision for families with financial difficulties or religious abstentions, and the cost for testing was a very nominal fee of $15 more for each student. "If we can save one kid's life, it is worth it," Smith said.

The Texas House Bill 76 is named "Cody's Law" in remembrance of 18-year-old Cody Stephens, who died from Sudden Cardiac Arrest while training for football in May 2012 at Tarleton State University. After nearly seven years and possibly 40 trips to Austin, Cody's Father, Scott, saw HB 76 (named after Cody's player's number) signed into law on the 14th of June 2019. Now, Texas students have the option of including the ECG as part of their physical exam.[52] Cody's Father, Scott, through his Son's foundation, Go Big or Go

Home, and Who we Play For provide EKG testing for young athletes across the state of Texas.

A staunch supporter of the bill is the family of 16-year-old Zachary Schrah, who died suddenly in 2009 when he collapsed at practice. The Living for Zachary Foundation has provided, 3,000 screenings in which 4 percent were found to have causes relating to SCD.[53]

What say the major Sports Organizations of the World?

In 2006, the U.S.'s very own NBA National Basketball Association became the first of our professional sports leagues to mandate cardiovascular prescreening for their players. The screening process includes a PE physical exam, family and personal history, blood workup, and three heart screening tests: an Electrocardiogram, a resting Echocardiogram, and a Stress Echocardiogram. "The standardized and systematic strategy that the N.B.A. is instituting is very reasonable and important," said Dr. Barry J. Maron, who served on a four-person panel that helped the league devise the program. "They should be given substantial credit for this initiative."[54]

Of the big 4 U.S. sports organizations, the NBA is the only one who has established standardized heart screenings, which also includes the Echocardiogram. Other majors, the National Hockey League, and Major League Baseball do not currently have heart screening programs. The National Football League consists of an EKG as part of its annual sports physical but does not require an Echocardiogram screening unless they feel their results warrant one. When I approached Adam Silver, the Commissioner of the National Basketball Association, and asked him why his national sports organization of all the majors in the U.S. had chosen to provide mandatory heart screenings for their players, I am happy to share his answer which CHAD is privileged to grace the back cover of his book. I know there are two stellar basketball athletes, Reggie Lewis and Hank Gathers, who are also cheering the NBA for their decision.

"Player health is one of the most important issues to the NBA, and Cardiac screening is a critical part of our player health program. We've worked to create the best cardiac screening program in professional sports, and we've used that program to support research that will improve doctors' understanding of cardiac conditions in athletes. The NBA is proud to be working with NBA players, team physicians, and leading cardiology researchers to reduce sudden death in athletes and welcome efforts from others in the community on this important issue."

Sincerely,

Adam (Silver)
Commissioner, National Basketball Association

Internationally, FIFA (Fédération Internationale de Football Association) and the IOC (International Olympic Committee) have adopted prescreening programmes to prevent Sudden Cardiac Death in their sportsmen. Spurred on by the tragic death of 28-year-old Marc-Vivien Foe who died of SCD while playing at a FIFA Cup match on 26 June 2003, the PCMA or pre-competition medical assessment was created which also included both the Electrocardiogram (EKG) and Echocardiogram (ECHO.) The PCMA was administered to all 32 teams participating in the FIFA World Cup in Germany in 2006. In 2007, it was added to the FIFA Women's World Cup with 100% player compliance and now is mandatory for all of its competitions.[55] (Of note: Chad was providing "Free Echocardiogram Screenings" for Players of 16 countries participating in the *"1st Homeless Streetsoccer World Cup in Graz, Austria"* just ten days after Marc-Vivien Foe's sudden death. It was found in the autopsy that the Cameroonian player died from HCM, hypertrophic cardiomyopathy, the abnormally enlarged heart muscle that is the leading silent killer of SCD in athletes. Players at this World Cup of the disenfranchised were still in shock at the recent tragedy and were especially anxious to receive the testing. For this moment in time, these athletes were part of the 'athletic family,' and their concern was more for their heart than the fact that many would return to their country without having a home.)

FIFA continued to grow its preventive heart program as once again, it was impacted by the sudden cardiac arrest of another player in 2012. This time it was Fabrice Muamba, a midfielder of the Bolton Wanderers who collapsed on the pitch. According to FIFA's Chief Medical Officer and Chairman of the FIFA Medical and Research Centre, Professor Jiri Dvorak, the world football's governing body will be studying cardiac arrest cases in football players to learn what causes sudden collapses like Muamba's. "We have been working on prevention since the Marc-Vivien Foe case in 2003 when we re-assessed the situation. It was the wake-up call that we needed to deal with this situation and do everything to mitigate the risk factor. We have invited all national team doctors to establish a worldwide database for cases of sudden cardiac arrest. This will lead to an analysis of the risk factors."[56]

And lastly, how does the Mother of All Athletic Competitions, "The Olympics," weigh in on the issue of Cardiac Testing for the elite athletes of the world? What they have to say is especially significant due to the sheer amount of athletes' hearts that participate in this global competition. In Beijing Olympics alone, 10,500 elite athletes gleaned from 204 countries competed to be the best of the best.

Here are some of the salient points drawn from The International Olympic Committee (IOC) Consensus Statement[57] on periodic health evaluation of elite athletes that focus on cardiovascular issues: A primary concern of the (IOC) is to 'protect the health of the athlete'; hence the need for PPE, preparticipation examinations or PHE, periodic health evaluations. Specifically, in the area of the CV cardiovascular and the current data available on SCD Sudden Cardiac Death, the document makes the case that the PHEs are most necessary as prescreening can detect medical conditions that may 'place an athlete at risk for safe participation,' such as HCM hypertrophic cardiomyopathy, or AVC arrhythmogenic right ventricular cardiomyopathy. In most athletes that die from SCD, the heart condition presents as silent and asymptomatic, leaving the PHE the best way to identify lethal anomalies early to effect strategy, which can prevent SCD and the progression of the disease. "Changes in lifestyle, appropriate medication, cessation of sports if necessary, implantable cardioverter defibrillators ICDs, are all therapies that can be utilized with early intervention and detection, which also gives the athlete a long-term, favourable outcome."[57]

The inclusion of the 12-lead Electrocardiogram by the IOC is based on scientific evidence that it increases the detection of unknown heart disease and reduces SCDs and is used for preventive strategy. It has been endorsed by "The Lausanne Recommendations" and the European Society of Cardiology (ESC), although not supported by the American Heart Association.

The document also recommends that questions that deal with cardiovascular risk factors be included in the Family History portion of the PHE, such as: Have any relatives died before the age of 50 of (sudden/unexpected) deaths due to heart disease? Is there a history of cardiomyopathies, Marfan syndrome, Long QT syndromes? And in the Personal History section, has there been an incidence of fainting (syncope), shortness of breath, or irregular heartbeat?

The IOC Consensus also recommended that 'sport organizations, together with scientific sport societies, should encourage and support educational activities intended to enhance the knowledge and skill of physicians involved in the cardiology part of the PHE process.'[57] Also, it answered a point that is often of concern when it comes to prescreening athletes, and that is the possibility of having to disqualify an athlete from playing due to the results of his or her screening. According to the IOC's position, "The main goal should be to reduce the number of unnecessary disqualifications and to adapt (rather than restrict) sports activity in relation to the specific cardiovascular risk."

Given this concern that can be both life-saving and life-changing, what would be the response of a player who had to endure and accept this restriction of ceasing his athletic career? Here's what Bolton Wanderers' player, Fabrice Muamba, who collapsed on the pitch in 2012 from sudden cardiac arrest had to say. "I'll watch something on TV, and it comes into my memory. I wish things could have been different, but it's something I can't control. I'm just more grateful and thankful that I have my life. Would you prefer to be dead forever, or not play football?" he asks.[56] After he announced his retirement from football, he made plans to wed his fiancé, Shauna. Today they live happily with their two sons in Wilmslow, Cheshire in the UK.[56]

The single thread that seems to tie all these entities together is the profound concern not only for the health of the athlete but for his/her very Life. What is the value of a Life? One Life. Countries, states, major sport, and health organizations all over the world have made their decisions to prescreen their athletes. Some such as Japan, even screen their school-age children. Buttressed now by decades of scientific research and bent on learning and creating best-practices in the field, they too go forward to find and implement ways to safeguard hearts and save lives.

Dr. Francesco Fedele, MD, is a professor in the department of cardiovascular disease at Sapienza University of Rome and president of the Italian Federation of Cardiologists. He was one of the experts at a screening debate that took place at the American College of Cardiology Scientific Session and said it best, "The purpose of screening is to save lives and not save money."[45]

Dr. Fedele also supports not only screening the athletes but also non-athletes. "Many children, adolescents, and young adults participate in various levels of conditioning programs," Fedele said. "More than 25 million children and adolescents who do not participate in school-related sports teams, but participate in various physical activities, will be overlooked if ECG screening is limited to athletes."[45]

Step by step we will get there together, to that state of mandatory heart screenings for our children led by committed supporters of screening in the medical, sports, scientific communities, and countries of the world that are leading the way. We prepare in every way we can to hand off our children to the future – theirs and the world. They are our greatest Gift and gravest responsibility; and, the heart? It is their preeminent gift because it is the Keeper of Life.

CHAPTER 28

"Heed the Warnings – Chain of Survival, AEDS, CPR"

Heed the Doctors who have knowledge and experience with Sudden Cardiac Arrest in Young Athletes! Dr. Michael Silka from Children's Hospital Los Angeles Heart Institute who oversees the "Annual CHAD Screening" program in Los Angeles, California, told us on camera why heart screenings are essential:

> **"The main thing we worry about is people who pass out from exertion.** That's why we always warn people who have passed out while you are exercising; they need to be evaluated by a cardiologist. Sadly, sometimes, the first symptom that someone may have is the only symptom, like Chad.
>
> What happens is the heart muscle has a subtle but very serious abnormality, and the right combination of circumstances causes the heart to start beating very irregularly and not pump blood effectively. After about 3 minutes of the heart, not beating effectively, vital organs are affected and no longer compatible with survival. There's not a long warning time or a lot of response time, so our efforts are to try to raise peoples' awareness to do some screening efforts. Our test for screening is an ultrasound which bounces soundwaves off the heart back to the receiver. It allows us to reconstruct a very accurate image of the heart and allows us to know if the heart muscle is weakened; if there are any abnormalities of the heart valves, and at times, if there are any problems with the coronary arteries. So it is a very comprehensive cardiac exam. It takes a little time

and expertise to do this; also, it takes special technicians who have special knowledge, trained to do this."

Warning Signs

Please pay close attention to the following Warning Signs. These are listed in the "Chad Foundation Pre-Screening Questionnaire":

- Become dizzy or passed out during exercise? Develop chest pain, shortness of breath, or wheezing?
- Become tired more quickly than peers during exercise?
- Have you been told that he/she has a heart murmur or heart disease?
- Have you been told that he/she has skipped heartbeats or racing heartbeats?
- Has anyone in the family developed heart disease or died from heart disease (Sudden death or cardiomyopathy) under the age of 40?
- Do you get any discomfort in your chest when you are active?
- Compared to others in your age group, do you feel tired when exercising?
- Have you been told you have high blood pressure?
- Chest pain or pressure: When? (__walking, __resting, __ exercising/sports, __ anytime)
- Palpitations: When? (__walking, __resting, __exercising/ sports, __anytime)
- Shortness of Breath: When? (__walking, __resting, __ exercising/sports, __anytime)
- Ankles/Leg Swelling: When? (__walking, __resting, __ exercising/sports, __anytime)
- Unusual Fatigue: When? (__walking, __resting, __exercising/ sports, __anytime)

- Light-headed/dizzy: When? (__walking, __resting, __ exercising/sports, __anytime)
- Girls: Fainting during the menstrual cycle or anytime____
- Boys: Fainting/blackouts anytime ____

Risk Factors

- Overweight for height/age? _____
- Drinking alcohol? How much? _____
- Smoking cigarettes? How many? _____
- Is there any family history (direct blood relatives) with a history of cardiomyopathy, Marfan's Syndrome, WPW, LQS or sudden death under 40 years of age?
- Taking drugs? What? How often? Performance-enhancing agents (e.g., ephedra, steroids)?
- Family history of high cholesterol?
- Family history of diabetes?
- Family history of hypertension?
- Family history of a "heart attack" or "Sudden Cardiac Death" at age less than 40 years? _____

According to the American Heart Association and the American Stroke Association, there are approximately 424,000 cardiac arrests that occur outside of a hospital setting in the U.S., and on average, just 5.2% of victims survive.[59] The American Heart Association has deemed the "Chain of Survival," a global guideline for the response to Sudden Cardiac Arrest (SCA). It is comprised of 5 steps, and the first responder's quick action may save a life.

Chain of Survival

1. **Early Access:** Call 9-1-1 or EMS Immediately[60]
2. **Early CPR: (Cardiopulmonary Resuscitation)** Provide **CPR** to help maintain blood flow to the brain and body until the next step.[60]
3. **Early Defibrillation: Defibrillation** is the only way to restart a heart in sudden cardiac arrest.[60] The device is known as a defibrillator and is used to deliver a shock. Electricity moves through the chest via paddles or adhesive electrodes.
4. **Early Advanced Care:** After successful defibrillation, an emergency team provides advanced cardiac care on-scene, such as intravenous medications. This care continues during transport to the hospital.[60]
5. **Advanced life support and post-cardiac arrest care**[60]

AEDs

An AED, short for an Automatic External Defibrillator, is a portable medical device that is user-friendly and can analyze the heart's rhythm during a cardiac arrest. It administers an electrical shock if necessary to stop the arrhythmia and restore normal heart rhythm.

It is essential to have an AED readily available, maintained, and updated with appropriately trained staff at the ready because, according to the Red Cross, 424,000 will suffer a cardiac arrest annually.[59] Every minute a person in cardiac arrest goes without successful intervention from the AED defibrillation device, their chances for survival decrease: 7 percent per minute in the first 3 minutes, and 10 percent per minute beyond 3 minutes.[61] Irreversible brain/tissue damage and death can also occur after this critical 3 to 5 minute period, which makes these life-saving tools crucial. The SCA death total annually is more than for breast cancer, lung cancer, and HIV/AIDs combined. Survival increased to 9% for patients who received bystander CPR, 24% for those who had an AED applied before EMS personnel arrived, and 38% for those who received an AED shock before EMS arrival.[62]

The National Safety Council says AEDs could save 40,000 Lives,[63] and we read every day how this medical device has saved lives. Yet, only 17 out of the 50 states require that some schools install AEDs as of February 2016.[80] All 50 U.S. states do have some regulations mandating AED access in place by 2001, such as public spaces, and AED access has been prescribed in federal buildings since 2002.[64] "Without an AED, the chances of surviving and leaving the hospital as a child are only 7 to 10 percent," Sherrid told Reuters Health. "So, these kids tend not to make it." But with a shockable rhythm, "your chances go up to 60 to 70 percent"[65] However, a study was done by Dr. Mark Sherrid et al. and revealed, "Nearly 35 million public elementary and secondary students attend school in U.S. states where there is no legislative requirement for a school AED," Sherrid said. And the states not requiring AEDS in their schools placed "a higher legislative priority" for AED placement in government buildings, "health clubs, gambling facilities, racetracks, and jails."[65] "If they've made the point of legislating to have AEDs in gambling facilities and race tracks, it would seem timely to move public access of defibrillation into schools as well," Sherrid said.[65]

Interestingly, an 18-year study that took place in Sports and Fitness Centers revealed that nine out of ten Cardiac Arrest victims survived in those facilities that had AEDs on the premises. Penela, one of the study's researchers, stated: "Our results clearly show that the presence of an AED saves lives. Out of 15 patients who suffered a cardiac arrest in centers with an AED, 14 survived and had no neurological damage (93%). That compares to just one survivor without neurological damage out of 11 cardiac arrests in centers without an AED (9%)."[66]

Daniela Aschieri, MD, chief of Progetto Vita, added: "We also found the quicker the AED was used, the greater the chance of survival. Additionally, the probability of survival was higher when a member of the public used the AED rather than waiting for medical assistance."[81,67] It was concluded that "Onsite AEDs provide an excellent neurologically intact survival rate for exercise-related cardiac arrest. An AED is a safe tool, even when used by an untrained citizen. In light of our results, we recommend that AEDs be acquired by amateur sports and fitness centers. Educational programs should be conducted to increase awareness about the issue of sudden death and provide basic knowledge about AED use."[67] "In cardiac arrest, every minute counts," said Dr. Robert W. Neumar, M.D., Ph.D., a professor and chair of the Department of Emergency Medicine for the University of Michigan Health Systems.[74] "If you consider the time it takes for a medical responder to arrive versus a co-worker or bystander, it can mean the difference between life and death."[74] He also reminded people not to be afraid of them. They are user-friendly so that bystanders with no training can use them efficiently when they come upon an emergency. "The defibrillator automatically measures the heart rhythm and only advises a shock when it recognizes the abnormal rhythm it was designed to treat."[83]

However, it is in the area of schools that parent advocates, many who have also lost children to Sudden Cardiac Death, have made their voices heard to change legislation and mandate AED in schools. Below, I share with you the story of 13-year old David Deuel, who died of Sudden Cardiac Arrest while playing basketball. His mom, Kathy, reached out to me in the early days of our cause when the land was still barren of knowledge on Sudden Cardiac Death in Young Athletes, and there were few people to talk to. Kathy was one of the first to advocate for the importance of AEDS, and she had the David Deuel Bill passed into law in Nevada – a Good Samaritan law that would relieve the trained user of fear of liability when using the defibrillator device to try and save a life. David's picture and story always travel with us from heart screening to heart screening. It's like the young honour guard that reminds every young athlete who reads their stories to take the opportunity that had not been available to them.

David Deuel
7/13/85- 2/6/99

"For where your treasure is, there will your heart be also."

It was like any other Saturday afternoon, maybe even better for David. His buddies came early, knocking at his window. They rode bikes, played Nintendo 64, and I saw David smiling with his friends as he shot hoops.

We always looked forward to Saturday afternoons as we all piled in the car to watch David play basketball. But within two minutes into the game, our perfect lives turned to blackness as we helplessly watched as David suffered a cardiac arrest on the gym floor. If a defibrillator had been on the scene, David could have survived, and with treatment, he could have lived a long life.

I would like to share David's short autobiography written for a church youth group and others' words about him.

I was born on July 13, 1985, in Las Vegas. I started playing sports when I was seven. I played youth soccer for three years. I started playing youth basketball when I was eight. I started playing little league baseball when I was eight. My teams finished first or second all but one year in both baseball and basketball. I played youth football for the first time last year. I was the tight end. My football team finished second.

My favorite teams are all the teams from Detroit - The Lions, the Red Wings, Pistons, & the Tigers. My favorite sport is basketball. Saturday, I scored twenty points in three ten minute quarters. My second favorite sport is baseball- my Dad coached my team three times. I have played six seasons of basketball and five seasons of baseball. My favorite college team is the UNLV Rebels. I went to their game on Saturday. They were playing Air Force.

David's Grandpa, who was terminally ill at the time: "Dear Lord, what happened on that Saturday my grandson passed away?" "Many hearts were full of rage. How could my grandson leave at such a tender age?" (Their graves are now next to each other).

David's Grandma's letter of encouragement to David before his departure: "I am happy to have such a good grandson. I think you are a "winner," and so does Grandpa. Always remember the song you love, "We are the Champions," because it is what you will always be. Whether you win or lose if Jesus is for you who can be against you? You will always keep on fighting till the end. And you'll always be a "champion."

Coach Rick Hughes: "I could write pages upon pages of what a tremendous young man David was, but I think all I will say is that I have never been associated with anyone with higher integrity, morals, or a more courageous heart."

Janet - His Sunday school teacher: "When I suffered from M. S. and would have to use a cane, he would hurry to get the door to open it for me. During class, he was the first with an answer, and he could read better than I do. He was definitely wise beyond his years. I know of no other thirteen year old who touched so many lives with his goodness than David did."

Randy Fultz (our friend): He was the only person I know that memorized John Chapter 3 of the Bible, and he was only six. I remember the first basketball game Desi and I went to, and David was the hero for sure making three, 3-point shots and several 2-pointers winning the game in the last seconds, beating the first-place team to take the lead.

Mom:

The David Deuel Bill has passed here, in Nevada, enabling automated external defibrillators at public facilities without fear of liability to the trained user. Sudden cardiac death is called the "silent epidemic," and much more needs to be done to save lives. We are heartbroken, and we miss our David every moment. His enthusiasm for sports and life was contagious. Through Jesus Christ, we know we will be with him again. In the interim, we are suffering, missing him.

"We love you, David." Thank You for a glimpse of Heaven.

Parent advocates continue the crusade to mandate this life-saving device in schools. The Gregory W. Moyer Defibrillator Fund was created by Greg's parents, John and Rachel, when their 16-year-old son Greg died from Sudden Cardiac Death just minutes after he left the basketball court. Greg's organization also includes a 10 step program incorporating sound principles and best practices for creating a successful AED program. 'It is not enough to have an AED in a locked sports closet without a plan of action; it requires just that, a cohesive plan of action, and staff who have been trained appropriately in the operation of the AED and can implement it.'

On the 4th of June 2019, the Pennsylvania Senate gave final approval to Bill 115, which would help save lives 'by strengthening academic guidelines in schools for CPR training in grades nine through 12, while adding hands-only CPR instruction to Pennsylvania's education curriculum.' Senator Scavello, who co-sponsored the bill, gave a shout out to John and Rachel Moyers. "I want to also recognize the efforts of local constituents Rachel and John Moyer for their tireless work in advocating for this bill and for AEDs in every school. Through their foundation, the Greg W. Moyer Fund, they continue to honor the life of their son, who tragically passed while playing basketball during a sporting event at his school. They have worked ever since to ensure schools, businesses, and community organizations have defibrillators accessible to save lives when every moment counts. This legislation is a top priority of the American Heart Association and the American Stroke Association."[69]

And in 2006, the Helgeson Family dug in their heels, and the state of Maryland enacted "Andrew's Law," which placed AEDs in Maryland high schools and at all school-sponsored sports events.

Their son, Andrew Helgeson, was but 18 when he died suddenly from Sudden Cardiac Arrest, just days before his high school graduation. He was an all-star lacrosse player who hailed from Silver Spring, MD. (Jennifer Helgeson shares her story of her beloved brother in Chapter 24 – "Brothers and Sisters.")

On the 7th of May 2002, Governor George Pataki implemented Louis' Law requiring all public schools in New York State to be equipped with AEDs in their buildings as well as sporting events.[16] New York agencies are required to have AEDs in public buildings. The bill honours Louis J Acompora, who died on March 25, 2000, at the age of 14 yrs. old. Louis was playing goalie on the freshman lacrosse team at Northport High School and went to make a routine save. The ball hit him in the chest, and Louis died of commotio cordis, a lethal disruption of the heart's rhythm.

However, young Louis' legacy lives on through his foundation. Grandparent, John Ronan, was watching his grandson perform at Longwood High School in NY, went into Sudden Cardiac Arrest (SCA), and collapsed. "We are very proud of the fast actions demonstrated by bystanders Kevin, Marie, and of course, by Kayla. The availability of AEDs at schools and John's life saved is proof that having these devices readily available can make a difference in the lives of students, staff, and attendees of school-related events. Louis's legacy will live on in the many lives that have and will be saved in New York State as a result of AEDs in schools," said Karen Acompora, Founder of The Louis J. Acompora Memorial Foundation (and Louis Acompora's Mother).[85]

Mother, Rhonda Harrill, fought hard for a decade to get her AED bill passed honouring her 13-year-old son Tanner. Tanner died in 2009 from cardiac arrhythmia after collapsing during basketball practice. In 2019, her perseverance paid off: "mandatory placement of at least one automated external defibrillator device in every Tennessee public school. The state House of Representatives finally made it happen with the sponsorship and guidance of state Rep. Bob Ramsey, R-Maryville."[86] Because of an undaunted Mom, 1800 schools will have this lifesaving equipment.

Dr. Fernando Di Paolo reported at a FIFA Medical conference in Zurich that both prevention and response are crucial. "Above all, we asked ourselves how we could best fight against young athletes dying like this," he said. "We identified two main approaches: prevention through PCMA, and reaction when it happens by an effective emergency response, including defibrillation." A quick and effective reaction in the wake of a cardiac arrest is paramount when it wasn't prevented in the first place, but the survival rate still remains terribly low at just 16 to 17 per cent.[68]

CPR

According to the American Heart Association, about 92,000 in the U.S. are saved by the CPR technique. However, only 32% of Sudden Cardiac Arrests receive CPR due to the lack of training in the lay population. Some schools across the country are mandating CPR certification as a requirement for graduation. One big brother, Jeffrey Hall, saved his younger brother Skylar who was drowning in the backyard pool. Trained in CPR, he put it into action and saved a life, his baby brother Skylar's. He hails from a small city in Tennessee, called Cookesville, which stipulates CPR certification as a requirement for graduation.

CPR, Cardiopulmonary Resuscitation, is an emergency, life-saving technique used to restore blood flow and oxygen to vital organs until the AED and Emergency Response team arrive for advanced care. CPR technique is simple to learn. Today, the American Heart Association (AHA) places emphasis on using the "Hands-Only CPR" on adults who suddenly collapse, rather than integrating chest compressions with clearing air passages and alternating with mouth-to-mouth rescue breaths. Bystanders can save a life wherever they may be. Drowning victims may still benefit from the traditional breath rescue/chest compression technique.[70]

When the person is not responsive, or breathing is when to immediately begin chest compressions with the appropriate CPR hands-on procedure, which starts a flow of blood into vital organs. This technique is done continuously while the AED is being located and brought to the victim in a 3 minute response time.[71] Survival increased to 9% for patients who received bystander CPR, 24% for those who had an AED applied before EMS personnel arrived, and 38% for those who received an AED shock before EMS arrival.[72]

The American Heart Association offers both CPR/AED training in a classroom setting or online. At many of the "Chad Preventive Heart Screenings," nurses or health practitioners will offer hands-on CPR demonstrations to students and parents as they await their screenings. At a recent screening event, Steve Tannenbaum, a Cardiac Arrest Survivor, believes in giving back. He came to demonstrate the CPR technique and how an AED works to the student-athletes of Port Richmond High School in Staten Island, NY. It was gratifying to see both parent and child on the floor practicing this life-saving technique on the individual dummies.

Students as early as the sixth grade have been certified in CPR/AED training. Sixth-grade students who attended Blanchard Memorial School in Boxborough MA were trained by the local Boxborough Fire Department. Officials felt the students were mature enough to learn the technique utilizing the designated dummies and learning the proper placement of the hands and fingers. One rationale for training younger students is that high school seniors who have acquired the training will be leaving, while these students have six years on campus to possibly save a life – a win-win for the school, the family and the community.[73]

What steps can parents, educators, coaches, communities take?

First, **awareness**: be aware of what Sudden Cardiac Arrest is and that it can occur at any time or to any age. SCA occurs when the heart has a severe abnormality, which can suddenly and without warning or symptoms cause the heart to start beating very irregularly and not pump blood effectively. After several minutes of vital organs not receiving critical blood supply, life is no longer sustainable. A Heart Attack occurs when there is a blockage to a heart valve, which prevents blood flow to the heart. If that part of the heart does not receive nourishment, it will begin to die; the longer the non-intervention, the more serious the consequences.[74,75] Unlike the Sudden Cardiac Arrest victims who may be asymptomatic, heart attack victims may experience intense pain immediately or for hours and days.

Parents invite your local health organizations, such as the fire department or EMS, to give a talk on Sudden Cardiac Arrest and the importance of AED/CPR training in schools, which can then save a Life anywhere, anytime. Director of Athletics/Coaches, Educators can do the same. Invite a parent heart advocate in your area to come and speak to your school, your coaches, your teachers. Many parent advocates who have lost their own child or relative to SCD know the warning signs, how vital preventive screenings are, and the reactive responses of AED/CPR, which are included in the AHA's 5 step "Chain of Survival." At PTA meetings, have a special meeting to discuss SCD, preventive and response measures, and how to disseminate this vital information to all parents. Let your children get involved. It may save their own life or the life of a family member.

Share that awareness of Sudden Cardiac Death, its warning signs, and preventive measures with anyone you know or meet. It's like a small pebble, which has a life-saving ripple effect. Take my friend who knows all about Chad and his Foundation. She went to the movies with a young friend in her late 20's. The young woman indicated she had been having chest pains. My friend told her not to wait and told her all about Chad and what we do. The woman made an appointment with a cardiologist and, within two weeks, was having surgery to repair a hole in her heart (which she was unaware of.) And for another example, remember the young military friend aforementioned that accompanied his friend to one of the *"Annual Chad Volleyball Tourney and Heart Screenings"* in Hermosa Beach, CA. He took advantage of the free Echocardiogram and EKG screening that Saturday and brought the Chad Result Form to his medical people at the base. The serviceman was in the hospital that Tuesday having surgery for a mitral valve prolapse problem, which he also never knew he had.

I live in New York City. I carry my Chad business cards with me. Many Lyft, Uber, and Taxi drivers have my card. They want the 'awareness' – they have one of the most stressful, demanding occupations, and they, in turn, share awareness with friends, family, and colleagues.

Have the "Chain of Survival" poster up in schools, offices, and your homes. Make sure everyone knows what it is and that understanding those five steps can save a Life. Teach them to your children and family members.

Second, **education**: Have an openness to finding out about heart health for all ages, including diet and exercise, preventive heart screenings, and CPR/AED Life-saving response tools. Make this a family heart affair. Initiate a "Heart Healthy Campaign" in your child's school or camp. Invite local cardiologists and or first responders to speak about Sudden Cardiac Arrest, Preventive Screenings, and the importance and implementation of response measures, CPR/AED. Have hands-on demonstrations that parents and students can participate in. Invite Nutritionists to recommend Heart-Healthy Diets. Initiate "Heart Healthy Fairs" in your school that begins the awareness by taking basic steps, such as height/weight and blood pressure readings, that can show premature cardiovascular risk factors. According to a 2017 NCHS data brief, the prevalence of obesity was 18.5%, and affected about 13.7 million children and adolescents; 20.6% among 12- to 19-year-olds.[76] And by age 7, more than 50% of those diagnosed with *hypertension* find the cause is due to obesity; this rises to 85-95% by the teenage years. Early intervention is critical to identify and prevent other serious problems.[77]

Third, **screening opportunities**: Firstly, do your due diligence in evaluating the ongoing debate of "To Screen or Not to Screen." Are those not advocating screenings, physicians? Cardiologists? What criteria are they using to make their case? Two newspapers used the obit section as an indicator of how many children died from SCD. These results became the basis of their conclusion that the mandated screening program in their country did not make a difference. Secondly, use the same diligence in selecting a screening organization. Do they have a history? Experience? Are they known in their community, their state? What protocols are they using? Is there a licensed, board-certified cardiologist on-site during screenings, with interest, specialty, training in sports medicine? I recommend accessing the Parent Heart Watch website listed in the next chapter, which lists heart screenings that are happening around the country. I'm sure that there may be other screening entities not on their lists, but in our 20 years of doing screenings, these are the organizations I know and rely upon for information.

If you would like to organize a heart screening in your child/ children's school or community, it is difficult.... Not impossible but not for the 'faint of heart.' Permission, liability, and waiver forms will need to be drawn up by an attorney. Enlist a cardiologist versed in sports medicine to advise your family history and screening questionnaire forms. For your event, licensed, board-certified cardiologists who are well-trained and committed to saving student's lives from SCD are necessary to read the Echocardiograms and EKGS in real-time. (These physicians are most often donating their most valuable time and service.)

Cardiac Sonographers, nurses/PAs will be needed to administer EKGs. State of the art Echocardiogram/EKG equipment that is maintained and calibrated is an obvious essential, as well as a dedicated place to host the event such as a school, college, or sporting facility. If you are planning on asking for donations, you should have applied for and received your 501 c 3 tax-exempt status (which is a daunting process in itself). Plentiful supportive volunteers are crucial to helping your screening run smoothly and efficiently. They will organize your stations, administer necessary paperwork, keep the lines flowing, and feed your medical and volunteer staff. And lastly, acquire knowledge of the best practices of running a screening by attending one. Be forewarned; this is often an uphill battle. However, if you are clearly determined, can do many jobs at once, have a supportive family and community behind you, or have lost your child or relative to SCD, you will find the perseverance, knowledge, and constitution to do it. Nothing will stop you from helping save another Child's Life.

As an alternative, I would suggest approaching your local hospital. There are now hospitals across the country who believe in the importance of preventive screenings for athletes and are offering heart screenings, such as the *"Play Smart Youth Heart Screenings,"* which take place at the Providence Heart Institute in Portland, Oregon. According to their website, this entity is the 'largest provider of cardiac services throughout Oregon' and has screened more than 22,000 hearts in the last 5-year period and identified 7% (over 1,200) young people who are needing further treatment.[78]

In the Midwest, *The Beaumont Healthy Heart Check Student Heart Screening* is located in Royal Oak, Michigan, and screens students 13 to 18 years of age. In their program, out of 16,180 kids that were tested, 1,646 required some type of follow-up (or 10.17%). Seven youths were found to have HCM, hypertrophic cardiomyopathy, the no. 1 silent killer in Sudden Cardiac Death in Young Athletes.[79] (Chad would be especially happy to hear about this heart screening program in the state where he was born.)

Lastly, parents can advocate for Public Access Defibrillation (PAD) Programs in your schools, community buildings, health clubs, and sports centers. A Public Access Defibrillation (PAD) program encourages within its state, the acquisition, and usage of more automatic external defibrillator AEDs to reduce deaths caused by sudden cardiac arrest. In NY, since this legislation was passed, "4,889 PAD programs were established, with over 156,167 people trained and 21,692 AED machines in public sites across the state. This program has been successful in saving many lives all across New York State.[84]

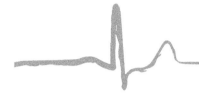

CHAPTER 29

"Resources, Testimonials, Letters of Support"

In our 20 years of heart screenings, *The Chad Foundation for Athletes and Artists* has been proud to be affiliated with so many of the excellent organizations listed below. They are ongoing sources of information, education, prevention, and inspiration in our common cause – safeguarding the Heart and Heart Health. These Guardians of the Heart have raised awareness of Sudden Cardiac Death in Adults and Youth, have protected hearts, and prevented deaths through Heart Screenings, CPR training, and AED presence. These parents and heart organizations are responsible for the preservation of thousands of Lives through prevention and awareness.

Resources for SCA, Preventive Screenings,
AED and CPR Training

-Parent Heartwatch
"Our Mission: Parent Heart Watch (PHW) is the only national voice solely dedicated to protecting youth from sudden cardiac arrest and preventable sudden cardiac death. PHW leads and empowers others by educating and advocating for change."
https://parentheartwatch.org

-American Heart Association/CPR
"World leader in CPR and Emergency Cardiovascular Care Training"
www.heart.org/en/cpr

-Red Cross
"Training + Certification, Fast, Easy Simple"
www.redcross.org/CPR-Training

-Simons Heart
"Protecting Hearts. Saving Lives." (providing heart screenings)
https://www.simonsheart.org/
https://www.screenacrossamerica.org/about-us/ (a map of screening organizations)

-Anthony Bates Foundation
"Screening Young Hearts. Saving Young Lives. https://www.anthonybates.org/

-Matthew Krug Foundation
"Protecting Children and Youth from Cardiac Arrest" (Education, AEDS, Screenings)
http://www.matthewkrugfoundation.org/

-Louis J. Acompora Memorial Foundation
"Taking Our Children Out of Harm's Way" (sports safety AEDS/Screening) https://la12.org/

-Gregory W. Moyer Defibrillator Fund
"Let the beat go on" (AED awareness and training)
gregaed.com/

-R. Andrew Helgeson Memorial Foundation
"spread awareness of sudden cardiac arrest"
www.andrewhelgeson.org/

-Sudden Cardiac Arrest Foundation
"you can SAVE A LIFE anywhere"
https://www.sca-aware.org/

-Heartfelt Cardiac Projects
"Dedicated to Saving Lives from Cardiac Arrest" (screenings) https://heartfeltscreening.org/

-Children's Cardiomyopathy Foundation
"focus on pediatric cardiomyopathy" https://dev.childrenscardiomyopathy.org/

-KEN (Kids Endangered Now) Heart Foundation
"education and prevention of Sudden Cardiac Death" (AEDs)
https://youthsportssafetyalliance.org/node/62

-Louis T. Savino, III Foundation
"AEDS Save Lives"
http://www.louissavinofoundation.org

-Travis R. Roy Sudden Cardiac Arrest Fund
"Raise awareness of Sudden Cardiac Arrest/Screenings/CPR" https://www.thetravisfund.org/

-Cody Stephens Go Big or Go Home Foundation,
(provides heart screenings)
https://www.codystephensfoundation.org/

-Quinn Driscoll Foundation
"Awareness, Education and Heart Testing" https://www.quinndriscollfoundation.org

-Eric Paredes Save A Life Foundation
(heart screenings, CPR training, providing AEDS) https://epsavealife.org/register

-Nick of Time Foundation
(SCA awareness, youth heart screenings)
https://nickoftimefoundation.org

-KEVS Foundation
(education SCA, AEDS, youth heart screening) https://www.kevsfoundation.com/index.html

-HCMA – Hypertrophic Cardiomyopathy Association
(Serving the HCM Spectrum Disorder Community Since 1996)
https://www.4hcm.org/

-Carolinas HealthCare System- Heart of a Champion Program
(sports specific heart screening)
https://atriumhealth.org/medical-services/specialty-care/heart-care/heart-of-a-champion

-PlaySmart Youth Heart Screenings
Free Youth Heart Screenings (Oregon)
https://oregon.providence.org/html/playsmart/index.html

-LIVING FOR ZACHARY HEART SCREENING, BAYLOR SCOTT & WHITE THE HEART HOSPITAL – PLANO
Screen youth ages 12-22 for heart abnormalities that may lead to sudden cardiac arrest (SCA)
https://www.bswhealth.com/locations/the-heart-hospital-plano/Pages/living-for-zachary-heart-screening.aspx
https://www.livingforzachary.org/heart-screenings/

-The Beaumont Healthy Heart Check Student Heart Screening
Free Student Heart checks (Royal Oak, Michigan)
Max and Debra Ernst Heart Center
(248) 551-4400

-The Chad Foundation for Athletes and Artists, -"The Gifts of Heart and Art" (heart screenings, premature cardiovascular risk

factors, AED placement) (The Gift of Art: books, film, theatre - reflecting the Celebration of Life - Healthy Body, Mind and Spirit," anti-substance abuse)
www.chadfoundation.org

Testimonials from Chad Heart Screenings

At the *CHAD Zuma Beach/Malibu Screening* Troy Wirth was found to have abnormalities of the heart:

-"I have been meaning to write and thank you for all the spectacular work The Chad Foundation has been doing across the country. I am especially appreciative because I am one of the lives you might have saved. Due to your echocardiogram screening at the Chad Foundation Malibu Benefit for Children's Hospital, Doctors detected an arrhythmia and advised immediate follow-up, which I did and ended up having surgery in October, with a diagnosis of Wolff-Parkinson-White Syndrome. All my life, I suffered from this undiagnosed physical challenge and played NCAA Division I volleyball at USC and never could play to my optimum. Now, I am playing sports better than ever, thanks to your fortuitous screening event. I would be honored to be a spokesperson for your cause, of which I am living proof!"

-Troy Wirth
Owner,
Orange Coast Insurance Solutions,
Irvine, CA

-"Dear Arista,

Thank you so much for your dedication honoring your beautiful son. I so admire how many children you have saved over the years. If it were not for your program, we might not have our beautiful granddaughter (Lindsay Shoaff). We have watched her grow into a thoughtful and caring person who I feel will dedicate her life helping others. She is dedicated to "The Chad Foundation," and is very proud to be a part of your organization. Thank you again for all you do to save others; my prayers are always with you."

Linda Lancaster Shoaff

Proud Grandmother of Lindsay Shoaff

-"I just graduated Magna Cum Laude from Middlebury College (Vermont) last month with a degree in Molecular Biology & Biochemistry with departmental honors. It all went very, very well. I will be starting a one-year position at UMass Amherst in September, working in a neuroscience laboratory. It's very hard to say what I plan on specializing in at this point, but Cardiology is definitely a huge interest for me. It's something I saw a lot of when I was undergoing all of the testing in high school for my enlarged left ventricle. Some type of surgery is also a major interest of mine. I am still very grateful for the work that the Chad Foundation did for me and many others. You and the Chad Foundation do incredible work.

All the best,
-Mack Hale, alumnus, Northampton High School
Northampton, MA

[Mack attended the Chad Heart Screening at Holyoke High School in Holyoke, MA and doctors found his anomaly. To give other students at his high school the benefit of heart screenings, Mack raised monies from a baseball tourney he organized to bring Chad Heart Screenings to Northampton High School, Northampton, MA.]

-Arista, I've been meaning to tell you I invited some friends to the "Chad Volleyball Benefit" last year. Another friend came with them, who was in the military. The doctors found a Mitral Valve Prolapse problem. The tourney was on a Saturday. He took the Chad Result Form with him and gave it to his doctors at the base. He was in surgery on Tuesday.

-Mike Nelson

(long-time Chad supporter)

[CHAD is proud to have now screened three generations of the Stuart Nelson Family: Mike, his Dad and Mom, his sister, and now his nephew! And any friends and relatives are most welcome. Men and Women of the Armed Forces we are proud to serve.~]

-"I've been playing water polo since I was 11 years old, and I never had any reason to believe I wasn't healthy or was in any danger other than an injury from the game. When I was 13, my Mom took some of us to the Chad 16th Volleyball fundraiser. She assured me the heart screening they were offering wouldn't hurt. She was right, but my life has changed forever after that screening. I like to think that was the moment I had to start being responsible for my future. I was diagnosed with aortic valve regurgitation and abnormality with stenosis. My doctor encouraged me to continue playing water polo to stay healthy, and I have continued playing it during my collegiate years at Whittier. I am currently majoring in Child Development and minoring in Business Administration and will continue on through Grad school, earning my Masters and credentials in education. After this, I hope to make my childhood dream since I was four come true and become a Kindergarten teacher.

I will continue to be monitored and have been told I will require a heart valve transplant at some point in my life, but because I am armed with this knowledge and have control and awareness of my body, this may not happen until I am much older. I don't know where I would be without the knowledge I have about my heart. My dreams may never have been possible or seen by my family. I will forever be thankful to Arista for bringing the CHAD Foundation to not only me but so many other people. My support and love will always be with this special group, and I will continue to share my experience and knowledge in hopes that I can help someone understand the importance of these screenings, especially in young children and young athletes. Thank you CHAD Foundation, I have great appreciation and love for being a part of your community!

With love,"
Lindsay Shoaff

Supporters of The Chad Foundation for Athletes

-"My association with Arista and the Chad Foundation has been outstanding, their honest, no-nonsense approach to education and screening of young people in sports; promote healthy heart living and inform the public. Collective data from their screening resources may yield a further understanding of heart-related illnesses in the young and causes of sudden death. The people associated with the program are of the highest quality. For these reasons, I give my unreserved support."

-Jim Gosset,
Head Athletic Trainer
Columbia University
in the City of New York

~   ~   ~

-"Arista, your mission to raise the awareness of sudden death in young athletes is a wonderful crusade. Thank you for enlightening us and arranging for the screenings here at our school. With the equipment supplied by Agilent Technologies [now Philips] and the doctors from Children's Hospital Los

Angeles Heart Center, these screenings were made possible. You are doing a wonderful thing keeping Chad's spirit alive with your foundation. Chad's lifestyle of not using drugs or alcohol should serve as a model for many young athletes today."

-Dr. John Hyland, Principal
Dave Smith, Assistant Principal
Brad Ratcliff, Football Coach
North Hollywood High School
North Hollywood, California

~ ~ ~

"Dear Arista, On behalf of the Port Richmond High School Athletic Program and Principal Timothy Gannon, I would like to thank you for providing complimentary heart screenings on December 5, 2015, for our Varsity and Junior Varsity Football Teams. We do hope to work with The Chad Foundation again to service our track, basketball, and other teams who would greatly benefit from this heart screening. We would like to extend our sincere thanks to Heather Butts, co-founder of HEALTH for Youths, the doctors, nurses, technicians, and volunteers who were a crucial part of this event. With sincere gratitude,"

-Nancy Cena, Athletic Director
Port Richmond High School
Staten Island, New York

~ ~ ~

-"This award is presented to The Chad Foundation for Your Leadership Efforts And Your Outstanding Contribution Towards Miles KT Kirkland Thomas 1st Annual Day of Remembrance May 3, 2015." – Remember the love, the warm embrace, Remember the touch, the smiling face. Remember the person so gentle and kind, who was caring in action and mind."

-Tanza Kirkland
Mother of Miles KT Kirkland

[The Chad Heart Screenings in 2015, 2016, and 2019, held at Curtis High School in Staten Island, NY, honoured 16-year-old Miles Kirkland, who died suddenly of undiagnosed hypertrophic cardiomyopathy while at football practice.]

~   ~   ~

-"On behalf of the INSP, International Streetnewspapers, and the 26 teams of homeless athletes who participated in the "1st and 2nd Homeless Streetsoccer World Cup," we thank you and The Chad Foundation for Athletes and Artists for providing this lifesaving test for our impoverished athletes of the world. Your heart screening event has become a necessary part of the World Cup, and we look forward to The Chad Foundation's participation in forthcoming events."

Bernhard Wolf
Managing Director,
Homeless Streetsoccer World Cup
Graz, Austria

~   ~   ~

-"Hi Arista, … I feel compelled to help out with the CHAD event every year. A very good friend of mine has three children. When the oldest was about 19, he was in the back seat of his car with his Mom and Stepdad when his Mom turned around to say something to him and saw that he was turning blue. They pulled the car over into the first building parking structure they came to and pulled him out of the car onto the ground. At that very moment, the parking lot elevator doors opened, and two nurses stepped off the elevator, saw what was happening, and immediately jumped in to give my friend's son CPR and keep him alive until the paramedics arrived. He has since been given a second chance and a pacemaker. This would have been a tragedy if not for the incredibly lucky circumstances. The other two children are twin girls. When they were about ten years, the parents started noticing that one was not growing as fast as the other. Because they were not identical twins, it wasn't immediately obvious that there was anything unusual going on. But since they were twins, it eventually did become evident that they were just growing at very different rates. It turned out one of the twins had a heart condition, which then required surgery to correct. Both these instances could have turned out very; differently, these were the fortunate and blessed ones. The CHAD event reminds me that the heart screening done during this event can hopefully help others to also land in the category of the "fortunate ones." Thank you, Arista, for the good work you do."

God bless,
Martha (H.)

~   ~   ~

-"As Governor of California, I commend the efforts of The Chad Foundation to raise public awareness of health issues. Heart health is an important concern in California, and I will continue to support efforts that encourage early screening and detection to prevent Sudden Cardiac Deaths. As such, I am grateful for the support that your foundation has provided to young athletes, the homeless, and the Children's Hospital of Los Angeles."

-Governor Arnold Schwarzenegger
Governor of the State of California

~   ~   ~

-"The Division of Cardiology at Children's Hospital Los Angeles has collaborated with The Chad Foundation for the past 16 years to perform echocardiographic screening of young athletes. We in the Heart Institute are enthusiastic in our support of the endeavors of the Chad Foundation.

Alan B. Lewis, MD
Children's Hospital Los Angeles
Professor of Pediatrics

~   ~   ~

-"Cardiac screenings provide an invaluable service to young people, their families, and their communities. They detect potentially fatal heart problems that were previously invisible. They save lives. They keep families intact. They make it possible for the dreams of young people to become reality."

Be well, –
Michael
Michael Willers, MD
The Children's Heart Center of Western Massachusetts

~   ~   ~

-"As a physician, especially one who specializes in pediatric cardiology and also as a father, it has been my privilege to participate in cardiac screening events such as those sponsored by the Chad Foundation. I feel very strongly that every young athlete should receive cardiac clearance prior to participating in competitive sports. Testing is non-invasive; results can be obtained quickly, and taking these types of preventative measures can potentially save lives."

-Jared LaCorte, MD, FAAP, FACC
Staten Island Pediatric Cardiology

~   ~   ~

-"As part of Philips goal to improve the lives of 3 billion people a year by 2025, Philips supports the communities in which we live and work through corporate social responsibility programs. Programs like Save An Athlete and the CHAD Foundation for Athletes and Artists, are cornerstones of these efforts, helping to organize cardiac screening events for kids in our communities. Healthcare is moving from reactive, sick care within the hospital, to more pro-active care in the community, avoiding health issues before they start. At Philips, we understand that it takes leading healthcare technologies, combined with great people and programs at organizations like CHAD, to identify kids at risk for cardiac events, and direct them towards the right care at the right time. Together, we can help improve outcomes, lower healthcare costs, and make a meaningful impact in people's lives, one community at a time."

-Kevin Geary
Save An Athlete Leader
Philips

~   ~   ~

-"Dear Friends,

It is a pleasure to welcome everyone to the Harlem YMCA, where the Chad Foundation for Artists and Athletes is offering preventative screenings for young athletes throughout the day.

From determined distance runners to high-flying basketball stars, New York City's student-athletes show a lot of heart every time they put on their uniforms – and today, the Chad Foundation is making sure their hearts are healthy. By taking small donations in exchange for screenings that would normally be too expensive for many families to afford this organization is helping our young people look for potential risk factors and make the healthy choices that will keep them in the game.

On behalf of the City of New York, I thank all those whose generosity and dedication has made these screenings possible. I wish all of the athletes participating in these screenings the very best for an informative day, and for a healthy, happy future.

Sincerely,"

Michael R. Bloomberg
Mayor
City of New York

The Gift of Art

-"Arista, I wanted to let you know how much I enjoyed working with The Chad Players in the *Days of Wine and Roses* production in NYC off-Broadway at the Lion Theatre. I have been a performer for nearly 30 years, and the production was top-level in artistic direction, and the staff was top-notch. It was nice to see seasoned actors working with some beginners, on and off the boards, all learning from each other. There was a lot of heart in this performance because Chad was always with us too. It would be a pleasure to work with your company again, and I applaud you for your preventative heart screenings. Thank you for offering these lifesaving tests to members of the Screen Actors Guild-AFTRA. - I was a willing and fortunate recipient. We have lost so many of our members to heart-related problems.

I hope you can offer these life-saving screenings to more of our performing unions. Wishing you the very best in all your important work. Hope we can work together soon,

All the Best,
John Haggerty,
NYC Actor,
SAG-AFTRA, AEA

~ ~ ~

"At the age of 40, I remember telling my young family I wanted to move to New York City and to become an actor. In 2009, after a number of years singing, dancing, miming, clowning, and acting in a number of wonderful upstate plays, Arista offered me the part of 'John' in *All About Sneakers* - off-Broadway, no less. Now, we're heading to Broadway with another of Arista's ideas. Thank you, Arista, for keeping my dream alive."

-signed Philip M. Oberlander

~ ~ ~

-"We would like to thank the CHAD Players for bringing their wonderful production of *Days of Wine and Roses* to Atlantic City. This production helped immensely in heightening awareness of the impact substance abuse has on the family. This memorable performance resonated with both adult and adolescent viewers. The Atlantic County Commission on Abused and Missing Children/DYFS Community Advisory Board would be happy to support The Chad Foundation for Athletes and Artists and the CHAD Players for their efforts in raising community awareness so that this group can continue their mission of enlightening audiences for years to come.

-Betty Sherman
Commission/Community Advisory Board Member,
Atlantic Commission of Missing and Abused Children"

CHAPTER 30

"The Journey of the Heart Continues ...And the Beat Goes On..."

When I began to write this book, it was to be about my son Chad's journey on Earth recounted through *A Mother's Memories*, but with the turning of each page, I began to realize the three words in its title - *A Celebration of Life* - is really its central theme. It heralds the greatest Gift we are given, Life: the recognition thereof, and celebration of each intrinsic moment that comprises its voyage, and the careful and responsible safeguarding of its ultimate Keeper - the Heart. In making the most of each moment he was given, Chad taught me the meaning of Life, the sacredness of every heartbeat...which only comes once and is never repeated.

If we ponder the steps that make up the journey of our Lives and ask ourselves, what really is important? What are the most valuable things in my Life? I know many of us will answer – it is that little human being who is attached to your hand, who is looking up at you learning about Life through your eyes, your heart, your mind. Or the mate who walks along beside you experiencing the many steps of joy and angst that you make and take together, or the parents, siblings, friends who enrich your path daily. It is all the Celebration of Life. However, long or short the duration, its preciousness is marked by each beat of your heart.

We now know we can and do die of a broken heart. The evolution of science and medicine acknowledges there are chemical changes that occur when a loss occurs, so we are more open to the Guardians of Life – the preventive healers and physicians of the mind, body, and spirit to help us bridge the gap. When a parent loses a child, it is for many the most significant loss of their lives. And the loss of a parent by a child is equally traumatic and life-changing, especially if that child is young. The bond between parent and child is inexorable and eternal.

Many parents whom I have met through this odyssey have had far fewer moments than we had with Chad. I am keenly aware of that. - I wish they too could have had millions of moments more, and collectively, that's what our work is trying to do for all the other children out there. That is what we are trying to give to you and them, the millions of moments we had and those lifetimes of moments we didn't. Here is where the transcendence of *Beyond A Mother's Memories* imperceptibly occurs: You are well into your heart screening endeavours. And one day you screen 200 youths. You are absolutely ecstatic that 200 athletes will have the best chance of not becoming a tragic statistic. And for a moment you forget who brought you here, why you are here.—It had gone way beyond my own child, it was for every child here, all children everywhere.

In searching for hearts to protect, I became aware of each child's soul and humanity and knew better what I was striving to protect. There was a face, a body, a heart, and a soul standing in front of me, not a number. There was nothing sentimental about it, that's the future of our planet, and it's not a robot, so you can't replace it. It's a miraculous young human being… and guess what? It's under our care. The adage reminds me: "If it takes a village to raise a child, it takes a village to save a child."

But it was a tall young athlete with dark hair at Holyoke High School in Holyoke, Massachusetts, that crystallized the reason for doing what we do. As I sat immersed in the paperwork at the exit station of the screening, I looked up to see a bright, young athlete standing before me. His Mother had just thanked me so sincerely, and the son was now extending his hand to shake mine. "I'm sorry you lost your son," said he, and I was taken aback for a moment, unprepared for that exquisite utterance. It caused me to look directly up at him, giving him my absolute attention. And after a moment which allowed me to gather my thoughts, I said, "Young man, -this is about You, your Life. - My son is no longer here. This is his Gift to You. – You go out and lead a long, healthy, happy Life. You play your 'heart out' and make the very best of Life." He agreed with his heart as I started to see a tear well in his eye as I was holding back my own. I knew he would, I knew he would always remember our moment together as would I. Sometimes moments can inform and change a Life. It did mine. This young man's Life was the reason I was here, we all were here. –His hopes, his dreams, his happiness, his health, and his future were the most essential things in the world. The value of one Life, his Life – was the most valuable thing we have on Earth. We are the parents of the Universe. It doesn't matter that our children aren't coming home anymore. It matters that *he is* that every single one we screen will have a better chance at a long, healthy, productive Life and can make their cherished dreams reality.

These phenomenal people I have witnessed: John Walsh, Amber's Mother, Sharon Bates, Linette Derminer, Stewart Krug, Laura Friend, John and Karen Acompora, John and Rachel Moyers, and 1,000's of other parents who have lost their children. Most already have full-time jobs and families. Why do they take on another full-time job for Life?? Most of our organizations are volunteer, all the proceeds going into the programs. Why would one do that when your plate is already overflowing, especially with the demands of your own family and today's society? The number one answer may sound cliché, but it is not. It is the truth: *We do not want any family to ever lose their child and endure what we have suffered through. The loss of one's child is like no other. What is the value of a Life? Everything. There is not a price that can replace it.*

It never ends, you know, I can best explain it by summoning the image of our battle-scarred Vets again. The horrors of war and its attendant memories and losses are unforgiving, even though they may have occurred 60 to 70 years ago. But ask a Vet to tell you about it, his comrades, his eyes flood instantly with tears – it is involuntary. It is as fresh as it just happened yesterday. My good doctor friend, who lost his son in a car accident just before he was to begin college, said to me at one of Chad's screenings which he has been faithfully performing for the past 20 years, "We belong to this exclusive club that we never asked to belong to." And for those of us who have been doing these preventive screenings for the past 19 years or so, it is really our intent never to have another member again. Close up shop– when preventive heart screenings are mandatory for all athletes and school-age children. I go one step further, for <u>All of Us</u>. Many of us have learned the value of Life paradoxically as Life has been taken away from us, and that Life is not sustainable without the heart. The heart nourishes the soul of the universe. -With our moment on Earth, let us celebrate and appreciate every beat it makes and protect it as our Life because it is.

For years, I have had this reoccurring dream where Chad is piloting some grand futuristic vehicle through space (a larger version of the SST). It is moving gracefully and slowly through the vast blackness. The passengers all seem to be young, and their wide-eyed anticipation is visible as their noses press firmly against the windows. He has a copilot who sits next to him, a little older than the younger ones but who shares their exhilaration. And though it is apparent Chad is still learning how to pilot this enormous transport vehicle, there is an air of wanderlust about him and joy in his eyes for the mission he has been chosen to undertake. For wherever it is, his soul is forging new horizons on its own and pioneering lands unknown. We were honoured to be your Family on Earth for 26 years and always will be, and I was given the highest honour of all, to be your Mother.

Perhaps it is a Land where the Heart is respected as the sustainer of Life, where we have evolved as a species so that we don't kill each other, and thus the Life we are given – is truly our greatest Gift. With Chad at the controls – maybe the children are heading toward something we have not yet reached –the state of Love where the Heart reigns free. A place where the Heart is revered for what it is – the Keeper of the two greatest Gifts we possess, Love and Life.

... The journey of the heart continues. And as the beat goes on, what are the next steps in *The Chad Foundation for Athletes and Artists?* For many years I have also seen another image – the image of the *"Chad Heart Mobile"* making its way up and down both coasts and crisscrossing the nation. The fleet could be sponsored by corporations, philanthropists, athletes, artists, musicians, and families honouring their children who are SCA Victims or Survivors, – all who care deeply about 'the heart.' I have found great 'heart' in this country of ours. When I was working with our homeless population, corporations gave so much back. Their employees were encouraged to volunteer, and they did so with a genuine, caring heart. I saw a CEO sitting next to a man without a home, teaching him Excel, and a young Vice President coming in on his lunch hour whenever he was free to help these individuals update their resumes. CHAD exists because of 'the heart' of Volunteers. We could not do our work without them.

With such a heart fleet, we could expand screenings in a big way. Just think of how many hearts we could screen in a year, how many schools we could visit. At least 52 a year, we could cover with each mobile unit. They would need only one cardiologist, one cardiac sonographer, one nurse, two echocardiogram machines, two EKG stations, and a cholesterol and diabetes station. We could invite other cardiologists in the community to join us for an hour or so while the "Chad Heart Mobile" is at their local school: Effective, efficient, economical with a database of informative results to draw from regarding young hearts of this generation.

The heart pumps blood into every organ of our body, nourishing its purpose. A kernel of an idea takes birth in that strange, convoluted organ called the brain, and we manifest it like a seed that grows from the Earth into skyscrapers to flying ships that break beyond our horizons, and medicine that heals and prolongs longevity and science that creates bionic parts. It also loves and atrophies without it. We can help safeguard this vital organ for a generation of young Lives with a small fleet of Chad Heart Mobiles.

It is Chad's original mission to promote "Healthy Body, Mind, and Spirit," experience Life unceasingly and honor each of the people in it as was the namesake's way. A foundation project that has always been dear to my heart is *Chad's Place*, a homey, welcoming space where young people can go to learn about Life and express it – through books, films, video, the performing arts and athletics. A place where they could take out equipment and film Life in their own way under the auspices of talented, experienced people who can guide them. A platform where they could create The Spoken Word, Poetry, Screenplays, Theatre, and perform it on a living room size stage. Upstairs there might be a room where once a month, cardiologists and cardiac sonographers would volunteer their time to perform Echocardiograms and EKGs. And a quiet place would exist where they could watch films on the history of the world, exploring its culture, its people, and what is to-be. Downstairs they could serve healthy food and drinks that they may have created with the counsel of a nutritionist and up and coming chefs. A place where at least once a year a Volleyball Tournament, a Baseball Benefit and Dance Marathon would take place, for they brought great happiness to Chad's Life—the joy of Dance, the Love of Sport. A place where all cultures, religions, and orientations could come together for meet and greets, and they would have a comfortable setting to get to know each other. They could discover/uncover other sicknesses, deprivations of the heart, often resulting in overwhelming substance abuse and suicide in youth. Here, they could discuss the issues of substance abuse, bullying, suicide, life-meaning issues –where all of us together can listen, learn and help find keys to solutions…get to the *'the heart of the matter.'* A place where high school and college students might work at the Café after classes to serve those healthy creative drinks and snacks, they have created.

Trust me, Chad would be there too monitoring the whole program: sitting and watching their minds, laughing with them, and being the peacemaker. Like a flashlight within, he would show them the great potential each has and help them gain the confidence to fulfill their dreams and goals. Their hearts, minds, bodies, and spirits will be nourished by Art and Athletics the universal language, which we can all understand, which brings us wholly together – The Body, Heart, and Soul of the Universe.

He and his young Friends with whom he walks now look down from wherever their vantage point is. They know that through their parents and supporters who have become advocates of the Heart and thus of Life, many more children will live. By raising the awareness of Sudden Cardiac Arrest in Youth and all ages, by providing preventive heart screenings, and teaching life-saving methods and tools such as CPR and placement of AEDS, children will live and thrive.

When CHAD first started 20 some years ago, the land was bleak, and it was a solitary journey. Now when I look back, I see there is an entire flotilla of ships all dedicated to one cause –safeguarding young hearts and saving Lives. Chad is only the masthead now, joined by thousands of dedicated parents who are screening and educating and changing legislation across the nation. Science and research have taken up our cause all over the world to refine the techniques and make screening cost-effective: legislation is being passed. Countries have spoken and mandated screenings for their athletes and some even for their school-age children. At the highest level, sports organizations are supporting our cause. The health of the young heart and the importance of its Life have been heard and acted upon. For the parents and supporters, this is an ongoing crusade. There is nothing more important than the Lives of all our Children.

This book is dedicated to Life: breathing, laughing, loving, observing, enrapture, growth, enjoining the eternal spirit of youth that fuels us on making momentous moments that rally the dawn. Chad and all his young Friends who are with him capture that essence that will always be with us even though their physical presence is not. They, each one of them, have taught us the meaning of Life –each moment is a Gift to be lived to the fullest.

Thank you for letting me share my journey of the Heart with you. It is not over and, in many ways, has just begun on a new, all-encompassing level. It has been my greatest joy and gravest responsibility to borne and raise 3 children of the Earth, who will leave their individual footprints for others to ponder and follow atop those of ancestors. Each enriching and evolving the Human Race with Wisdom, Truth, Compassion, and Growth. With every beat of their Heart, they honour the supreme Gift we are given – Life. The Heart is the Keeper of those two most majestic Gifts –"Life and Love." We cannot exist long without either. Love is the Sustenance of Life and the Heart its Keeper until its last beat frees it to beat forever. "Love is eternal." [Arista 28 July 2018]

Chad's "Gift of Heart and Art" is my Son's Gift to you – to protect the Heart and nourish the Mind and Spirit. - You are in our Hearts forever.

With Love,

From my Heart to Yours,

Arista
Chad (and Curt and Collin's Mom) – the most important role in Life

CHAD Foundation's first steps were Gifts to the renowned Children's Hospital Los Angeles Heart Institute. Mrs. J. Wilson, COB, Sean Smith, founding member CHAD, Collin Butrum, Chad's brother, Susan Lapis, Dir. Dev., Dr. Alan Lewis, Dr. Pierre Wong, Head of Echocardiography, Dr. Arno Hohn, Head of Cardiology. In the years to come, these fine cardiologists would provide hundreds of Chad Heart Screenings.

L., Peggy Ritch, (Reggie Lewis's Mom, Arista, and Dr.Theodore Abraham, Director

R., Baltimore's H.S. Jr. Olympics, Morgan State U.
The Hopkins Heart Hype Program

Johns Hopkins cardiovascular staff volunteering to screen "All-Star High School Athletes" at Morgan State University, Baltimore, MD.

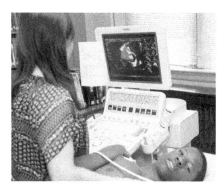
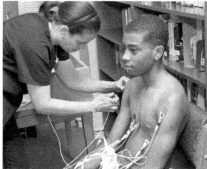

L. Top, Student receiving Echocardiogram, Rice High School, Harlem, NY. R., Top, Student receiving EKG, thanks to Doctors and Staff from Mt. Sinai Medical Center NY, led by Dr. M. Geiger and Philips.

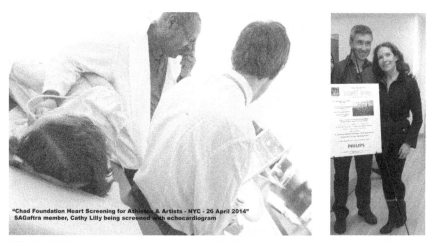

"Chad Foundation Heart Screening for Athletes & Artists - NYC - 26 April 2014" SAGaftra member, Cathy Lilly being screened with echocardiogram

"SAG-AFTRA member being screened by Teddy, ultrasound tech and NY cardiologist Dr. Francesco Rotatori in Manhattan at GEB. R., SAG-AFTRA actors, John Haggerty and Cathy Lilly, support "Chad Heart Screening for NYC Athletes and Artists."

Nurse, Gloria Mabry, provides cholesterol and diabetes testing to student at "YMCA- Harlem Chad Heart Screening." The student will then proceed for blood pressure testing, followed by an EKG, and culminating with the Echocardiogram screening.

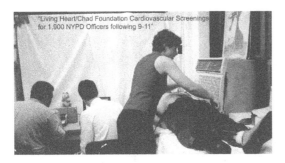
"Living Heart/Chad Foundation Cardiovascular Screenings for 1,900 NYPD Officers following 9-11"

CHAD was privileged to join Living Heart at The Police Academy in midtown to provide crucial cardio-vascular screenings. For 3 weeks, cardiologists from major hospitals in NY came to volunteer services in reading echocardiograms when their own shifts ended. We found patients that Dr. Arthur Roberts, who organized the event, sent straight to the hospital after their exams. The exposure to these pernicious chemicals and fumes would have long-term if not life-taking effects

NYPD - New York's finest -Police Academy "Livingheart/Chad Foundation Cariovascular Screenings" for 1,900 NYPD Officers following 911

R., Two of NY's Finest escort us to Ground Zero, a sacred site never to be forgotten. Here, 2,977 Citizens of the World lost their Lives while working at the World Trade Center, New York City, September 11, 2001.

THE CHAD FOUNDATION FOR ATHLETES & ARTISTS

On 30th Sept., CHAD went home to Malibu, CA, to screen the Malibu Sharks Football Team. Laura Suico, Ms. California, joined us. Doctors from Children's Hospital Los Angeles performed the echocardiogram screenings at Zuma Beach.

Athletes filling our screening questionnai...
"Chad Heart Screening, Zuma Beach, CA"

CHAD Screening Questionnaires are very important in determining family health history and contain questions that pertain to cardiovascular health in the patient to be screened. As the Result Form is signed by a physician in real-time, it acts as a referral if further testing is recommended by the screening cardiologist.

Holly McPeak

3-time U.S.
Volleyball Olympian

CHAD was honoured to have 3-time Volleyball Olympian, Holly McPeak as a co-host and "player." Holly believes in the importance of pre-screening athletes and encourages athletes to take advantage of this test when it's offered, as it could prevent a death.

R., The lifesaving CPR technique is often demonstrated at CHAD Screenings. Both students and parents learn the "Hands-on Method" which could save the life of one of their own family members. Holyoke High School, Holyoke, MA.

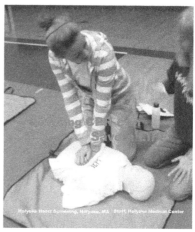

L., Jonathan "Jonno" Gray had graduated Holyoke H.S. a few months before the CHAD Heart Screening. In January, he was home from college training on his rowing ergometer and collapsed and died from an unknown heart anomaly. His brother, Mackenzie, R., credits his brother for saving his own life, as he was screened immediately after Jonno's death. A quarter size hole was found in Mack's heart which required open-heart surgery. Mack was a marathon runner. Today, he is studying to be a PA (Physician's Assistant.)

Patrick Ulias

Patrick was a runner and hiker. He was a gifted musician and Athlete and hailed from Holyoke, MA. He died at 27 years old from a sudden fatal arrhythmia. "Noble man of the earth." Pat's Family bequeathed CHAD gifts for heart screenings at his service.

Miles Kirkland was only 16 years old when he collapsed and died from HCM while at football training. Miles was a beloved friend and teammate. CHAD has honoured Miles by screening his football team at Curtis High in Staten Island for 3 years.

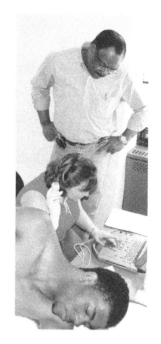

Above, Kevin Major's motto was, "No excuses, Play like a Champion." He died of undiagnosed HCM while swimming on the 11th of July 2011. He was only 19 yrs. old. Chad was honoured to co-sponsor his 1st heart screening in Westfield, MA. R., a few weeks before Dr. Robert Brown of Lincoln Hospital in NY led the CHAD screening at the Harlem YMCA, he was called to care for a H.S. football player who collapsed. He revived him but a few days later the young man succumbed to undetected HCM, the leading killer of Sudden Death in Young Athletes.

L., When a Junior, Mack Hale braved a blizzard to come to the CHAD screening at Holyoke, H.S. An anomaly was detected. So appreciative was he that he planned a baseball derby to raise funds to bring a CHAD screening to his own Northampton H.S. in western MA. Mack is now pursuing a career in science and medicine.

R., When Lindsay Shoaff was 12, she had her heart screened at the CHAD Volleyball event. She was found to have stenosis of the carotid artery. Under the watchful guidance of her cardiologist, Lindsay is now in her last year of college and will soon fulfill a child-hood dream of becoming a kindergarten teacher.

"CHAD Annual Volleyball Tourney at Hermosa
Beach CA, benefiting Chad and CHLA"

For 17 years, the Najarian Family hosted this event which raised monies for CHAD Heart Screenings and our annual gift to the Children's Hospital Los Angeles Heart Institute. Thanks to the generosity of CHLA physicians and staff, Philips and Mortara, 10 to 20% of anomalies were found in screenings, such as holes in the heart, Wolf Parkinson White Syndrome, Aortic Valve problems, and enlarged ventricles, some requiring surgeries. Above R., Co-chairs, Michael Tidik and Dave Najarian.

Dr. Alan Lewis, Hui Gao, Dr. Masato (Mike) Takahashi, Novell Castillo, and Dr. Michael Silka, Children's Hospital Los Angeles Heart Institute

Above., When this youngster was 6 months old, he was screened at the CHAD event and a hole was found in his heart requiring surgery. Now he comes with his siblings to be screened. L., Lady Raiders Basketball team await their heart screenings at Port Richmond High School, Staten Island, NY.

Dr. Lacorte reading EKG's with Wagner Nurse & CHS students
CHAD Heart Screening - Curtis High School - 5 May 2016

Dr. Jared Lacorte, pediatric cardiologist, instructs student nurses on EKG placement. Dr. Lacorte has led 5 CHAD Heart Screenings: 3 at Curtis H.S and 2 at Port Richmond H.S. in Staten Island, NY. He is a staunch supporter in preventive heart screenings for athletes.

L., Sixteen countries of athletes participated in the "1st Homeless Streetsoccer World Cup" in Graz, Austria. The CHAD Foundation, Philips, and Dr. Carlos Luna, then of CHLA, provided echocardiogram screenings to the athletes. Just weeks before, Cameroonian soccer player, Marc-Vivien Foe collapsed and died suddenly from a heart-related problem.

Below, Abteilingfur Kardiologie, LKH, Dr. Josepha Binder, of Graz, Austria is screening athletes participating in the "1st Homeless Streetsoccer World Cup."

L., The "2nd Homeless Streetsoccer World Cup," took place in Gothenburg, Sweden. There were 26 countries of athletes CHAD was able to provide echocardiogram screenings for, such as Canada, Russia, Japan, Nambia, Slovakia, the UK, Spain, the USA, South Africa, Brazil, Ireland, Scotland, and Switzerland.

R., Dr. Odd Bech Hanssen and Staff, Chief of Echocardiography Lab, Sahlgrenska University Hosp., Gothenburg, Sweden. The doctors and staff had just begun their summer holiday, but devoted an entire week to providing screenings for the disenfranchised of the world.

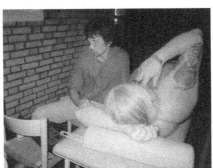

"The Gift of Art"

"Days of Wine and Roses"
Dante Hall - Atlantic City, NJ

This CHAD production of *Days of Wine and Roses* was sponsored by the "Atlantic Commission on Missing and Abused Children/ Department of Family and Youth Services" as the community event of the year to show how substance abuse can have deleterious effects on the family. Denial, alcoholism and the journey to find one's way in this maelstrom of powerful addictive forces can challenge love to its core. It resonated powerfully in teens as well as adults.

L. CHAD Players, Jon Furey and Patrick Kleeman

"All About Sneakers" - Wings Theatre, off Broadway, NYC

Above, *The CHAD Players:* Belgrave Fitzgerald Henderson, Steven Consentino, Arista, Matt Derek, Michael Durell, and Philip Oberlander. Directed by Tony Macy-Perez. *"All About Sneakers,"* is an original play and old-fashioned Love story - the discovery that loving oneself first precedes loving another. CHAD promotes multi-cultural art which includes stories about All of Us – the hopes, the dreams, the angst, the challenges of All Americans.

"The Chad Foundation Classic Concert Benefit" was held at The National Opera Center Recital Hall in NYC. Harpist, Eric Sabatino, classical pianist, Javor Bracic, and Mezzo-soprano, Caterina Secchi, collaborated in an exciting program of operatic and classical favourites, featuring the music of Saint- Saens, Bizet, Ponchielli and Tosti. The benefit supported The Chad Foundation for Athletes and Artists programs to safeguard young hearts and create Art that challenges the mind and heals the spirit.

"Chad Honour Roll of Safe Drivers"

In "Chad's Life is a Gift Safe Drivers Campaign" students /adults in 11 states and 6 countries have taken the pledge: **"Life is a Gift, don't text/drink and drive."**

They carry their Chad Key Shield in their car and belong to the *"Chad Honour Roll of Safe Drivers."*

Chad loved all people. He cared about their hopes and dreams. He never drank, smoked or did drugs, and he always did the driving when he and his friends went out clubbing and dancing. And you always had to wear your seatbelt in his car or it didn't go. "Healthy Body, Mind and Spirit."

Rose, volunteer photographer, Gia Farda, Arista, and Peter Joubert, Volunteer. *The "CHAD Dance for the Gifts of Art" at McGettigan's – NYC. Finale: (singing Chad's fave, "New York, New York" by Frank Sinatra)*

ACKNOWLEDGMENTS

I wish to thank our Creator for giving us the beauty and the joy of Chad for as many years as we were given. Every moment was a Gift embedded in our Hearts forever. In witnessing the days of my son's Life, I saw the presence of a young, old soul who was enriched by so many Lives on his voyage of Life. I thank Chad's Family and each Friend who made his short journey on this Earth so memorable. As an artist mother, I have tried to celebrate the moments and chronicle the memories that make up a Son's Life, which each of you made possible because you were such an integral part of it. The words of this book are informed by each one of you. I am especially thankful to the Mothers, Fathers, Sisters, Brothers, Friends, and Relatives, who opened their hearts and shared the precious, poignant stories of their beloved Child, Sibling, Relative, Friend who is no longer with them. Their life-long pain and determined quest to save young lives show unequivocally, the need for preventive measures we must have knowledge of and be prepared to act upon to safeguard the hearts and Lives of All our Children.

For Part II, Beyond A Mother's Memories. - "The Gift of Heart"

My gratitude to our Researchers: Erin Dunn, Joyce Oates, Gabe Krivenko, and Mary Grace Centeno, MD, Pathology Resident, all who volunteered their time and service to do research on the heart, cardiovascular risk factors, substance abuse, and texting/drinking while driving, often working simultaneously on theses, grad course work or residencies, and a shout-out to Lauren Emmett, Grantwriter, and Alexie Basil. We are forever grateful to our Chair, Michael Tidik, The Dave Najarian Family, and the loyal Supporters of *The Annual Chad Foundation Volleyball Tourney and Heart Screening Benefit for Children's Hospital Los Angeles Heart Institute and CHAD's Gifts of Heart & Art,"* in Hermosa Beach, CA which has made possible thousands of heart screenings in the Los Angeles area and across the U.S. To the following Doctors, Cardiac Sonographers, PA's, Nurses, and hospital manufacturers we extend our heartfelt gratitude for safeguarding the hearts of every child, student, and athlete of every age who received life-saving heart screenings thanks to each of you. <u>In California,</u> for their 20 years of unfailing support, our deepest gratitude goes to the *Children's Hospital Los Angeles Heart Institute*: Dr. Michael Silka, MD, Dr. Pierre Wong, MD, Dir. Echocardiography, Dr. Alan Lewis, MD, Dr. Masata (Mike) Takahashi, MD, Dr. Arno Hohn, MD, (in memoriam), their entire Staff, Residents, Fellows and Cardiac Sonographers; and Dr. David Porzio, *Hoag Hospital*, in Newport Beach, CA, and Monica Potter, RN and Debra Rivie, RN. <u>In Washington, D. C.,</u> thanks for your support Dr. Craig Sable, MD, and the *National Children's Medical System.* <u>In Baltimore, Maryland,</u> my special recognition for his support and dedication goes to Dr. Theodore Abraham, MD, Dir. of *Heart Hype, The Johns Hopkins Hospital, and Cardiovascular Staff,* who always made time to pick me up from the train station. <u>In Massachusetts,</u> express gratitude to Dr. Arthur (Archie) Roberts MD, my first partner, and his Family for their amazing support, and the exceptional support of *Holyoke Medical Center, Division of Cardiology*, and Staff, and Dr. Michael Willers, MD, *Children's Western MA Cardiovascular Ctr.,* who always came with extra backup toting his own Echocardiographic machine behind him. A big shout out to all the wonderful Nurses at *Capuano Home Care* for your care and great service and also hiring a bus from Holyoke to come and see The Chad Players perform *Welcome Home Kelly!* Off-Broadway in NY. To *Pioneer Valley Cardiology of Springfield* and *Bay Path PA Program, Hampden County Cardiology Associates of Holyoke,* we thank you for always staffing our screenings with such professionals and spirited graduates. To my dear Friends of the Heart, *Kev's Foundation,* and the *Jonno Gray Foundation,* you travel with me always. And Melanie Martin, Dir. of Athletics at *Holyoke H. S.,* you made every screening a success, and still there to pick up my Volunteer, Peter and I at the train station. In New York, my heartfelt gratitude goes to the following medical professionals for your belief and support in the importance of preventive screenings for athletes, and students: Cardiologists - Dr. Robert Brown, MD, *Lincoln Hospital,* Dr. Ben Co, MD and Staff, Dr. Stephen Duvvuri, MD and Staff, Dr. Ayman Farid, MD, *NYU Langone Health,* Dr. Miwa Geiger, MD and Staff at The *Mount Sinai Hospital Cardiovascular Division,* Dr. Jared LaCorte, MD, Dr. Francesco Rotatori, MD, and Dr. Samala Swamy, MD, and all the NY Cardiologists who read Echos at the *Living Heart-CHAD 9-11 Screening Event,* as well as, techs, Nurses volunteers and NYPD support. A debt of thanks to our N.Y. Cardiac Sonographer Technicians who worked tirelessly in assisting their physicians: George Beyzman, Tamara Underwood, Darlene Mariano, Olga, Elle W., Ginette Lamberti, Azam Bayati, Sal Modica, Natalie Concepcion, Brian Boyle, Eduardo Colon, Chris Ferlisi, Cintia Rengel, Lilian Pereira, Pakriti Smrilo, Percy Kayla, Nina Ramos, *New Jersey Institute of Ultrasound,* Dr. Sylvia Priori, MD, *Dir. Cardio Genetics Lab Cardiovascular Genetics Program at NYU. School of Medicine,* Michele Costa, RN, Gloria Mabry, RN, Johanna Martinez, RN, the *Evelyn L. Spiro School of Nursing of Wagner College,* Connie Cordero, Stacey Dayee, Stacey Momo, Latisha Carter, Jennifer Panzella Crews, Nina Ramos, Ana Puzie, Irene Treadwell, Laura Allison, *Black Nurses Rock, Community Health Center of Richmond,* partners: Dr. Bruce Paswall, DC, *GEB Solutions,* Heather Butts, *H.E.A.L.T.H. for Youths, C.H.A.S.I., Staten Island Borough President, James S. Oddo,* and Dr. Ginny Mantello. Thanks to Steve Tannebaum for teaching students and parents how to use the invaluable AED. We are forever grateful to the following Hospital Equipment Manufacturers for making it possible to screen children's hearts with state-of-the-art equipment: *Acuson, Cardiac*

Science, GE, Mortara, Philips, and *SonoSite.* In Sweden, heartfelt thanks for giving up a portion of your summer Holidays to screen 26 countries of homeless athletes, Dr. Odd Bech Hanssen, MD *Chief of Echocardiography Lab, and Staff, Sahlgrenska University Hospital Sweden.* In Austria, great thanks to Prof. Klein, am L.K.H., Dr. Josepha Binder, *Abteilung fur Kardiologie,* for working an entire week to screen 16 countries of homeless athletes participating in the *1st Homeless Streetsocce World Cup.* Exceptional thanks to Carlos Luna, MD, and his Family for traveling from Italy on vacation to Graz, Austria, to help Dr. Binder screen the disenfranchised athletes of the world. Lastly, Volunteers in Administration provide the nuts and bolts of our heart screenings and events. We are supremely grateful for your Gifts of Service: In LA, Tammy McMeekin (6 years), Martha Hammer (5 years of service), Erin McGlew, David McNamara, and Kennedy. In NY, Peter Joubert (10 years of service) Lorelei Stevens, Christine Tersero, Reethee Prakriti, Vanessa Asiamah, Tomasita Negron and Jennifer Snowdon, great Friends and Supporters, as well as in Event Planning - Gia Farda and Kirsten Joyce and Ekuko (Ekko) at the CHAD Dance.

The Gift of Art

We are proud to honour and acknowledge the following Artists, for your excellent *Gifts of Art* in theater, music, visual arts, media, performance, and production. Thanks to each of you, CHAD provided 10 Off-Broadway performances and one in Atlantic City, New Jersey, that not only entertained but often challenged the mind and became a vehicle for healing and understanding. Though we all make our home in N.Y., it is our multi-cultural heritage that we bring with us through our ancestors that enrich every performance. May your careers and hearts flourish in excellent health, longevity, and abundant success!

The Chad Players

Katy Apostolico, Muriel Borst, Nick Bosco, Louis Changchien, Tony Cheng, Sam Chan, Dina Ann Comoli, Steve Cosentino, Dan Doby, John Fukada, Ree Davis, Matt Derek, Michael Durrell, Gia Farda, Jon Furey, John Haggerty, Belgrave Fitzgerald Henderson, Robert L. Haber, Kenji, Jeff Knapp, Patrick Kleeman, Shannyn Kleeman, Evan Lai, Michael Manning, Jackson Ning, Philip Oberlander, Frank L. Parker, Kaipo Schwab, Erik Colin Smith, Lu Yu, Len Weiss

Directors: Tony Macy-Perez, (8 Chad Off-Broadway productions), Victor Maog, Annette Jolles

Production: Christine Chaya, *Asst. Graphic Design*, Ana Cortils, *Graphic Design*, Steve Cosentino, *Set Designer*, Annmarie Duggan, *Lighting Designer*, Erin Elliott, *Lighting Board Operator*, Charles Foster, *Lighting Consultant*, Charles Garbowski, *Sound Designer*, James "Reddz" Graham, *Asst. Stage Mgr./Prop Master*, Peter Joubert, *Asst., Props*, Noreen Maiolini, *Asst. Production Mgr./Makeup Artist*, Michelle Malavet, *Set Design*, Zulma Mejia, *Stylist*, Mimi O'Donell, *Costume Design*, Jung Hyun Park, *Intern*, Angela Ranieri, *Makeup Artist*, Betsy Rhodes, *Sound Design*, Betty Sherman, *Associate Producer*, Latrina Stokes, *Graphic Artist/House Manager*, James Wiggins, *Sound Technician*. (*Chad Dance NYC*- Nicholas Wood, *DJ, and Crew*.)

Graphic Artists: John Gehringer *(Designer-Chad Book Cover-, CHAD, A Celebration of Life – Beyond A Mother's Memories.)* Aree W., *NYU., (Designer Chad Dance Event poster)*, Ralph Andre *(Designer Chad logo)*. Video Editors: Stevie, Anna Chen; Gabrielle LeGendre, Lorena Marques, Michael Pryzytarski

Media Production: Jake Downey, *Field Producer*, Dave Parker, *co-producer*, Collin Butrum, *Producer*, Rik Nyburg, *Camera Operator*

Motion Graphics: Ariel Saulog; PR: Emily Owens, Barry Alexander

Music (*CHAD Classical Concert*:) Javor Bracic, *Classical Croatian pianist*; Eric Sabatino, *Classical solo harpist, U.S. Air Force*; Caterina Secchi, *Mezzo-Soprano, U.S. & Italy;* Rick Della Ratta, *Pre-show Entertainment-by Pianist, (...All About Sneakers*), James Wiggin, *Guitar Solos*

Photographers: Mark Skelly – *"Days of Wine & Roses"* performance stills in N.Y. and Atlantic City, N.J.; Kenn Vick, *Chad Harlem Y.M.C.A. Heart Screening*, Joe Connors – *Chad Life is a Gift Keychain Shield* photos and photo restoration, *CHAD, A Celebration of Life – Beyond A Mother's Memories;* Rose Cirrincione, *CHAD Dance-McGettigan's NYC*; Caryssa Ramirez, and Ed Deavers – *Chad Volleyball Benefit* – Hermosa Beach, CA; Allan Gilmore - Photography Exhibition, *Sneakers, Wings Theatre NYC,* Kaitlyn Helwig, *S.V.A.,* formatting and photo retouching, *CHAD, A Celebration of Life – Beyond A Mother's Memories,* Fred Canpolat, *Author's Photograph.*

Webmaster and Design: Opher Segev; Liza Luzod, Nate Luzod, Ralph Andre.

To all of Chad's Friends and Supporters, Carolco Pictures who gave us our 'foundation,' to each and every one of our Donors and Grantors, your Gifts and Grants are our fuel; we bestow our highest appreciation to every single one of you (and those I may have missed; my apologies, I'll catch you the next edition). You All are what makes Chad's **Gifts of Heart & Art** possible.

In Memoriam
John Gehringer
Designer Extraordinaire
(CHAD Book cover)
Thank you for
your beautiful Gift before
you went 'Home...'
R.I.P. dear
Artist/Husband
Father/Grandfather

4ᵗʰ August 2020

WORKS CITED

Chapter 4 *The Bridge Days*

1 https://www.accessgenealogy.com/vermont/biography-captain-alden-partridge.htm

Chapter 17 *Baltimore's Favourite Son, Reggie Lewis and The Johns Hopkins Hospital*

2 https://www.hopkinsmedicine.org/news/media/releases/young_athletes_need_dual_screening_tests_for_heart_defects_study_suggests, *Release Date: November 15, 2009 (Abstract #877, Room #W230ab, Orange County Convention Center, Orlando, Fla.)*

Chapter 20 *Western Massachusetts ~ A lot of 'Heart'*

3 http://kevsfoundation.com/kevins-story.html
4 National Association of School Nurses. (2016). Diabetes management in the school setting (Position Statement). Silver Spring, MD:
5 https://www.aacap.org/AACAP/Families_and_Youth/Facts_for_Families/FFF-Guide/Obesity-In-Children-And-Teens-079.aspx

Chapter 26 *"The Gift of Art" and "The Chad Safe Driving Campaign"*

6 https://www.reuters.com/article/us-cellphones-driving-idUSTRE68M53K20100923

7   Harmon KG, Drezner JA, Wilson MG, Sharma S.Incidence of sudden cardiac death in athletes: a state-of-the-art review.Br J Sports Med.2014;*48*:1185–1192. doi: 10.1136/bjsports-2014-093

8   NIH National Heart, Lung, & Blood Institute WISQARS, National Vital Statistics System, CDC.

9   The Michigan Department of Community Health (MDCH)] http://www.michigan.gov/documents/mdch/SCDYReportfinalJan09_269478_7.pdf.

10   Drezner JA, Owens DS, Prutkin JM, Salerno JC, Harmon KG, Prosise S, Clark A, Asif IM. Electrocardiographic Screening National Collegiate Athletic Association Athletes Am J Cardiol. 2016 Sep 1;118(5):754-9. doi: 10.1016/j.amjcard.2016.06.004. Epub 2016 Jun 1https://www.ncbi.nlm.nih.gov/pubmed/27496294.

11   Corrado D, Basso C, Rizzoli G, Schiavon M, Thiene G. Does sports activity enhance the risk of sudden death in adolescents and young adults? *J Am Coll Cardiol.*

12   Corrado D, Pelliccia A, Bjørnstad HH, Vanhees L, Biffi A, Borjesson M, Panhuyzen-Goedkoop N, Deligiannis A, Solberg E, Dugmore D, Mellwig KP, Assanelli D, Delise P, van-Buuren F, Anastasakis A, Heidbuchel H, Hoffmann E, Fagard R, Priori SG, Basso C, Arbustini E, Blomstrom-Lundqvist C, McKenna WJ, Thiene G. Cardiovascular preparticipation screening of young competitive athletes for prevention of sudden death: proposal for a common European protocol. Consensus statement of the Study Group of Sport Cardiology of the Working Group of Cardiac Rehabilitation and Exercise Physiology and the Working Group of Myocardial and Pericardial Diseases of the European Society of Cardiology, *Eur Heart J,* 2005, vol. 26, (pg. 516-524).

13   Corrado D, Basso C, Schiavon M, Thiene G. Screening for hypertrophic cardiomyopathy in young athletes, *New Engl J Med*, 1998, vol. 39 (pg. 364-369).

14   Domenico Corrado, Antonio Pelliccia, Hans Halvor Bjørnstad, Luc Vanhees, Alessandro Biffi, Mats Borjesson, Nicole Panhuyzen-Goedkoop, Asterios Deligiannis, Erik Solberg, Dorian Dugmore, Klaus P. Mellwig, Deodato Assanelli, Pietro Delise, Frank van-Buuren, Aris Anastasakis, Hein Heidbuchel, Ellen Hoffmann, Robert Fagard, Silvia G. Priori, Cristina Basso, Eloisa Arbustini, Carina Blomstrom-Lundqvist, William J. McKenna, Gaetano Thiene, Cardiovascular pre-participation screening of young competitive athletes for prevention of sudden death: proposal for a common European protocol: Consensus Statement of the Study Group of Sport Cardiology of the Working Group of Cardiac Rehabilitation and Exercise Physiology and

the Working Group of Myocardial and Pericardial Diseases of the European Society of Cardiology. *European Heart Journal*, Volume 26, Issue 5, March 2005, https://academic.oup.com/eurheartj/article/26/5/516/2888062

15 DomenicoCorradoMD, PhD*CristinaBassoMD, PhD†MaurizioSchiavonM D‡AntonioPellicciaMD§GaetanoThieneMD†Pre-Participation Screening of Young Competitive Athletes for Prevention of Sudden Cardiac Death, Journal of the American College of Cardiology, Volume 52, Issue 24,9 December 2008, Pages 1981-1989. https://www.sciencedirect.com/science/article/pii/ S0735109708031811.

16 Legislation - la12.orgla12.org - Louis J. Acompora https://la12.org/her-campaign-to-make-lacrosse-safer-goes-on-20-years-after-her-sons-death/

17 James A. Colbert, M.D, Polling Results. N Engl J Med 2014; 370:e16); Cardiac Screening before Participation in Sports —http://www.nejm.org/ doi/full/10.1056/NEJMclde1401118#article_citing_articles March 6, 2014, N Engl J Med 2014; 370:e16, DOI: 10.1056/NEJMclde1401118.

18 Barry J.MaronMD, Tammy S.HaasRN Caleb, J.MurphyBS, Aneesha Ahluwalia Stephanie Rutten-RamosDVM, Ph.D., Incidence and Causes of Sudden Death in U.S. College Athletes, https://www.sciencedirect.com/ science/article/pii/S0735109714010870.

19 Maron BJ[1], Doerer JJ, Haas TS, Tierney DM, Mueller FOSudden deaths in young competitive athletes: analysis of 1866 deaths in the United States, 1980-2006., 1 Hypertrophic Cardiomyopathy Center, Minneapolis Heart Institute Foundation and Abbott Northwestern Hospital, Minneapolis, Minn., USA. hcm.maron@mhif.org, https://www.ncbi.nlm.nih.gov/pubmed/19221222.

20 Rebecca M. Cunningham, M.D., Maureen A. Walton, M.P.H., Ph.D., and Patrick M. Carter, M.D, The Major Causes of Death in Children and Adolescents in the United States, N Engl J Med. 2018 Dec 20; 379(25): 2468–2475.doi: 10.1056/NEJMsr1804754.

21 Centers for Disease Control and Prevention, National Center for Injury Prevention and Control, https://www.cdc.gov/injury/wisqars/LeadingCauses. html., https://www.cdc.gov/injury/images/lccharts/leading_causes_of_ death_by_age_group_2018_1100w850h.jpg.

22 Vigneron, Peter. (2014, November 14). Inside the debate on athlete heart screenings. http://www.outsideonline.comhttps://www.outsideonline. com/1928286/inside-debate-athlete-heart-screenings.

23 American Heart Association News. (2015, May 22), Screening young athletes for heart disease. http://www.news.heart.org/ screening-young-athletes-for-heart-disease/.

24 Halkin A, Steinvil A, Rosso R, Adler A, Rozovski U, Viskin S. Preventing sudden death of athletes with electrocardiographic screening: what is the absolute benefit and how much will it cost? J Am Coll Cardiol. 2012;60(22):2271-6, https://www.ncbi.nlm.nih.gov/pubmed/23194938.

25 Azimi NA, Welch HG. The effectiveness of cost-effectiveness analysis in containing costs. J. Gen Intern Med. 1998;13:664–9.

26 Christopher Schmehil, Devika Malhotra, Dilip R. Patel. (2017, July). AME Publications. TP Translational Pediatrics. Cardiac screening to prevent sudden death in young athletes. http://www.ncbi.nlm.nih.gov/pmc/articles/PMC5532197/.

27 Teresina Vessella1, Alessandro Zorzi2,Laura Merlo1,Cinzia Pegoraro1,Flaviano Giorgiano1,Michele Trevisanato1,Mirella Viel1,Pietro Formentini1,Domenico Corrado2,Patrizio Sarto1,Author affiliations: 1.*Center for Sports Medicine and Exercise, 2. Prescription, Treviso, Italy Department of Cardiac, Thoracic and Vascular Sciences, University of Padova, Padova, Italy,* The Italian preparticipation evaluation programme: diagnostic yield, rate of disqualification and cost analysis, http://orcid.org/0000-0002-3578-0583.

28 Latest research by CRY leads to major advance in the future of heart screening for young people. *Published research funded by the charity CRY is improving the way young people are screened and leading to significant cost savings.* https://www.c-r-y.org.uk/latest-research-by-cry-leads-to-major-advance-in-the-future-of-heart-screening-for-young-people/.

29 Interpretation of Cost-Effectiveness Analyses, J Gen Intern Med. 1998 Oct; 13(10): 716–717.doi:10.1046/j.1525-1497.1998.00211.x.

30 Christopher Schmehil, Devika Malhotra, Dilip R. Patel. (2017, July). AME Publications. TP Translational Pediatrics. Cardiac screening to prevent sudden death in young athletes. http://www.ncbi.nlm.nih.gov/pmc/articles/PMC5532197/.

31 Weiner RB, Hutter AM, Wang F, Kim JH, Wood MJ, Wang TJ, Picard MH, Baggish AL., Author information[1]: 1Division of Cardiology, Massachusetts General Hospital, Boston, MA 02114, USA, Performance of the 2010 European Society of Cardiology criteria for ECG interpretation in athletes.

32 SHARON M. BATES, J A C C: CASE R E P O R T S VOL. 2, NO. 3, 2020[a] 2 0 2 0 THE AUTHOR. PU B L I S HED B Y E L S E V I E R ON B E H A L F OF THE AME R I C A N C O L L E G E OF CARDIO L O G Y FOUNDATION. THIS IS AN OPEN AC C E S S ART I C L E UNDE RT HE CC BY -NC-ND L I C ENS E (h t t p: / / c r e a t I v e c o m m o n s. o r g / l I c e n s e s / b y - n c - n d / 4.0/).

33 Hill AC[1], Miyake CY, Grady S, Dubin AMJ Pediatr.Author information[1,] 1Department of Pediatrics, Stanford University, Stanford, CA, USA. Accuracy of interpretation of preparticipation screening electrocardiograms 2011 Nov;159(5):783-8. doi: 10.1016/j.jpeds.2011.05.014. Epub 2011 Jul 14.

34 Mei-Sing Ong and Kenneth D. Mandl, National Expenditure For False-Positive Mammograms And Breast Cancer Overdiagnoses Estimated At $4

Billion A Year, HEALTH AFFAIRSVOL. 34, NO. 4: COST & QUALITY OF CANCER.

35 NIH NATIONAL INSTITUTE ON HEALTH, PrinciplesofDrugAddiction Treatment: A Research-Based Guide (Third Edition) Is drug addiction treatment worth its cost? https:// https://www.drugabuse.gov/publications/ principles-drug-addiction-treatment-research-based-guide-third-edition/ frequently-asked-questions/drug-addiction-treatment-worth-its-coste.gov/ publications/principles-drug-addictiontreatment-.

36 https://www.drugabuse.gov/about-nida/legislative-activities/budget-information/fiscal-year-2017-budget-information-congressional-justification-national-institute-drug-abuse.

37 https://www.cdc.gov/sids/data.htm,www.babywill.org/sids-information/ what-is-sids/sids-research.

38 NIH and CDC Launch Registry for Sudden Death in the Young., https://www. sca-aware.org/sca-news/nih-and-cdc-launch-registry-for-sudden-death-in-the-young; Submitted by SCAFoundation on Thu, 10/24/2013 - 2:14 pm.

39 Grazioli G, Merino B, Montserrat S, Vidal B, Azqueta M, Pare C, Sarquella-Brugada G, Yangüas X, Pi R, Til L, Escoda J, Brugada J, Sitges M.Rev Esp Cardiol (Engl Ed). 2014 Sep; 67(9):701-5. doi: 10.1016/j.rec.2013.11.023.[6].Epub 2014 Apr 13. Usefulness of echocardiography in preparticipation screening of competitive athletes.

40 Victoria L. Vetter, MD, MPH, Noreen Dugan, RN, BSN, Rong Guo, MS, Laura Mercer-Rosa, MD, Marie Gleason, MD, Meryl Cohen, MD, R. Lee Vogel, MD, and Ramesh Iyer, MD Philadelphia, PA, A pilot study of the feasibility of heart screening for sudden cardiac arrest in healthy children. https:// www.yh4l.org/wp-content/uploads/2014/06/A-pilot-study-of-the-feasibility-of-heart-screening-for-sudden-cardiac-arrest-in-healthy-children.pdf

41 John Hopkins Medicine, Young Athletes Need Dual Screening Tests For Heart Defects, Study Suggests, Using just one popular test or the other could miss serious cardiac abnormalities, Release Date: November 15, 2009*(Abstract #877, Room #W230ab, Orange County Convention Center, Orlando, Fla.)* https://www.hopkinsmedicine.org/news/media/releases/young_athletes_need_dual_screening_tests_for_heart_defects_study_suggests.

42 Kerkhof DL, Gleason CN, Basilico FC, et al. Is There a Role for Limited Echocardiography During the Preparticipation Physical Examination? PM R 2016;8:S36-44. 10.1016/j.pmrj.2016.01.004.

43 Eckart RE[1], Scoville SL, Campbell CL, Shry EA, tajduhar KC, Potter RN, Pearse LA, Virmani R., Author Information: 1 Brooke Army Medical Center, San Antonio, Texas, USA. Robert.Eckart@us.army.mil, Sudden death in young adults: a 25-year review of autopsies in military recruits.1Ann Intern Med. 2004 Dec 7;141(11):829-34, https://www.ncbi.nlm.nih.gov/ pubmed/15583223.

44 Fedele F. ECG Screening in Athletes: The Great Debate. Presented at: American College of Cardiology Scientific Session; March 17-19, 2017; Washington, D.C. https://www.healio.com/cardiology/arrhythmia-disorders/news/online/%7B3c9d7dbb-ab1b-4357-b74d-a9c89e3581ac%7D/debate-necessity-of-ecg-screenings-in-young-athletes-still-uncertain.

45 Debate: Necessity of ECG Screenings in Young Athletes Still Uncertain, https://www.sca-aware.org/sca-news/debate-necessity-of-ecg-screenings-in-young-athletes-still-uncertain, https://www.healio.com/cardiology/arrhythmia-disorders/news/online/%7B3c9d7dbb-ab1b-4357-b74d-a9c89e3581ac%7D/debate-necessity-of-ecg-screenings-in-young-athletes-still-uncertain?page=1.

46 M Brosnan - ʃ2014 - ʃJun 27, 2013 -BACKGROUND: In *2010*, the *European Society* of *Cardiology* (*ESC*) ... with the aim of improving the *specificity* of *ECG screening* in *athletes*. OBJECTIVES: First, to assess the *prevalence* of *ECG* abnormalities in a ... CONCLUSIONS: The 'Seattle *Criteria*' *reduced* the *false-positive rate* of *ECG screening*, pubmed www.ncbi.nlm.nih.gov.

47 https://onlinemasters.ohio.edu/cost-of-school-athletics-are-increasing/

48 Steve Berkowitz, Christopher Schnaars and Mark Hannan of USA TODAY; Mark Alewine, Jennifer Brugh, Rebecca Harris, Jessica Hunt, Cynthia Maldonado Perez, Luis Ulloa Rodriguez, Zhancheng Wu and Kellon Thomas of the Indiana University-Purdue University Indianapolis' Sports Capital Journalism Program. http://www.businessinsider.com/ncaa-schools-college-sports-revenue-2016-10, http://sports.usatoday.com/ncaa/finances.

49 Importance of Youth Sports: Statistics that will Scare and Inspire by Bo Hanson – 4x Olympian, Coaching Consultant & Director of Athlete Assessments. Source: Women's Sports Foundation.

50 The Benefits of an Interscholastic Athletic Program, https://www.section6.elb.org/cms/lib/NY19000854/Centricity/shared/ad_tool_kit/BenefitsofAthleticsBrochure.pdf.

51 Kaori Shinagawa, MD, PhD Pharmaceuticals and Medical Devices Agency CSRC Think Tank: Prevention of SCD in the Young February 20th, 2015, https://cardiac-safety.org/wp-content/uploads/2015/03/S2_2_-Shinagawa_Peds.pdf.

52 Elliott Lapin, Staff writer, Governor Greg Abbott signs HB 76, Cody's Law, fulfilling 7-year crusade for Crosby man, Updated 2:59 pm CDT, Monday, July 8, 2019, https://www.chron.com/neighborhood/lakehouston/news/article/Governor-Greg-Abbott-signs-HB-76-Cody-s-Law-14026608.php.

53 https://www.bswhealth.com/locations/the-heart-hospital-plano/Pages/living-for-zachary-heart-screening.aspx.

54 By HOWARD BECK -SEPT. 17, 2006, *The N.B.A. Is the First League to Begin Standardized Cardiac Screening,* https://www.nytimes.com/2006/09/17/sports/basketball/17nba.html.

55 DEVELOPMENT Dvorak discusses FIFA's role in heart monitoring, (FIFA.com)29 Mar 2012, https://www.fifa.com/who-we-are/news/ dvorak-discusses-fifa-role-heart-monitoring-1607788

56 Bringing Fabrice Muamba back from the dead, @Anna_Kessel Sun 5 Oct 2014 09.33 EDTFirst published on Sun 5 Oct 2014 04.00EDT, https://www. theguardian.com/football/2014/oct/05/bringing-fabrice-back-from-the-dead.

57 Br J Sports Med 2009;43:631-643 doi:10.1136/bjsm.2009.064394, Downloaded from http://bjsm.bmj.com/ on June 17, 2015 - Published by group.bmj.com.

58 FullerCMCost-effectiveness analysis of screening of high school athletes for risk of sudden cardiac death, Med Sci Sports Exerc2000, vol.32, (pg.887-890)10.1097/00005768-200005000-00002Med Sci Sports.

Chapter 28 *"Heed the Warnings - Be Prepared & Be Proactive"*

59 Go, AS, et al. Heart Disease and Stroke Statistics – 2014 Update: A Report From the American Heart Association. Circulation. December 18, 2013. https://www.heart.org/idc/groups/heartpublic/@wcm/@adv/documents/ downloadable/ucm_462303.pdf.

60 Cummins RO, [1].1. Emergency Medical Services, University of Washington Medical Center, Seattle 98195, The "chain of survival" concept: how it can save lives.
https://www.ncbi.nlm.nih.gov/pubmed/1344085
https://cpr.heart.org/en/resources/cpr-facts-and-stats/out-of-hospital-chain-of-survival.

61 https://www.heart.org/idc/groups/heart-public/@wcm/@adv/documents/ downloadable/ucm_301646.pdf.

62 Survival After Application of Automatic External Defibrillators Before Arrival of the Emergency Medical SystemEvaluation in the Resuscitation Outcomes Consortium Population of 21 Million Myron L. Weisfeldt, MD, Colleen M. Sitlani, MS, Joseph P. OrnatoMD, Thomas Rea, MD, Tom P. Aufderheide, MD, Daniel Davis, MD, Jonathan Dreyer, MD, Erik P. Hess, MD, MSc, Jonathan Jui, MD, MPH, Justin Maloney, MD, George Sopko, MD, MPH, Judy Powell, BSN, Graham Nichol, MD, MPH, and Laurie J. Morrison, MD, MSc, for the ROC Investigators, https://www.ncbi.nlm.nih.gov/pmc/ articles/PMC3008654/.

63 Making Sure The Beat Goes On, https://americanhealthcarejournal. com/2020/02/28/making-sure-the-beat-goes-on/.

64 https://www.ncsl.org/research/health/laws-on-cardiac-arrest-and-defibrillators-aeds.aspx.

65 Sherrid MV, et al. Journal of the American College of Cardiology Source Reference: "State requirements for automated external defibrillators in

American schools: framing the debate about legislative action" J Am Coll Cardiol 2017; DOI: 10.1016/j.jacc.2017.01.033.

66 ESC, European Society of Cardiology, Automatic external defibrillators save lives in amateur sports and fitness centres, 27 Aug 2017, https://www.escardio.org/The-ESC/Press-Office/Press-releases/automatic-external-defibrillators-save-lives-in-amateur-sports-and-fitness-centres.

67 The Public Experience with Cardiac Arrest https://www.ncbi.nlm.nih.gov/books/NBK321502/.

68 Source: Getting to the heart of cardiac problems (FIFA.com) 05 Nov 2009, Fifa Medical Conference, 16-17 October, https://www.fifa.com/who-we-are/news/getting-the-heart-cardiac-problems-1121851.

69 https://www.senatorscavello.com/2019/06/05/scavello-applauds-final-passage-of-bill-to-expand-cpr-training-in-school/.

70 Alexis A. Topjian, Robert A. Berg, Joost J. L. M. Bierens, Christine M. Branche, Robert S. Clark, Hans Friberg, Cornelia W. E. Hoedemaekers, Michael Holzer, Laurence M. Katz, Johannes T. A. Knape, Patrick M. Kochanek, Vinay Nadkarni, Johannes G. van der Hoeven, and David S. Warner Brain Resuscitation in the Drowning Victim, PMC 2013 Jun 10.Published in final edited form as: Neurocrit Care. 2012 Dec; 17(3): 441–467.doi: 10.1007/s12028-012-9747-4.

71 http://www.wisegeek.com/what-is-cpr.htm.

72 Myron L. Weisfeldt, MD, Colleen M. Sitlani, MS, Joseph P. Ornato, MD, Thomas Rea, MD, Tom P. Aufderheide, MD, Daniel Davis, MD, Jonathan Dreyer, MD, Erik P. Hess, MD, MSc, Jonathan Jui, MD, MPH, Justin Maloney, MD, George Sopko, MD, MPH, Judy Powell, BSN, Graham Nichol, MD, MPH, and Laurie J. Morrison, MD, MSc, for the ROC Investigators Survival After Application of Automatic External Defibrillators Before Arrival of the Emergency Medical System, Evaluation in the Resuscitation Outcomes Consortium Population of 21 Million.

73 By Jennifer Fenn Lefferts, Boston Globe Correspondent / January 2, 2011.

74 Source: September 2014 issue of Occupational Health & Safety. By Jeff Walters https://ohsonline.com/Articles/2014/09/01/Importance-of-AED-CPR-Training.aspx?Page=2.

75 Heart Attack vs. Sudden Cardiac Arrest: https://health.clevelandclinic.org/heart-attack-or-sudden-cardiac-arrest.

76 CDC National Center for Health Statistics (NCHS) data brief[PDF-603KB] Suggested citation Hales CM, Carroll MD, Fryar CD, Ogden CL. Prevalence of obesity among adults and youth: United States, 2015–2016. NCHS data brief, no 288. Hyattsville, MD: National Center for Health Statistics. 2017.

77 https://www.healthychildren.org/English/health-issues/conditions/heart/Pages/High-Blood-Pressure-in-Children. August 21, 2017.

78 https://oregon.providence.org/html/playsmart/index.html.

79 https://www.beaumont.org/services/heart-vascular/student-heart-check.

80 Few States Require AEDS in Schools/Medpage, https://www.medpage today.com.

81 Posted by Sarah McLoughlin, Increasing Survival Of SCA In Sports September 8, 2017
    https://www.thedefibshop.com/blog/2017/09/08/increasing-survival-of-sca-in-sports.

82 Wheeler MT[1], Heidenreich PA, Froelicher VF, Hlatky MA, Ashley EA, Author information,1Stanford University, California 94305, USA, Cost-effectiveness of preparticipation screening for prevention of sudden cardiac death in young athletes, https://www.ncbi.nlm.nih.gov/pubmed/20194233.

83 https://ohsonline.com/Articles/2014/09/01/Importance-of-AED-CPR-Training.aspx?Page=5.

84 Public Access Defibrillation, https://www.health.ny.gov/professionals/ems/policy/09-03.html.

85 Students Save a Life During High School Concert, Cardiac Science, https://www.cardiacscience.com/students-save-a-life-during-high-school-concert/.

86 Source: Robert Norris, the daily times, Harrill's battle won: AEDs for every Tennessee school, bobn@thedailytimes.com
    https://www.thedailytimes.com/news/harrill-s-battle-won-aeds-for-every-tennessee-school/article_354bfc2b-4783-5d44-9043-f0d76feecbc1.html

NOTES FROM THE AUTHOR

In some passages, I have used initials instead of names to respect the privacy of some individuals whom I discern would appreciate the nondisclosure. But for Chad's close Friends and Family, I have included their names as it would have seemed strange not to.

The words Love and Life, you will find often capitalized throughout because, for me, they have become the two most essential words in the English language, perhaps any language. Similarly, the words, Son, Gift, Family, Friend or Heart I have capitalized in specific contexts to give them the prominence they deserve.

Though a 3rd generation American, borne and bred in America, my strange fascination with the Old World beyond the pond is reflected by some of my words which have a British spelling. As long as I have been writing, that's the way they emanate from my pen. Perhaps it is my way of connecting the old with the new.

I have respected the Childrens' Stories written by their Parents, Relatives, and Friends, as well as my own Son, Chad's authorship, and refrained from any editing. It is the purity and heart of their words that are most significant. Some photos, due to age, are not as perfect as we would like. Restoration is on our list.

The pages are sprinkled with Artists and their Gifts because they have always been such an intricate part of our Lives and culture. They have influenced, informed, documented, and inspired our Lives from the beginning of time. The Sounds of Music alone can get us through times, it might be unendurable without. And being a member of that artistic corps, I am most grateful for the entirety of their Gifts, which also brought joy to my Son, Chad's Life, and continue to carry me through without him.

Through my Son Chad's book, I have discovered the many layers of the Heart, and perceive many yet to be uncovered. Maybe, that is what our Children have left us ~ the legacy of their Hearts ~ to instill and ensure that Life and Love will continue to their fullest measure... and beyond for all future generations...

ABOUT THE AUTHOR

Arista is an actor/writer/voice artist living in New York City. Her Art celebrates the Human Spirit. She is the author of two Off-Broadway produced plays, ..*All About Sneakers* and *Welcome Home Kelly,* a children's book, *The Gemini Kiid,* and her screenplay, *Ew-Ess-Ah* (USA) which heralds the real-life event of, the 1st "Homeless Streetsoccer World Cup," in Graz, Austria. She deems her most important role as mother to her sons Chad, Curt and Collin, and has dedicated her life's work to "Chad's Gifts of Heart and Art - Healthy Body, Mind & Spirit" ~ a tribute to her son, Chad's motto in Life.

Jacket photos of Chad
by Jon McKee
Author's photograph
by Fred Canpolat
Jacket Design by John Gehringer
Chad logo by Ralph Andre

CPSIA information can be obtained
at www.ICGtesting.com
Printed in the USA
BVHW071146200820
586901BV00001B/122

9 781982 250782